The Cultivators Handbook of Natural Tobacco
By Bill Drake

Cover Design

"Tobacco Spirit" by Lisle Drake

www.mermaidsprings.com

Based on an original from a pamphlet by

German Kali Works, Havana, Cuba 1924

Copyright © 1981 - 2010 by Bill Drake

Illustrations by Pat Krug & Terry Rutledge

Photos by Lisle Drake & Tim James

All Rights Reserved

EAN13 9781451514643

ISBN 1451514646

Second edition: February 2010
www.cultivatorshandbook.com

Dedicated to Donna Childs & Richard Meiners of Pinetree Garden Seeds

www.superseeds.com

Without Whose Encouragement & Support This

New Edition Could Not Have Been Created

Grow Where You Are Planted

Table of Contents

Introduction 1

SECTION ONE: Growing Natural Native American Tobacco 3

Basic Misunderstanding At First Contact 5

Native American Natural Tobacco 6

Native American Growing Methods 9

Tobacco in Everyday Native American Life 14

Grow Your Own Natural Tobacco? 15

A CAUTION TO HOME GROWERS 19

Starting Natural Tobacco Seed 19

Caring For Seedlings 21

Planting In Containers 22

Lighting Indoor Tobacco Plants 23

Preparing For Outdoor Planting 25

Transplanting Tobacco Seedling Outdoors 26

Fertilizing Your Tobacco Plants 27

Watering Your Tobacco Plants 27

Dealing Naturally With Bugs 28

Deficiency Signs In Tobacco 30

Effects Show on Lower Leaves Only 30

Effects Show on the Entire Plant 30

Effects Show on New Bud Leaves 31

Suckering Natural Tobacco Plants 31

Topping Natural Tobacco Plants 32

Which Leaves For Which Purpose 32

Harvesting And Curing Natural Tobacco 33

Priming And Air-Curing Natural Tobacco 34

Flavoring Naturally- Cured Tobacco 35

Making The Flavor Essences 36

Home-Grown Smoke 38

Making Rolling Tobacco 39

Making Pipe Tobacco 41

Making Natural Tobacco Snuff 42

A Few Words On Chewing Natural Tobacco 45

Growing Natural Tobacco Hydroponically 45

Section Two: Advice From Old-Time Master Tobacco Growers 50

General Advice 51

Tobacco And The Growing Environment 55

Types of Soil Favorable for Tobacco Growing 58

Methods of Treating, Fertilizing & Tilling The Land 63

Growing & Preparing Tobacco Seed 75

Methods of Sowing & Starting a Tobacco Crop 79

Transplanting or Setting Out The Young Plants 87

Cultivating The Growing Crop 91

Insects That Damage Tobacco & How To Control Them 93

Suckering & Topping – Critical Practices for a Quality Crop 103

Harvesting and Drying Ripe Tobacco Leaves 110

Curing and Flavoring 116

Online Access To Master Tobacco Growers 125

SECTION THREE: WHO ARE THE TRUE TERRORISTS? 128

The Problem With The Lawyers 133

Maybe It's Not The Tobacco Killing People 138

Pesticides Currently On US Tobacco Products 141

A Piece Of Good Advice 143

Pesticides mean tobacco profitability 144

Contamination Of Third World Tobacco 147

Smoking-Related Disease And Agrichemicals 149

The Cigarette Pesticides 150

The Low Tar Game - And You're It 151

SECTION FOUR: Native Natural Tobacco and the European Mind 156

Love It or Hate It 156

King James Sees The Devil 157

Didn't Work Then, Doesn't Work Now 160

Tobacco Inspires Poetry & Song 161

Distinguished People Who Inhaled 164

How Tobacco Arrived & Conquered 166

A Blessing For Many; A Curse For Some 171

A Good Woman Was Worth A Lot Of Tobacco 175

Pipes & Other Great Inventions 178

Up Your Nose 183

The (Dis)Graceful Art 187

The Gentleman's Smoke 188

A Long Way, Baby? 190

A Novel Strategy for Natural Tobacco Growers 190

Introduction

I first began growing native, natural tobacco in the late 1970s while living in Northern New Mexico. I had a Native American friend who brought me a handful of tobacco seeds that he and his friends had found in an ancient burial site. John knew that my wife and I enjoyed growing unusual herbs and other plants and thought that tobacco plants would interest us. The native tobacco of New Mexico is called Punché but John was pretty sure that these seeds were of a different variety from very long ago – he estimated that the burial site dated to the 12th-14th Century.

I wasn't sure that the seeds would even be viable after all that time, but we planted them and in just a few months we had a plot full of seven foot high tobacco plants that glistened with crystal clear resin and attracted swarms of insects to their bright yellow flowers. This is a photo of the crowning top of an N. Rustica about to go into full flower, which is the point at which you should pinch it off – called 'topping'.

As the insects landed on the plant they died – it was clear that there wasn't going to be a problem with bugs eating these plants! We later discovered that while insects are not a problem once the N. Rustica plants matured, when it is young there is a wide range of critters like deer and rabbits who love the tender, sweet leaves, so we had to guard our young plants carefully until they matured enough to produce their own potent Nicotine. (Please keep in mind that this was my experience growing in New Mexico's high desert environment, where there are none of Tobacco's traditional enemies – especially the notorious "Tobacco Hawk" moth whose offspring, the Horned Tobacco Worm, creates so much destruction in most regions where Tobacco is typically grown. (We'll discuss detailed traditional methods of dealing with this voracious tobacco predator, and other destructive pests, in Section Two.)

As the summer ended the leaves began to turn first light brown and then golden brown on the plant, and on the afternoon we harvested our first few leaves we invited John to come over for a smoke. Crumbling the tip of a dry leaf and packing it into a water pipe we each took a hit and sat back.

Bazoom! This sure wasn't like any tobacco I had ever smoked before. More like excellent sinsemilla, maybe combined with a shot of tequila. Right away my mind began turning over the idea of growing this stuff commercially. Why not, I thought, work with John and some of his friends who lived on Native American land in San Juan Pueblo, where they couldn't be touched by the Federal Government who at that time tightly controlled tobacco production in the US, to grow native tobacco using pure, natural methods and then sell that tobacco by mail order all over the country (this was before the internet).

That's how Santa Fe Natural Tobacco Company was started, and with the help of a few friends we began packing natural native tobacco into baggies and selling it around the southwest. I called our tobacco "American Spirit" in honor of its origins, and had big plans to create a high value business that would benefit Native American communities throughout the southwest. But I was pretty naïve and soon lost the business to a group of slick folks who did a great job of turning it into a commercial success but who never followed through with the original intent to create wealth for Native Americans from a plant that was theirs in the first place.

I walked away from Santa Fe Natural and never looked back but have continued to grow small plots of tobacco for my friends who smoke commercial cigarettes (I stopped smoking anything except for the occasional miraculous gift I receive from friends years ago) and have continued to believe that hand-grown native natural tobacco could be a wonderful source of wealth for thousands of growers – Native American or not. Especially now with the internet anyone who grows a small plot of truly excellent boutique tobacco and who hand-processes it into pure, natural roll-your-own, cigarettes, cigars, snuff can, I believe, look forward to finding a devoted following worldwide.

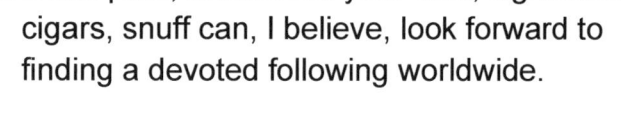

Fortunately there is also an excellent, FREE source of hundreds of varieties of exotic varieties of completely natural, native tobacco seeds – I'll tell you where that is shortly.

And equally fortunately you don't have to plant acres and acres of native natural tobacco in order to be able to harvest enough to sustain an excellent small business – as little as a quarter-acre will produce hundreds of mature tobacco plants that will yield a pound or more of finished leaf each. If you can sell your tobacco at a profit of $10 an ounce – a very reasonable price – that translates to $16,000 per hundred pounds. You do the math. It won't take much land or labor to support a small family farm very nicely with a crop of native, natural tobacco sold over the internet and distributed in nearby cities. Since the Feds are no longer in the tobacco quota business you have nothing to worry about from that angle and as long as you pay your taxes you have nothing to worry about at all – tobacco is a completely legal crop, unlike our beloved Marijuana.

In short – maybe now, almost forty years after my original experiments with native natural tobacco seeds from an ancient Shaman's grave the time has come for the original dream to come true. That is the inspiration for this book, which began as a little pamphlet first printed when I started Santa Fe Natural Tobacco Company to promote the idea that those who enjoy smoking tobacco could grow their own and share it with others.

I hope that this book will inspire you to become a native natural tobacco grower and, even if only in some small way, help to take back for all people one of the great sources of wealth and pleasure in the world, long ago stolen by the white race from the Native Americans and later stolen by giant corporations from its rightful owners – all people who live on and work the sacred soil of Mother Earth. If you are Native American, or are a non-Native person who understands what it means to a people to lose a critical part of their heritage to predatory conquerors and exploiters, then the simple act of growing your own Tobacco, and using it with respect and moderation, enables you to make a powerful statement. Ultimately, many such voices joined together, can bring down the strongest walls that these evil institutions have erected to protect themselves from their destiny, which is their destruction.

SECTION ONE: Growing Natural Native American Tobacco

"It is a curious fact that while the Whites took the material tobacco from the Indians they took with it no fragment of the world that accompanied it, nor were they at first aware that there was such a world. After all of the generations that have elapsed since its introduction among the Whites, it has woven itself scarcely at all into their psychology and mythology. Nicotine is enshrined among the Whites only as a drug, as a taste, as a habit, along with the seeking after mild and tasty forms, while the Native peoples make tobacco a heritage from the gods, a strange path which juts from there into this world and leads to the very ends of magic."

An early anthropologist, Ralph Linton, left one of the best descriptions of Native American tobacco use:

" At the time of the discovery of America, tobacco was in use over the greater part of the continent. It was not used in the sub-Arctic regions of North America or in the extreme southern part of Southern America. On the west coast of South America and in the Andean highlands it was replaced by another narcotic Erythroxicum coca, from which cocaine is extracted. The coca leaves were dried and chewed with powdered lime.

"Tobacco was smoked throughout most of its range, but the tribes of the northwest coast of North America mixed it with shell lime and made it into small pellets which were swallowed or dissolved in the mouth. The tribes of Washington, Oregon and a great part of California used it in the same way, but also smoked it. Along the eastern side of the Andean highlands in South America tobacco was both smoked and chewed. The chewing tobacco was prepared like the Andean coca, and the idea was probably borrowed from coca chewing.

"Although Europeans learned the custom of smoking from the Indians and even copied the Indian smoking appliances rather closely, the modern American custom of tobacco chewing may not be of Indian origin. None of the North American Indians east of the Rocky Mountains chewed tobacco, and the only point at which South American tobacco chewing reached the Atlantic Coast was a small region in northern Colombia. Modern chewing tobacco lacks the powdered lime, which was considered necessary by all Indian tobacco chewers and seems to have been an invention of the white frontiersmen. It is possible, however, that the idea of tobacco chewing was carried to the English colonies by the Spaniards, who may have learned it from the South American Indians.

Basic Misunderstanding At First Contact

First contact between tobacco and the White race took place during the first voyage of Admiral Columbus in 1492. After touching land at San Salvador, Columbus steered south by southwest and, after a few hours, spotted a canoe in the open sea. Pulling alongside the canoe, the Europeans saw a single Carib rower with a cargo of dried leaves. The Europeans were transfixed by what they saw the Indian doing.

On a long sea voyage the rowers of Carib merchant canoes kept a small brazier of coals going amidships. Every 30 minutes or so, a small wad of tobacco leaves was placed on the brazier and, as the smoke began to rise, the rowers would put a forked nose pipe made from the breastbone of a seabird into the fumes and draw them in. After holding the smoke for awhile, a rower would exhale powerfully with a shout like high school players breaking a football huddle and then go back to the awesome task of single-handedly rowing a fully loaded commercial canoe over the open seas.

We can only imagine the feelings of this Native American, alone in his canoe on the ocean where his ancestors had traveled forever as lords, suddenly being appraised by strange white beings leaning over the rails of the biggest ship he had ever seen.

If there was ever a time for a smoke, that must have been it. Luckily for that Carib none of the Europeans spoke to him to ask what he was doing, so he didn't have to deal with their ignorance of what must have been a commonplace experience to him.

The next landfall of this first European expedition was the island of Hispanola, which today is called Santo Domingo where Columbus, sweeping the south side of the land mass, detected signs of an organized civilization. He anchored and sent ashore two men, one of whom could speak Italian, Spanish, Chaldean, Hebrew and Arabic, insuring that he would be able to communicate with the local deputy of the Grand Khan of Cathay.

Upon landing, this deputy and his guard were met by a party of Caribs, who came to the beach with torches, and held out strange objects to the two amazed White people. Lighting one end of these objects in the torch, the New World People sucked the smoke out the other end, explaining by both sign and voice that it relaxed them, intoxicated them, and lessened their weariness. The Indians called the objects "tobacos." To the Carib, "tobaco" was not the herb itself, but the object that was created by rolling the leaves of the herb. Columbus' deputy, however, took tobacco to be the name of the herb rather than the rolled object, and recorded it that way for posterity.

So, we get our word tobacco from the very first encounter between the New World and the Old, perhaps from the first word spoken. Ironic that this first communication creates such a fundamental misunderstanding, the beginning of a long series of wrong conclusions which come down to our own times, about tobacco, about the Native Americans, and about the New World.

Native American Natural Tobacco

There are over 100 varieties of the tobacco plant, all of which contain the psychoactive principle Nicotine in the leaves, though in varying degrees of concentration. Besides native Virginia tobacco, Nicotiana tabacum, for which the genus was composed, there are many other kinds of tobacco that are far more interesting for a personal garden of organic, natural homegrown tobacco and for specialty natural tobacco grower/producers. Since many of these native varieties are rare and unavailable commercially, you'll be happy to know that you can get seeds for just about any type of tobacco you can imagine completely free from the U.S. government. The National Plant Germplasm System maintains an inventory of seeds from every variety of plant ever grown commercially or ever considered of potential commercial importance, including 100's of kinds of tobacco collected from around the world.

Every variety is carefully bred true, and upon request you can receive between 100-1000 seeds for any kind of tobacco you want to grow.

The address of the NPGS homepage (as of February 2010) is:

http://www.ars-grin.gov/npgs/acc/acc_queries.html

Go to this page and use the search box to locate the tobacco seed files –they are extensive so be prepared to do some enjoyable browsing. For the native, natural tobacco varieties you'll find details on where and when they were first collected in the field, as well as who did the collecting and any comments they made at the time. It takes NPGS about a month to process requests. If you prefer to deal with a private company rather than the Federal government there are several excellent tobacco seed sources, including: www.superseeds.com, http://www.newhopeseed.com and http://www.crosscreekseed.com.

Among the many kinds of native natural tobacco seed available from NPGS or the others are:

- Nicotiana rustica, a species cultivated in Mexico, India, the Middle East, Turkey, and found native and escaped in many parts of the U.S. Nicotiana rustica is a hardy species with yellow flowers, and was grown by the tribes of the United States and Canada as far west as the great plains and as far north as agriculture was possible. Rustica leaves are more oval than lance-shaped. Grows 3' – 8' tall depending on strain & conditions. You'll find over 75 kinds of Rustica available on NPGS. Be careful - it's very potent & can be dangerous.

Nicotiana rustica was the first tobacco grown for the European trade, but was soon supplanted by the smoother, less savage N. tabacum. N. Rustica is still cultivated by many Native Americans who use it ceremonially, and also as a specialty smoking product.

- Nicotiana palmeri or tree tobacco grows wild in Arizona, and probably will do well in any low humidity, long-season environment. **Palmeri is highly toxic in its natural environment and should only be grown as a specimen – never smoked**.

- Nicotiana attenuata flourished historically as a sacred smoking tobacco over a larger area than any other species. Its natural range was the southwestern United States and southern plains, and northward into western Canada and British Colombia. It was also cultivated on the lower Colorado, but anthropological literature says that many Pueblo tribes preferred Rustica for everyday smoking. Night-blooming attenuata will be quite easy for most people to raise either in a summer garden or as an indoors/outdoors potted plant.

- Nicotiana quadrivalvus, cultivated by Native Americans from the Northwest through the Mississippi Valley, this tobacco has small leaves and delicate flowers, and can be found growing wild today throughout the midwest. It produces a sweet, almost minty smoke when properly cultivated, and it loves pots.

- A related species, Nicotiana multivalis grows in Washington and Oregon, and was the tobacco preferred by the Crow who lived on the western edge of the great plains.

•Nicotiana chinensis is both cultivated and wild in China and Japan. This is a small, hardy plant with very potent resins and a harsh smoke that calls for a water-pipe. Probably a Rustica variant.

•Nicotiana trigonophylla, a highly potent species with attractive flowers and small leaves which grows wild in Southern California, Arizona, Utah, and New Mexico, where it is gathered for smoking and for religious purposes. **It can be very dangerous – significant numbers of people die in the southwest from smoking small doses.**

•Related species Nicotiana biglovii (old botanical print on left) and N. Glauca were/are used by the California tribes and by the Hupa. **They are also very potent and therefore quite dangerous - not recommended except as specimens.**

•Yaqui tobacco is cultivated in Arizona by the Yaqui Indians and others and is a wildly potent smoke. Many believe that Yaqui tobacco is simply a variety of N. Rustica that has adapted to the arid, high plateau of the interior southwest.

• Nicotiana tabacum, the species to which practically all the modern commercial tobaccos belong, was originally grown throughout Mexico, the West Indies, and in northern and eastern South America. It was unknown north of Mexico until its introduction into Virginia by the English colonists trading with the Spanish from the Caribbean. In its natural non-hybridized state it is a hairy, sticky, potent plant that reaches 7-8 feet in height and is covered with showy pink flowers.

•Nicotiana clevelandi is a low-profile tobacco with somewhat rounded leaves that grows wild all over southern California, and **can be extremely potent to the point of being very, very dangerous if mis-used**. Its flowers are a favorite food of nectar-gathering insects. Grow it primarily as a specimen.

•Nicotiana fructicosa is a beautiful plant with sharply pointed seed capsules and is used primarily for ornamental purposes - not smokable, although the dried flowers make a nice addition to smoking tobaccos.

•Nicotiana persica or shirazi (shown above left potted at 10 weeks) is a fragrant plant from Iran, easy to grow almost anywhere in the world, responds very well to hand cultivation, and is **one of the best of the tobaccos for taste, attractiveness, and**

manageable potency. Shirazi flowers are creamy white and the leaves are slender and pointed.

•Nicotiana rapanda is a wild tropical tobacco, producer of fine Cuban smoke, grows bountifully in soil and pots, produces a profusion of flowers and is very high in flavor.

• Burley tobacco is a highly disease resistant, hybridized tobacco that grows well indoors or outdoors. It has broad leaves with fine veins, and cures easily for smoking in any form.

Tobacco belongs to the elite order of dark knights, the Solanaceae. It is definitely a plant to be respected as both potent and toxic. The darkness of the Solanacae is illustrated by the three princes who share the order with tobacco:

•First: black henbane, Hyoscyamus niger also called Hyoscyamus lethalis. Deadly if barely misused, often lethal anyway. A lot of lives have been taken by this plant, through both deliberate misuse and through mistaken use as a salad herb.

•Next there is Solanum nigerum, or deadly nightshade. A very painful, messy death. Even if you changed heart halfway down, jumping from a bridge would probably be easier than taking this black prince to heart.

•Finally, there is Datura stramonium, jimson weed. It won't kill you but it will snuff out the bright part of your lights. It used to be a common adulterant in street marijuana, and still is in some areas. It gets dried, chopped, mixed with real marijuana seeds, bagged and sold - a very poisonous smoke. Jimson weed grows wild in vast patches, especially in the South.

Native American Growing Methods
The North American Native Americans used at least nine species of Nicotiana, most of which were cultivated rather than gathered wild.

As you'll see in Section Two, there is a wealth of information on the Native American methods of tobacco culture in the eastern United States. Here we'll just look at a few of the more relevant points for the home gardener. Almost all tribes used some kind of digging stick at various points in the planting process (Crow stick at left), whether to poke holes for transplanting, to root out destructive insects, or to aerate the soil.

Early writers generally say that Tobacco was not grown with other crops by Native Americans, as it was believed to be injurious to them, and was usually cultivated by men. The Cayuga in New York State had permanent tobacco beds in which the plant was grown year after year. These beds were cultivated and lightly manured from time to time before planting after which the plants were left to propagate themselves. When the crop had matured, the golden leaves were gathered but the stems, with the maturing seed pods attached, were left standing in the patch.

The Seneca, another tribe of the Iroquois confederacy, had a very strong religious prohibition against anyone cultivating the plant. They simply scattered the seeds on the ground in a sacred place and took what the Great Spirit gave back.

The Kickapoo and Potawatomi were known for making large brush piles fifty or more feet long and ten or twelve feet wide which they fired about the middle of June. When the fires were cold the ground was hoed up, mixing in the rich ashes, and were then planted using a digging stick (left). These tobacco gardens were made in the woods, remote from the villages, and were always surrounded by dense, tall brush fences.

The Sauk also planted their tobacco in the ashes of brush fires, but did not break the ground or fertilize the crop. In some cases they simply threw a handful of seeds on the ground near the lodge in the ashes of an old cooking fire site.

The Kickapoo, Potawatomi and Sauk all gathered the leaves of the plant in late August. They spread them on hides or blankets, and when they had wilted but not yet dried, they rolled them between the palms of their hands into little rolled-up tubes, much like tea-leaves are handled after harvesting. When these little rolled-up leaves were dry, the leaves were crushed. The reason given by the Sauk for the rolling was that leaves treated in this way did not crush to fine powder like those that had been dried flat. Most of the eastern tribes grew only enough tobacco for their own needs, but the Tionontati raised large quantities of it for export and were called Tobacco People (Nation de Petun) by the French.

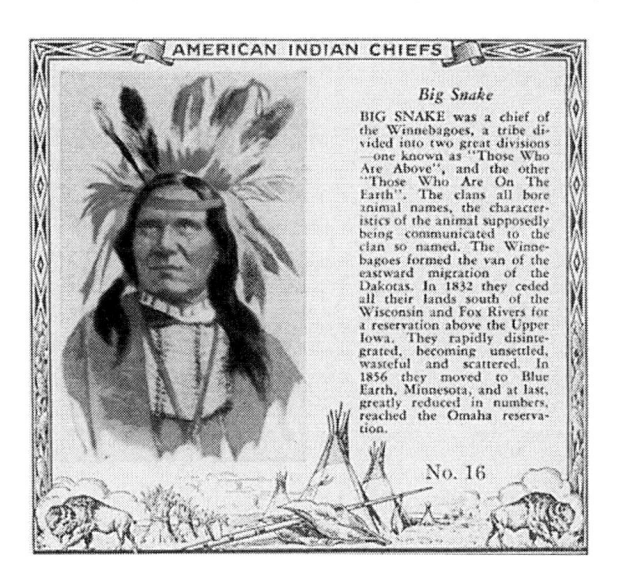

One of the best published account of Native American tobacco culture is that given to G. L. Wilson by Buffalobirdwoman, an elderly member of the Hidatsa tribe. The Hidatsa and Winnebago raised a different species of tobacco from the eastern Indians (N. quadrivalvis), and their methods were somewhat different. She tells us:

"The old men of the tribe who smoked each had a tobacco garden planted not very far away from our corn-fields, but never in the same plot with corn. Tobacco gardens were planted apart, because the tobacco plants have a strong odor that affects the corn; if tobacco is planted near the corn, the growing cornstalks turn yellow, and the corn is not so good.

Tobacco seed was planted at the same time sunflower seed was planted, as early in April as the soil could be worked. The grower took a hoe and made soft every foot of the tobacco garden; and with a rake he made the loosened soil level and smooth. He marked the ground with a stick into rows about eighteen inches apart, and sowed the seed very thickly in the row. He covered the newly sowed soil very lightly with earth that he raked with his hand.

When rain came and warmth, the seed sprouted. The plants came up quickly so they had to be thinned out. The owner of the garden would weed out the weak plants, leaving only the stronger standing. The earth about each plant was hilled up with a buffalo rib into a little hill like a corn hill. A very old man, I remember, used a big buffalo rib sharpened on the edges to work the soil and cultivate his tobacco. He caught the rib by both ends with the edge downward; and stooping over, he scraped the soil towards him, now and then raising the rib up and loosening the earth with the point at one end. He knelt as he worked.

Tobacco plants begin to blossom about the middle of June, and picking then began. Tobacco was gathered in two harvests. The first harvest was the blossoms, which we reckon the best part of the plant for smoking. Blossoms were picked regularly every fourth day. If we neglected to pick them until the fifth day the blossoms would begin to seed. Only the green part of the blossom was kept. When we fetched the blossoms home to the lodge, my father would spread a deer hide out on the floor in front of his sacred objects and spread the blossoms on the hide to dry. The smoke hole of the lodge being rather large, would let through quite a strong sunbeam, and the drying blossoms were kept directly in the beam.

When the blossoms had quite dried my father fetched them over near the fireplace and took a piece of buffalo fat, thrust it on the end of a stick and roasted it slowly over the coals. (N.B. – you can buy buffalo meat in many markets like Whole Foods these days if you would like to try this method. Buffalo ribeye steaks have great fat content. I have tried this, and it's a delightful smoke.) He touched it lightly here and there to the piled up blossoms, so as to oil them slightly, but not too much. Now and then he would gently stir the pile of blossoms with a little stick, so that the whole mass might be oiled equally. When my father wanted to smoke these dried blossoms he chopped them fine with a knife, a pipeful at a time. The blossoms were always dried in the lodge: if dried without, the sun and air took away their strength.

About harvest time, just before frost came, the rest of the plants were gathered. He dried the plants in the lodge. For this he took sticks, about fifteen inches long, and thrust them over the beam between two of the exterior supporting posts, so that the sticks pointed a little upwards. On each of these sticks he hung two or three tobacco plants by thrusting the plants, root up, upon the stick, but without tying them. When the tobacco plants were quite dry, the leaves readily fell off. It was the stems that furnished most of the smoking. They were treated like the blossoms, with buffalo fat. We did not treat tobacco with buffalo fat except as needed for use, and to be put into the tobacco pouch ready for smoking. Before putting the tobacco away into the cache pit, my father was careful to set aside seed for the next year's planting. He gathered the black seeds into a small bundle about as big as a baby's fist, wrapping them in a piece of soft skin which he tied with a string. He made two or three of these bundles and tied them to the top of his bed, or to a post nearby, where there was no danger of their being disturbed.

Told by: Buffalo Bird Woman, 1914

As the late Sioux Medicine Man, Lame Deer, used to say,

"The pipe is the Indian's blood and flesh. Its red pipe bowl is the blood, the opening the Indian's mouth, the stem the Indian's spine, the smoke his sacred breath, wafting up the smoker's prayers to Wakan Tanka, the Grandfather Spirit above. With the pipe in your hand, you can speak nothing but the truth."

True herbal tobacco can be very potent if misused. The following account is from a description of a Native American tribe who loved the pure, potent plant – probably N. trigonophylla.

" He feels good over all his meat when he takes it into his lungs. Sometimes he rolls up his eyes. And sometimes he falls over, backward he falls over backward. He puts his pipe quickly on the ground, then he falls over. Then they laugh at him, they all laugh at him. Nobody takes heed, when one faints from smoking, but if he faints because he is sick, then they throw water on him. When it is from tobacco that he faints, he does not lie there stiff long.

" Sometimes when the tobacco is strong the man himself when he smokes does not know when he faints away. Sometimes he falls to the ground and does not know it. Somebody else says "Look, he is fainting". They see his hands shake. He feels good for a long time after he smokes, if he likes to smoke he feels good for a long while. Sometimes he falls on the ground he feels faint.

" They say that some old men have to walk with a cane when they have finished smoking, they feel it so over their whole meat. I used to see them, the old men. It was the strong tobacco, that was what they liked. They fall on the ground. They awaken, and they smoke again. People always laugh at the old men smoking. When they smoke they talk in the sweathouse. All at once one man quits talking. That is the way they used to do in the old times. They used to like the tobacco so well. They used to like the tobacco strong. Whenever they faint from tobacco, they always get ashamed. They used to do that way, get stunned.

" Sometimes one fellow will have so strong tobacco that nobody can stand it without fainting, it is so strong. He feels proud of his strong tobacco. Some were fainters when they smoked, others never did faint. Some faint when the tobacco gets strong from them, and others do not.

" Vaskok was a fainter when he smoked. Everybody knew that Vaskok was a fainter. Vaskok used to faint, but he liked it. When he first starts to smoke he does not fall. It is when he finishes smoking a pipeful of tobacco that he falls; it is then as it gets strong for him that he falls."

Tobacco in Everyday Native American Life

Ralph Linton's early writings contained this excellent description of the place of tobacco in Native American spiritual and everyday life.

" An Indian warrior was rarely without his pipe and tobacco, and special tobacco-bags were used by all the tribes east of the Rocky Mountains. In early times, these bags were usually made from the skins of small animals taken off whole. The Eastern Woodland tribes used a rather small bag that was tied to the belt. The Plains tribes used a larger bag, often made from a fawn skin, in which they carried both the pipe and tobacco. In historic times the northern Plains Indians have used long, flat rectangular bags decorated with beads or porcupine quills, but this type apparently is not an ancient one.

" Several of the Plains tribes also had special boards on which the tobacco was cut up and elaborate pipe tampers. These accessories were used mainly in ceremonial smoking. In Pawnee ceremonies the pipe was always tamped with an arrow captured from the enemy. It was forbidden to pack it with the fingers, as the gods might think that the man who did so offered himself with the tobacco and take his life. The tribes of the Northwest Coast crushed their tobacco in mortars. These were usually made from whale vertebrae, and were often elaborately carved.

" Even if documentary evidence of the New World origin of tobacco were lacking, its importance in the religious and ceremonial life of the Indians would leave little doubt of the antiquity of its use among them. Among all the tribes east of the Rocky Mountains tobacco was the favorite offering to the supernatural powers, and among the Central Algonquians no ceremony could take place without it. As a sacrifice it might be burned as incense, cast into the air or on the ground, or buried. There were sacred places at which every visitor left a tobacco offering, and during storms it was thrown into lakes and rivers to appease the under-water powers.

" Smoking was indulged in on all solemn occasions, such as councils, and was a necessary part of most religious ceremonies. In such ceremonial smoking the methods of picking up, filling, and lighting the pipe were usually rigidly prescribed, and the first smoke was offered to the spirits. The methods of passing and holding the pipe were also prescribed and differed with the ceremony and even with the personal taboos of the smokers. In the religious ceremonies of the Hopi, the head chief was attended by an assistant of nearly equal rank, who ceremonially lighted the pipe, and with certain formalities and set words handed it to the chief, who blew the smoke to the world quarters and over the altar as a preliminary to his invocation.

" The medicine-bundles, collections of sacred objects around which the religious life of many of the Central Algonquians and Plains Tribes centered, often contained pipes which were smoked in the ceremonies attending the opening of the bundle. In some cases the pipe itself seems to have been the most important object, and the palladium of the Arapaho tribe is a straight pipe of black stone.

" Among some of the eastern Siouan tribes each clan had its sacred pipe which was used at namings and other clan ceremonies. The stems of these pipes were covered with elaborate wrappings and other ornaments which symbolized the various supernatural powers invoked in the ceremonies, and the sanctity of the pipe lay in its stem rather than its bowl.

Grow Your Own Natural Tobacco?

So what happened? That 15th century tobacco sure doesn't sound like anything we see around here today, does it?

It isn't. It's taken the last 60 years and more of science and technology, and hundreds of years of trying, but now the tobacco industry has the tobacco plant pretty close to where it wants it. Maximum leaf size. Maximum ease of processing. Maximum growth. Minimal nicotine content. Minimal variation between plants. Minimal character. Genetically altered. Tolerant of pesticides.

It used to take only one or two puffs of pure, natural tobacco, as it existed before the tobacco industry became one of the great 20th century commercial success stories, next to oil and guns--and a person would not want another puff, or two, for a half hour or more. That way, in an afternoon or an evening, a person might smoke a pipe bowl of tobacco, probably less. There was a thriving business on European streets in the early days consisting of house servants selling and trading tobacco remnants from the bowls of gentlemen's pipes, left only partially smoked after an evening's reading or discussion.

Well, you just don't build the kind of economic empire which tobacco has become from a product which people use only in tiny, inexpensive amounts. What you have to do is change the product, and the people's use of it, so that they use lots of it, tiny, expensive amounts at a time.

It's a complex story--how the effect of tobacco has been transferred, by deliberate biochemical, genetic, and agricultural manipulation, from the realms of consciousness into the deep physiological networks of our bodies. Today's commercial tobacco is a remarkable success--it retains tobacco's effect, but transfers that effect so that we keep on using, but never quite get high.

It's also curious that growing our own tobacco is an idea so absent from our minds. We pay high prices without ever gaining satisfaction. We respond like zombies to advertising that consists largely of our own images, living out wealth and love fantasies. We know we're being manipulated, insulted, assaulted by exotic chemicals, sneered at, and robbed by commercial tobacco interests--but somehow we've never really considered growing our own. We grow our own vegetables, we grow our own herbs, and many of us grow our own Marijuana; but our own Tobacco? It just doesn't seem to occur to us. Isn't that curious? Perhaps not, if one considers how otherwise perfectly the tobacco industry designs its products.

A lot of folks who are involved in growing tobacco on a commercial scale are small farmers whose relationship to the tobacco companies is like that of the coal miner to the company store. And the tobacco they grow is so raunchy in the raw state, before elaborate chemical and industrial processing, that even those who grow tobacco for a living generally feel that the plant is nothing but a stinking weed. Most of these farmers have never grown anything but the hybridized, genetically neutered, swollen freak plants that the tobacco industry demands.

The internet changes everything. Commercial tobacco products bring such high prices and give the smoker so little quality in return that anyone with a dedication to quality and even a quarter acre or so of land can grow native strains of natural tobacco and then produce, package and sell their products at their local farmers market or on the internet.

I can't imagine that the market for organically-grown heirloom strains of the great native tobaccos doesn't number in the hundreds of thousands of smokers, if not millions.

Growing your own tobacco, as well as growing and selling to others, not only makes ethical and practical sense for today, but for the future, which increasing numbers of people see as a time when survival itself may depend on one's self-sufficiency. In all wars and times of chaos, tobacco has been one of the sure commodities of value in trade for just about anything. In any severe hard times to come, surely tobacco, and now Marijuana, will show this historical capacity to endure grim circumstances and retain value. Thus, it makes great sense to be self-sufficient unto your own needs, and to be able to grow tobacco for trade if times demand.

Then there's the interest and satisfaction which growing tobacco brings. Tobacco is a fascinating plant, its history aside. As it goes into flower, it will grow as much as three inches a day. A plant that is brushing your chin with the tip of its highest head in the evening will, by the next afternoon, be tickling your nose with its topmost little bell-shaped flowers. The tobacco plant starts life as a seed almost microscopic, pokes its head into the world almost invisibly, grows painfully slowly for the first few weeks, and then suddenly, and with increasing tempo, the great surge of vegetative growth occurs. During this 2-3 month period, the tobacco plant can gain a full five feet, and more, in stature, depending on the species, the growing conditions, and the cultivation techniques that apply.

There is a spirit to the tobacco plant, particularly evident under a full moon when the plant nears maturity. Tobacco is a high order plant, with such orderly genes and chromosomes that it is the darling of plant geneticists, the white rat of the plant kingdom. Its very highly evolved genes represent not only its evolutionary glory, but also its greatest vulnerability. It has been a plant easily enslaved and altered, but it can be a plant that is intimately cared for as well. Those of us who have been growing tobacco over the past several years have found that we get very close to our plants, and that they respond with high qualities and properties.

Tobacco is also a legal plant. I've been told that there are several states, and jurisdictions within states, where there are laws that might limit an individual's rights to grow tobacco without registering and paying taxes, and agreeing to grow only the permitted strains and species of tobacco. But in most cases nobody is going to know that you're growing tobacco unless you tell them, and even then there will probably be no local or state ordinances that apply. However, do your own checking and be sure that you're legal before growing.

The federal government not only has no laws against you growing your own tobacco for personal consumption, but USDA and other Federal agencies want to regulate the sale and distribution of tobacco, so if you decide to use the internet to sell you may be breaking some legal ground, either in the US or wherever you reside.

But as far as personal consumption is concerned, with your own personal tobacco, you grow it, you cure it, you flavor it, and you age it. You know what's going into your body, and you control potency. Nobody can raise prices on you and nobody's got hooks in your psyche.

You can grow tobacco plain and simple, or you can grow it fancy. You can grow it indoors, or you can grow it outdoors in a garden, or in pots. Indoors, you can grow it in pots, in beds, or hydroponically. You can grow it in Moosejaw as well as in Miami. A tobacco plant has simple, but specific needs. In the garden it needs good rock-free Ph neutral soil that is well-drained, rich but not heavy, light and airy, and warm. Tobacco also needs good strong light and fresh air, and a light but regular watering.

All these factors promote success in growing tobacco, and all are either free in nature, or easily established in an outdoor growing situation.

If you have no room inside or outdoors in a yard, and have no terrace or porch to grow plants on, it is a simple matter to raise a few tobacco plants indoors to about 6" high, and transplant them to a secluded location away from where you live. It's simple to prepare a fertile plug or two on some well-drained, little traveled land in the country, or in the back of a vacant lot in a city, and plant out your little plants at the appropriate time in June. Tobacco is not like Marijuana. It doesn't get ripped off early because you can't use it until it has ripened. Anyone stealing immature tobacco and smoking it will suffer a terrible justice.

Tobacco needs no fancy fertilizers or treatments, and it can be grown organically or not. It does have some pest problems in most of the country, but with only a few plants, these pests are easy to control by non-chemical means. If you're planting in an unprotected spot your plants are vulnerable to rabbits, deer and other browsing animals until it reaches 24" or so – the beginnings of resin production. And as mentioned earlier, unless you're growing in a high desert environment like New Mexico or parts of California or Oregon, you will probably have to deal with the Tobacco Hawk moth and other traditional predators like aphids/whiteflies even if you grow one of the potent strains of Native American Tobacco.

Tobacco is also vulnerable throughout its life cycle to frosts, to water collecting around its roots, to hail, heavy rain, and high winds.

A CAUTION TO HOME GROWERS

In its native, natural state tobacco can be among the most deadly plant on earth if ingested wrongly, whether accidentally or for lack of knowledge or respect. When working with a growing plant, use discretion. After touching the plant, wash your hands (not where you do dishes) with soap before touching your eyes or mouth. Lightweight cotton gloves, worn just for tobacco work, help a great deal in preventing accidental contact. Children and pets are vulnerable to contact with, or chewing on, tobacco plants grown in a home environment. This can seriously injure or kill a child, or pet. Tobacco plants should be grown in a secure area.

Finally, it's the collective experience of those involved with this book that natural tobacco is potentially harmful if overdone or abused or used by someone with other pre-existing health issues. My personal opinion is that nobody should smoke natural tobacco who isn't already smoking commercial tobacco products. Switch but don't start.

If you are currently using commercial cigarettes, cigars, chewing tobacco or snuff, natural tobacco is a less contaminated, more natural, but not necessarily less harmful alternative for you and those around you. Smoke is, in itself, full of potentially harmful substances whatever the origin of the smoke.

Starting Natural Tobacco Seed

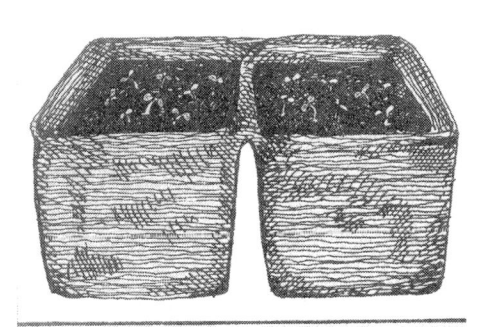

You will need several dozen small pots – I like the square peat pots that measure about 3" on a side, but any kind will do. Make a soil mixture of 75% good garden soil and 25% sand, along with a bit of coarse-ground pumice if you can find it in a local nursery. If you have access to a garden that has been well tended for a season or two, and the soil pH checks out to 6.5 – 7.0 you have a perfect soil for most of the native tobaccos.

Commercial potting soils are all right too as long as their pH is in this range. If you are digging up your soil and don't know the pH, almost any nursery will have a pH test kit available. If you are using a commercial potting soil, cut it with 25% clean sand a bit of coarse-ground pumice.

Fill a number of small pots with your soil mixture. Lightly water the soil in these pots, and sprinkle a few seeds evenly around the surface of each pot. Lightly pat the seeds into the soil, then sprinkle just a little more earth on top of the seeds--just barely enough to cover them. Pat this earth down, then lightly mulch the top of each pot with finely-cut straw. Only put a little mulch on – leave room for light to get through to the seeds.

Set the pots in a warm, sunny place where they will get at least 8 hours of direct sun every day. Be sure they don't cool down below 70°F. Mist the pots very lightly several times a day as needed to keep the surface just barely moist. Depending on how dry your environment is, you will need to deep-water the pots every day or two, enough to wet the soil in the pot, but don't let the soil become waterlogged. If you have your pots sitting in a tray or saucer be sure that water doesn't stand around the bottom of the pots.

If you are starting your seed under fluorescent grow-lights, the lights should be right down almost to the soil surface. If using other kinds of light, such as the HID systems discussed later, your light source will have to be further away to avoid heat damage to the delicate seedlings as they appear.

If you are going to plant your Tobacco out in a garden for the season, you should start your seedlings about 6 or 7 weeks before the date you plan to plant out. If you are growing your plants indoors in containers for their whole life, you can start them any time you want, since they will not be dependent on the natural seasons for their growth.

Within a few days to a couple of weeks, your Tobacco seedlings will appear. They will be extremely tiny, bright green, with delicate little twin leaves the size of a pinhead.

Caring For Seedlings

Different varieties of native tobacco seedlings each grow a bit differently at first, but all need the same sort of care. The surface of the soil in the pots should be kept barely moist.

Beginning with the second week of seedling growth, lightly water once a week with a water-soluble fertilizer – a 6-6-6 or a 12-12-12. If more than one watering a week is needed, use plain water the other times. If you want to go to just a little extra trouble, you can get superior results by soaking ½ oz. of alfalfa seed in a quart of room temperature water overnight, straining out the seeds, and using this soak-water on your seedlings instead of plain water.

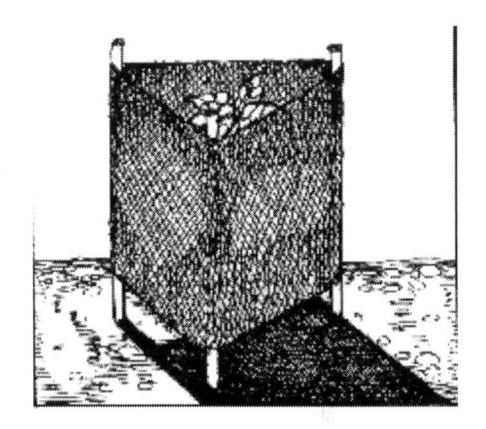

Tobacco plants are very sensitive to chlorine, so it's important to watch two things. First, if your tap water is chlorinated, at the very least fill a container and then set it aside overnight before using the water on your plants. This allows most of the chlorine to evaporate.

If you use a water softener system this makes your water very salty - don't use it on any plants unless you use Potassium Chloride rather than Sodium chloride for your softener! You must also be careful in your choice of fertilizers. Be sure that the brand you choose is low in chlorine. The principal source of chlorine in commercial fertilizers is muriate of potash as the potassium ingredient. Ask for a low-chlorine soluble fertilizer at a nursery if you are in doubt.

If you decide to set your seedlings out in the sun, you will need to rig a sunscreen for them, since intense, direct sun in the early stages of growth is harmful to Tobacco, though later in life it thrives on the sun and derives much of its potency and taste from intense solar radiation. A few layers of cheesecloth or a piece of plastic window screen will provide enough light shade to help your seedlings survive their first few weeks. As your seedlings appear, many will be growing close together.

Pull or thin the clusters of seedlings so that you are left with just 3-5 well separated seedlings per pot. Some kinds of tobacco will grow horizontally along the soil surface while developing their first few leaves, and then will begin growing erect. Go ahead and thin such crawlers or you'll have a tangled mess in a few days.

Rustica and the other desert-origin tobaccos begin growing vertically at once, so thinning is simple. As the seedlings develop more leaves, continue to thin the weakest-looking in each pot one at a time every few days until you have only one left per pot. This process should be completed by the third week after the plants first appear. This way you'll wind up with a good strong plant in each pot.

Planting In Containers

Even before planting your seeds, decide whether you want to grow your tobaccos outdoors or indoors. If you have decided to grow indoors you'll want to re-pot them when they are about 5" tall, with 4 to 6 leaves about the size of a dime and a healthy color. For each plant you intend to raise to maturity, you will need deep growing containers. We recommend ten gallon containers, minimum. You'll need one ten-gallon containers for each tobacco plant you'll be raising to maturity – the kind available almost everywhere nursery supplies are sold - made of soft plastic. Many nurseries give away used containers that work just fine when washed carefully first. You can also use plastic buckets – be sure to poke drain holes in the bottom.

While you are preparing your containers, if not earlier, think about where you are going to grow your Tobacco. A single mature tobacco plant will need at least 4 square feet of floor space and 6 feet of vertical space.

If you have the room to set your plants on a south-facing patio or terrace in the daytime, or in a south-facing window--so much the better. If you plan to move your plants from sun in the day to growlight at night, you'll probably want to set the heavy pots on roller platforms.

If you are depending on artificial light for part of the 16 hour day which produces the most excellent Tobacco, you'll need to consider locating your plants near an electric outlet, and near a source of fresh air.

Tobacco likes a warm, somewhat moist atmosphere, so if your indoor atmosphere is dry, consider a humidifier, steamer or vaporizer, or another means of adding moisture to the air.

To transplant the Tobacco seedlings you've been raising in little pots into their permanent home pot, simply tap the seedling plant out of its peat pot and set it into a hole in the soil of the large container. The soil in the home pot should have been thoroughly drenched with water 4 to 6 hours earlier. All that's left to do is to lightly water the seedling to settle it into its new home.

If you are pulling your transplants from a seedbed, gently wash off the soil surrounding the root ball, lower the washed roots into a prepared hole, and gently fill in around the roots, leaving a mound above the surface of the soil as shown in the cut-away (right). Then gently water the newly transplanted seedling, and the mound will settle to level with the surrounding soil as the water helps firm up the soil around the roots.

Lighting Indoor Tobacco Plants

The more sunlight your indoor plants can get, the better. If it's possible to give your plants direct sun, rather than sun through glass, your growing results will be that much better. However, even plants that get patio or terrace sun during the day will benefit from daylight extension indoors with any one of several indoor lighting systems.

The simplest, least expensive lighting option is a setup using 48" twin-bulb fluorescent fixtures with VHO plant bulbs, available nearly everywhere. A good minimal-investment set-up would include the fixture ($10-$15); the Grow-bulbs (@$15/2),and cord or chain to allow you to raise the fixture as the plants grow ($3-$5).

You will be able to raise 2-4 Tobacco plants to maturity under each 48" florescent fixture, but if you are interested in going to a higher light technology you will be able to raise up to 20 Tobacco plants per fixture. This higher technology is the High Intensity Discharge light system. Results obtained by friends using HID lamps on Tobacco and a wide range of indoor plants that have intense sunlight needs have convinced me that HID is the way to go. These systems come in 250, 400, 600 and 1000 watts – if you can afford it the 1000 watt system is ideal, although you can also get good results with the 600 watt system.

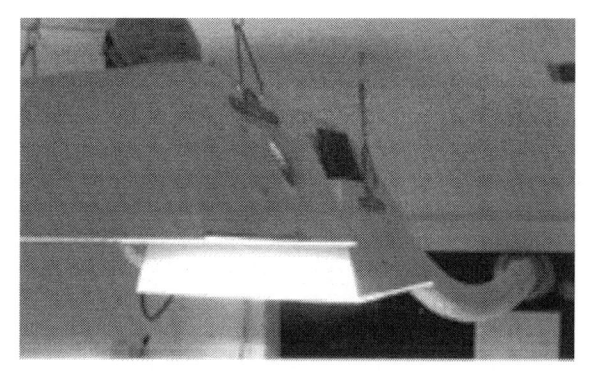

For HID lighting you will need at least 10-foot ceilings to avoid burning the top leaves of your plants, a sound electric wiring system in your house, some way to vent and/or utilize the heat the lights produce, and the ability to put out about $350 for a complete, ballasted system. For that, you get a light which is as close to sunlight as you'll get indoors, which effectively illuminates a growing area 12' x 12' with sun-like light, and which provides a halo growing area of another 6' on all sides where low-light plants such as culinary herbs, flowers and leafy vegetables thrive. The heat produced by a HID system can be a real bonus if it can be utilized to provide supplemental heat to a greenhouse or basement growing area; however, depending on your growing environment you may have to set up a venting fan on a timer to drain excess heat, which can injure your plants especially when they are young. Plan on venting every hour for 5-10 minutes if your growing space gets over 80° F.

Florescent systems don't produce enough heat for you to be concerned with burning the plants or with venting. Fluorescent light fixtures should hang 4 to 6" above the topmost part of the Tobacco plant, and should be raised as required to keep this distance. If you are raising two different Tobacco species under the same fixture--say, one Persica and one Rustica--you'll find that the difference in growth rate will require that you angle the light fixture, so hang it so that it can be tilted by raising one end or the other.

HID lights do not have to be raised during plant growth since the plants are growing toward the equivalent of the sun. You should install them high enough that the plants can grow toward the light without getting close enough to burn their tops. A good rule of thumb is that higher wattage lights should be at least four feet from where you expect the top of the plant to be. **Also, always place your ballasts somewhere where they won't ever have water accidentally spilled on them and where the heat they generate won't pose a danger.**

HID lamps are the best solution for most indoor growers. HID lamps come in 2 basic kinds: High Pressure Sodium (HPS) and Metal Halide (MH). Metal Halide is at the blue end of the light spectrum and is used for vegetative growth and the HPS is on the red end of the light spectrum and is used for the flowering period.

HPS lamps can be used to grow a crop from start to finish. Tests show that the HPS crop will mature 1 week later than a similar crop under MH, but it will be a bigger yield, so it's better to wait the extra week. Be sure to change your bulbs often since their light output diminishes over time. Normally most growers change their bulbs every 6-12 months.

HID system manufacturers give instructions of varying clarity for installation and operation of these powerful lights, so we recommend that you check with dealers in your area for ideas on your individual growing situation.

You should also be aware that people buying HID light systems frequently come to the attention of anti-drug police on the assumption that they are planning to grow Marijuana indoors. Be forewarned and please resist the temptation to grow anything illegal in your indoor tobacco growing space.

Preparing For Outdoor Planting

Unlike the complexity of indoor growing, a sunny location, protection from wind, a well-drained, light soil clean of rubbish, rocks, and other plant life; all are needed for ideal outdoor Tobacco growing conditions.

If you already have a garden. Consider giving your Tobacco the sunniest location, away from any tomato or potato plants, which harbor insects injurious to Tobacco because they are close relatives. If your soil is around pH 7.0 N. Rustica and Shirazi and many of the other heirloom varieties of tobacco will thrive.

Fortunately, this is the near-ideal for most gardening also. If your soil is too acid you can burn a pile of hardwood over the spots which are to become Tobacco beds, in the late fall, working the ash in either after burning or in the early spring. Fireplace ashes work great too – as long as you've been burning real logs and not the compressed sawdust variety.

If you have the opposite problem and your garden is a little too alkaline, you can correct most alkaline soil pH by working in compost at a rate of one pound per square yard. Ample applications of well-aged manure and/or compost can, over time, bind up much of the excess alkaline elements in organic processes – worm feeding, chelation, etc.

Either approach can shift the pH of a moderately sandy loamy soil between half a point and a full point on the scale in the course of a couple of months.

Transplanting Tobacco Seedling Outdoors

Let's assume that you want to grow five Tobacco plants to maturity. In that case you should start about ten little peat pots with a number of seeds each. You then thin the weaker seedlings as growth progresses so that by the time the seedlings reach 5" in height there should be only one seedling per pot. The reason you raise 10 seedlings for only 5 spaces is to assure selection – the same multiple applies to any number of individually-raised tobacco plants.

The best day to transplant from indoors to outdoors is an overcast moderately warm day after all chances of frost in your area have passed. Early in the day, take each of the little peat pots and carefully make deep scratches all over the outside of the pot. These scratches assure that once the peat pot is set in the permanent growing soil, whether garden, fertile plug, or indoor container, it will break up easily and allow the Tobacco roots to work their way out into the soil without interference. Next peel off the bottom of each peat pot, leaving the sides intact.

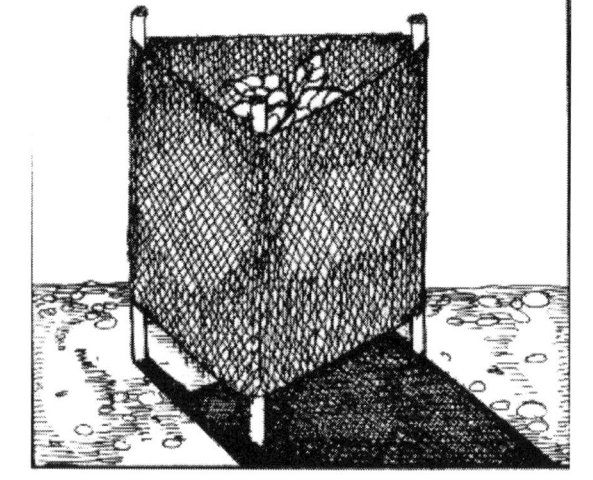

Scoop a hole in the soil the size of the peat pot, and set the Tobacco plant into the hole. Water with a root stimulating transplant solution, and set up a sunscreen. A simple sunscreen can be easily made by sticking 3 sticks in the ground in a triangular pattern around each plant, with each stick about 6" away from the plant. The sticks must be firmly planted in the ground, and should stick up about 12" above the ground. You then wrap a single layer of cheesecloth once around the outside of the sticks, and pin the cheesecloth in place with safety pins. This little triangle enclosure with an open space at the top is an ideal sunscreen and provides good bug protection as well, lasting several weeks into the plant's growth before it becomes unnecessary.

Even if you have only room for 3-5 mature plants, you should nevertheless set out several plants for each one you intend to raise to maturity. Transplant them into little groups of two or three plants where one will ultimately grow, and over the next couple of weeks cut down (don't pull – cut) all but the strongest from each growing area. This way you are assured not only of successful transplants, but also of thriving plants into maturity.

Fertilizing Your Tobacco Plants

Tobacco growing in even the most fertile garden soil needs a feeding every ten days of regular 12-12-12 or 20-20-20 fertilizer. In addition, tobacco needs a steady feeding of trace elements, so whatever approach you prefer, such as leaf-feeding with a trace element solution or side dressing your plants with an enriched compost, go ahead and give them a trace element feast every couple of weeks.

Tobacco growing in containers will benefit from either of the above fertilizer formulas, although in diluted form compared with the concentrations used for outdoor gardens, with every watering. Most nursery-style fertilizers give directions for use of the solution with potted plants and outdoor plants. (In Section Two you'll find extensive information on fertilizing methods used by the early 'master growers' who used primarily natural fertilizers from their farms, and who practiced the 'green manure' techniques of planting and plowing under a nutrient-rich crop like clover.)

Native natural tobaccos exert a tremendous drain on the soil as they go through their vegetative growth stage, so it's necessary to be vigilant in your fertilizing and watering routines. Depending upon your local environment and climate, you may have to water and fertilize much more or less than suggested.

Watering Your Tobacco Plants

You'll be concerned with two kinds of water needs of Tobacco. First, even in ideal Tobacco-growing weather-intense sun, some humidity, warm nights--your plants will need misting with a spray bottle of room-temperature water. Outdoor plants can be watered with a hose set on fine spray; indoor plants with a hand sprayer. In hot, dry weather, or in a hot, dry indoor environment, Tobacco may need misting or spraying several times a day. In rare mellow environments, once a day or less will do fine, just to wash off air pollution. This is important, because Tobacco is sensitive to airborne pollutants.

The second kind of water need is of course in the soil. Your Tobacco plants outdoors should be lightly mulched, and should be deep-watered as often as necessary to keep the top layers of the soil from drying out. Use an organic mulch like shredded cypress, cedar or poplar wood & bark, or use finely shredded straw. Tobacco should never be allowed to go to the wilt point, nor should the soil be waterlogged. In hot, dry areas you will need to water once or twice a day during the plant's growth and maturity. In mild, somewhat humid areas with intense sun, you may need to water only every three days. The soil condition you're looking for to indicate need for water is almost but not quite dry on top, and just moist when you probe 6" to the side of the plant with your finger as deep as it will go into the soil.

If you are growing your Tobacco in containers, in all but the driest environments the plant should be happy with 1/2 gallon of water/nutrient every 5 to 7 days for the first 4 to 6 weeks. The water requirements will increase radically as the plant gets well beyond 2-1/2' in height, and it can demand a gallon or more every day in its mature stage if the lighting is intense, the climate very dry, or if other factors require that the plant transpire large amounts of water.

When container-growing indoors, be sure to mulch the surface of each pot with a 1/2" fine-cut straw mulch to prevent the soil surface from drying out.

Dealing Naturally With Bugs

When you're only growing a few Tobacco plants you don't have the worries of a large-scale grower, and in most parts of the country your bug problems will be easy to handle. Even if you're in an area where the Tobacco Hawk moth lives, you'll be easily able to control its Hornworm offspring by walking your rows of plants and simply picking off these worms while they are still small and unable to cause damage. In Section Two you'll be able to browse the many creative methods for dealing with the Hornworm devised by the 'master growers' of earlier times. The hornworm is an expert at disguise and blends in almost perfectly with the color of the leaf, so look sharp! Old time growers relied on turkeys and even small children to go after hornworms but if the only turkeys around are people you know and if your small children are into video games rather than physical labor, you'll have to be the hornworm patrol yourself.

Another approach that's proven very successful is to use BT (bacillis Thuringesis), a bacteria that you can buy at almost any nursery or plant store. Simply mix it with water following the instructions and spray it on your plants – especially the undersides of the leaves. You will have to re-apply it after every rain during hornworm season. It doesn't affect smoking quality because it will be washed off in the fall rains after hornworm season has ended.

If you find a hornworm covered by little white fuzzy cocoons HARVEST THAT WORM! Place him in a jar with small holes in the lid and let those little cocoons hatch. They are a parasitic wasp that loves to eat hornworms, so as soon as the little critters have hatched release them into your tobacco garden at dusk and they will be an immense help in controlling Mr. Worm.

After you've harvested your first crop of tobacco you can set some aside to make a nicotine solution that is a very effective insect control agent. But until you have your own pesticide-free tobacco to make your bug spray with, I recommend that you buy a package of American Spirit organic tobacco and use about ¼ cup at a time to make yourself some nicotine bug tea. By the way, DO NOT be tempted to try this 'tea' yourself. It can make you very sick or even dead. ¼ cup of tobacco in a quart of water in a jar, set out in the sun for a couple of days, will make a very effective bug spray (after you filter out the cigarette residue).

Less toxic but almost as effective a bug spray can be made by blending 1/2 cup of fresh hot chili peppers and several peeled cloves of garlic in a quart of water by running the mix in a blender at high speed. After a thorough blending strain the mixture through multiple layers of fine cheesecloth and, using a large-aperture spray nozzle, spray down your tobacco plants whenever you see bugs causing a problem. Every part of the country has organic gardening groups and even if you're not a member a few telephone calls will provide you with a range of organic bug spray solutions that work in your area.

If you are growing in an outdoor garden, you may also want to interplant your tobacco with any of the aromatic insect-repelling herbs like basil or rosemary, and also create a border around your tobacco with insect repellent flowers like certain kinds of marigolds or sunflowers.

Deficiency Signs In Tobacco

Tobacco is an exhausting plant, demanding much from the soil, reaching perfection as a smoke or a snuff only when it has been properly fed throughout its life. If you are following the suggestions in this report for preparing and fertilizing your soil, whether indoors or out, you are extremely unlikely to experience nutrient or mineral deficiencies in your plants. However, there are situations and processes that can act to deprive your tobacco of an essential growth element. If your plants are deprived of any major or trace nutrient, they will develop characteristic symptoms. One caution: many of these deficiency signs can be caused by things other than actual deficiency, things such as abnormal soil pH, poor drainage, and over-watering. Don't, however, take this to mean that you should underwater. Tobacco plants are 80-90% water depending on the species, and the amount of water they receive radically effects leaf development, development of flavor and aroma, nicotine content, and other important qualities.

The deficiency signs of tobacco may be divided into several major groups of symptoms according to the parts of the plant on which they show.

Effects Show on Lower Leaves Only
Potassium Deficiency: Lower leaves mottled with dead spots at the tips and margins, which are curled under; in extreme cases the stalk is very thin and may show dead spots; in mature plants, an acute potassium deficiency may show first in the top leaves.

Magnesium Deficiency: The lower leaves will yellow without spotting, and their tips and margins will turn or curl upward; in extreme deficiencies the stalk will be very thin.

Effects Show on the Entire Plant
Nitrogen Deficiency: The plant turns light green. Lower leaves yellow, and dry to a light brown. If nitrogen deficiency develops in late life, growth ceases and the stalk is weak and thin.

Phosphorous Deficiency: The plant is dark green, and the lower leaves may turn yellow, then greenish-brown to black. The stalk will remain short and slender at maturity if the deficiency is felt at that time.

Effects Show on New Bud Leaves

Calcium Deficiency: The young leaves of the terminal bud hook up, then die back at the tips and margins so that later growth of new leaves appear cut-out at the tips and along the edges, and the stalk finally dies at the growing tip.

Boron Deficiency: The young leaves of the terminal bud turn light green at their base, and the stalk at the base of the young leaves withers. If leaf continues growing it is twisted. The terminal bud finally dies.

Manganese Deficiency: The young leaves turn markedly yellow, and dead spots appear. The smallest veins in the small leaves remain green, and the stalk remains thin and weak.

Sulphur Deficiency: The young leaves turn light green, but no dead spots appear. The veins turn a lighter green than the tissue between the veins, and the stalk is short and slender.

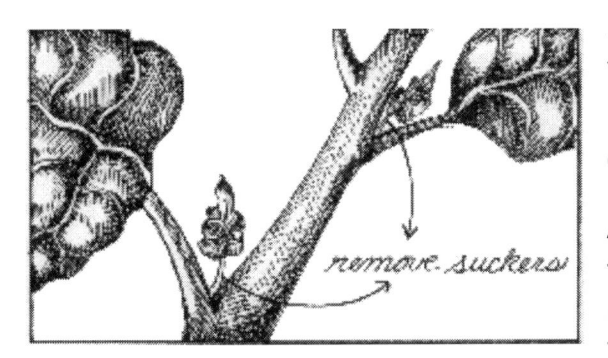

Suckering Natural Tobacco Plants

You'll read much more about this vital process in Section Two. For now, a brief explanation of what suckering is and why it's so important.

As your Tobacco plant grows it will produce two kinds of leaves. The first kind will be a large leaf that springs forth from the stalk. The second kind, called a sucker leaf, soon springs from the point where the main leafs' stem joins the main stalk.

All varieties of tobacco will keep trying to develop these suckers throughout their life, and each time the plant tries to put forth a sucker at any junction, that new growth must be cut away with a sharp blade. If you wish, the new sucker can simply be snapped off, but a clean sharp blade is vastly preferable.

Here is a close-up view of the developing sucker bud. Looks innocent, doesn't it? These little buds can put on 4-6" in a day and in doing so they will suck vital nutrients out of the plants largest leaves – the ones you are hoping to harvest and turn into most excellent smoke. From the plant's point of view this is a natural process – it is renewing itself, making more stalks from which to put forth seed heads, and the older leaves (quite properly) are merely nutrient storage vessels for these young shoots. But you must be vigilant, and merciless, or as the plant does its thing, it will undo yours in short order.

Topping Natural Tobacco Plants

As your plants grow and you keep removing the suckers, forcing growth into the main leaves and the unfolding bud at the top, keep an eye on that bud. At some point right around 3-1/2 to 4' of height, instead of unfolding new sets of leaves it is going to try to send up a cluster of flower buds on a rapidly-developing spike. As soon as you can reach the stalk underneath the flower cluster with a knife blade, remove the flowering top with a clean cut. This will end the plant's upward growth, and will force all the remaining growth and maturation energies into the main leaves. It's called topping, and it is vital to producing excellent leaf. Again, you'll read much more about Topping in Section Two, but for now let me just stress that it is one more area where you must stay on top of the exuberant growth of these remarkable plants. But be careful, because with the removal of the flowering top the plant will double its efforts to put out sucker leaves which, if you let them develop, would turn into great flowering spikes, completing the plant's development sequence.

Which Leaves For Which Purpose

In conventional tobaccos grown for cigar, pipe and specialty smoking mixtures, potency and aroma are concentrated more at the top of the plant than at the bottom, with the leaves on the top quarter of the plant the most potent in flavor and aroma while the leaves at mid-plant are often the most workable. Individual and family growers of high quality cigar tobaccos like N. Rapanda or Connecticut Broadleaf – an N. Tabacum variant- hand-pick individual leaves as they reach ripeness according to their intended use. Most people growing Rustica and the other native natural tobaccos like N. Shirazi will use the same process hand-selecting individual leaves for picking the moment they reach the right stage of maturity. Beginning near the bottom of the plant, as a leaf begins to show signs of yellowing it is picked and laid out on either newspaper or a screen to continue ripening and drying. This process is traditionally called Priming, and will be covered in greater detail in Section Two, for there are as many opinions about Priming as there are tobacco growers.

Basically, as the ripening process proceeds from the lower leaves upwards on the plant, first the lower, then the middle and then the top leaves are harvested. The top leaves can be extremely potent, so great care should be taken in smoking them. At a minimum they should be washed in a rum & water solution before final drying as described in the next section on curing.

This advice will vary depending upon the tobacco you're growing. Shrazi top leaves, for example, make excellent pipe and cigarette Tobacco as well as snuff, since they are not nearly as potent as Rustica. The top leaves of Rustica may simply be too toxic for smoking even after a good washing with rum and water. The leaves on the middle half of just about any kind of Tobacco plant make good smoking Tobacco or snuff, and take on flavors particularly well. They are also much larger than the top leaves, and cure much more slowly. The bottom leaves or plants from the garden are often beaten about by weather and holed by insects, and may or may not be worth curing and processing.

Harvesting And Curing Natural Tobacco

Harvest on a commercial Tobacco farm is a time of weather paranoia, churning adrenaline, and buckets of sweat. For the individual cultivator with a few carefully tended plants, the harvest is a leisurely, rewarding process.

Naturally-raised heirloom tobaccos will actually do most of the drying and curing work for you if you let them. You can simply let the leaves cure on the plant, harvesting them when they are dry and leathery. Since the process of yellowing begins on the lower leaves, these will also be the first ones to dry completely on the plant. Leaves cured on the plant tend to be much more harsh than leaves cured off the plant – but it is a lot easier.

In New Mexico my N. Rustica plants grew at an almost visible rate, with the Rustica reaching 6' and sending up flowering spikes within 8 weeks, and the Attenuata and Shirazi not far behind. These plants were started in a cold frame and set out at three weeks maturity just after last frost – in the high desert about June 15. By the middle of September many of the plants, both those I had kept topped and those I let run were beginning to develop the yellowing process on the lower leaves that signals the time to pick.

Nicotiana Rustica will grow to six feet tall in about 10-12 weeks if left untopped, (see left) or to four feet tall in the same time if you remove the flowering spike when it appears, and you will begin to see pickable leaves at about 12 weeks. Both Persica/Shirazi and Attenuata are smaller plants than Rustica but respond vigorously to a favorable growing environment and matures in 10-12 weeks so depending on growing conditions you'll see yellow/brown leaves at 12 weeks too. Burley and the other commercial cigarette/cigar tobaccos vary in height from 6' for Burley to well over 8' for some cigar tobaccos like N. Rapanda. These tobaccos tend to need 16-18 weeks to mature and develop the characteristic yellowish-brown spots appearing on the lowest leaves first, gradually enlarging and turning reddish-brown.

For several weeks before the spots begin to appear, the leaves on your plants will begin to show signs of maturity. These signs will be particularly obvious in plants which you have topped. The leaves will thicken. The principal and secondary leaf veins will become prominent. The edges of the leaf will begin to curl under, and the tip of the leaf can be broken if it is bent double. This is a time of great water need, and heavy nutrient draw on the soil.

The lowest leaves, first to develop spots, are also the first to be harvested. The process of picking leaf for drying and curing begins as soon as spotting is well-progressed on that leaf.

Priming And Air-Curing Natural Tobacco

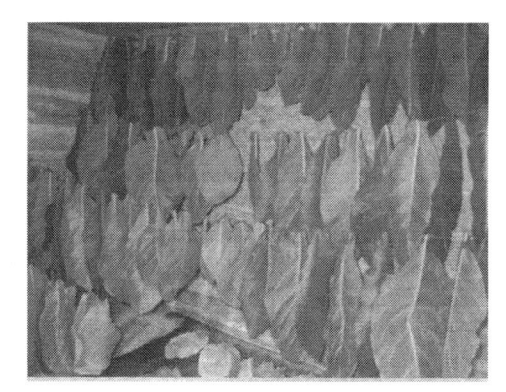

The best way to harvest a personal crop of natural tobacco is one leaf at a time, beginning with the lowest leaves on individual plants - a process called priming. It derives from the idea of picking each leaf in its prime. Tradition holds that it's best to begin priming as the harvest moon goes on the wane, and to pick only after the dew is off the plant.

The process of curing tobacco leaves entails keeping the individual leaves alive, breathing and slowly metabolizing their stored starches and enzymes. That's why it's important for leaves to be hung so that each one can get circulating air.

After you have primed the leaf from a plant, take it into a shady or semi-dark environment with a temperature near 75°F. String a simple cotton clothesline across the closet, basement, or wherever you will be hanging leaves to dry, and then attach the individual leaves to the clothesline with wooden clothespins, or tie them on with cotton twine. At the right is the traditional method of hanging tobacco on poles for barn-curing. More simply, you can thread them through the stems with a needle and some fishing line and hang them up.

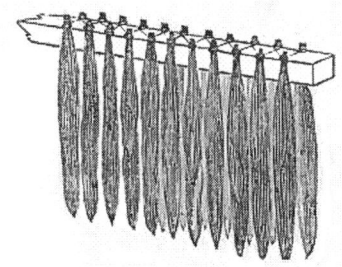

If your area goes through a spell of wet, cool weather during the curing process, which will take anywhere from five days to three weeks, depending on environmental conditions, when the leaf was picked, and other factors, be sure to add heat to the curing environment with a floor electric heater to keep the temperature up and the air unsaturated.

It's a good idea to have a circulating fan in your curing room, and since you don't want a build-up of moisture that could lead to mold you may want to vent your curing room as well. If you are bringing in outside air you should probably have a filter in the system that is capable of catching mold spores. And finally, some people have written to me to say that having a negative ion generator in both their growing room and their curing room has helped to create more vigorous growth, faster and better curing, and tastier leaf.

Your Tobacco leaves will be fully cured when they have turned a full golden yellow to golden brown, have turned crisp with curled edges, and give off a mild, hay-like odor. At this point, you have the option of flavoring your Tobacco before proceeding to make smoke or snuff, or of working with pure, natural Tobacco. It's fun to try both kinds of Tobacco experience.

Flavoring Naturally- Cured Tobacco
You've successfully cultivated and cured several plants, you now have a couple of clotheslines full of various-size, golden brown leaves which rustle when you touch them. So let's say that you want to divide your crop into a number of different batches and experiment with different flavors and aromas for smoking Tobacco and for snuff.

While just about every substance imaginable has been and is being used to flavor Tobacco, there are several basic flavors that work extremely well with both Rustica and the other desert tobaccos and with Burley and the commercial cigarette tobaccos.

Burley and the commercial varieties are generally light and mild, making good smoking Tobacco and a pleasant snuff. They take on flowery essences particularly well. The heavier flavors, such as Rum and Molasses, take Burley and the cigarette tobaccos over, but the mints, flowers and fruit essences work well.

Rustica and the other desert varieties are very potent and make wonderful snuff and very strong smoke. They do well with rum, vanilla, licorice and other heavy flavors. They also work very well as a snuff with mints, fruits and flowers. However, the lighter the scent, the more likely the desert tobaccos are to take over.

The method of applying flavors and aromas to your Tobacco is quite simple. Simply take a spray bottle that produces a fine mist, fill it with the solution, and mist the fully-cured leaf lightly. Then wait a day until the leaf is again fully dry, and mist lightly again. Before each spraying rotate the leaves in your little piles – inside leaves move to the outside, outside leaves to the center, etc. Continue this treatment as long as you like; the more you spray, the heavier the concentration.

Making The Flavor Essences

Two of the best Tobacco flavors are simply sprayed on full strength. You can do this with hard cider, and strong, black rum. Some folks enjoy adding a couple of teaspoons of sugar to each cup of rum or cider. This does sweeten the leaf and aid in penetration of the flavor, but it also produces a very dirty smoke and an irritating snuff. Molasses also produces a dirty smoke, but for some folks a molasses and rum Tobacco is all there is or needs to be. A cup of molasses to a quart of water is about the right strength for flavoring.

To extract herbal flavorings for Tobacco, you'll need a double-boiler, and either an electric plate or stovetop. **It's important to use only electric heat – never gas - because alcohol produces explosive fumes when heated and a gas flame will ignite these fumes while an electric element will not.**

Simply simmer the indicated amounts of the following herbs and spices in one cup of alcohol in your double-boiler for the time shown, then filter out the herb or spice, and you'll have a very nice extract. You may want to play around with the amount of herb you use, or the time you heat it, or with combinations of herbs in one extract, or with the use of sugar or honey to sweeten the leaf.

Caraway seed:	Lightly crush 1 teaspoon seed, simmer 20 minutes.
Chamomile:	1/4 cup bruised flowers, simmer 20 minutes.
Clove:	4 lightly crushed cloves, simmer 20 minutes.
Geranium:	1/2 cup fresh flowers, simmer 10 minutes.
Juniper:	4 to 6 whole berries, simmer 30 minutes.
Lemon:	Peel of 1/2 organic lemon, bruised, simmer 30 minutes.
Mints:	Any fresh mint, 1/4 cup leaves (and flowers too!), simmer @ r 20 minutes.
Orange:	Peel of 1/4 organic orange, bruised, simmer 30 minutes.
Pennyroyal:	1/4 cup fresh flowers, bruised, simmer 10 minutes.
Sassafras:	1 Tablespoon dried herb (available in many gourmet shops as "File" for making Gumbo), simmer 20 minutes.
Vanilla:	1 Vanilla Bean (Mexican if possible), simmer 45 minutes.

In addition to these extracts, which work well on either smoking Tobacco or Snuff, whichever you prefer, there are a great many herbal possibilities in any garden or, for that matter, on any walk through open country. Almost any plant flower, leaf, root, or seed can be extracted using alcohol and a double boiler. At the end of section two you'll find several downloadable books by old-time tobacconists who were considered the best in their day at flavoring the classic tobaccos – especially the mythical Cuban cigar tobaccos. Of course, some of the ingredients they used were so toxic that nobody in their right mind would use them today, but if you're interested in flavoring your tobacco leaves I'm sure you'll find lots to play with in these books.

As for the type of alcohol to use, we've worked with Brandy (mixed half and half with vodka), Vodka, Rum, High Proof Rum, and Grain Alcohol. I think that high proof rum is the best base when the Rum Flavor is desirable, and that Grain Alcohol is the most effective extract, but that it should be cut to half strength with distilled water before use.

You can also extract almost any herb in cold alcohol. Simply increase the ratio of herb to alcohol about 25% over the hot extract ratio, put the herb in a jar with a sealable lid, sprinkle a little pure Vitamin C over the herb, add the alcohol and seal the jar. If the jar is dark glass, so much the better. Just a pinch of pure Vitamin C will preserve the color of the extract. Without "C" it usually turns a muddy brown-green color. Pure Vitamin C means not to crush a pill and use it--try a pharmacy or health food shop for pure C crystals.

Home-Grown Smoke

Natural tobacco smoking requires a different technique. For those accustomed to cigarette smoking, a long, deep inhalation of natural tobacco is an invitation to purple-face disaster. For those accustomed to a pipe, with a slow, fairly shallow draw, natural tobacco smoking will be a familiar sort of experience. Cigar smokers, too--those that don't inhale--will find a mouthful of natural tobacco which has been well-cured no more difficult a smoke than a strong cigar.

It's tempting to say that natural tobacco is only for tough smokers, because it's true that the smoke of improperly cured, or hastily flavored, or poorly raised tobacco can be harsh on tongue, throat and lungs. If a person follows the simple steps outlined in this book for growing, curing and preparing homegrown tobacco, the resulting smoke will be smooth and powerful. In Section Two you'll find that there are as many curing and flavoring techniques as there are traditional Tobacco growers, as well as links to their original books that you can download and browse at your leisure.

But even well-cured natural tobacco will not be like the tobacco products most of us are used to. Natural tobacco smoke assaults your body with its heat, its alkaloids, and its power. Within seconds you can feel the effects in your head, and it's entirely possible, at first, that you will feel it in your stomach.

It's best to go slowly with natural tobacco, and to consider mixing it with smoother, more familiar smoking herb, to get used to the dynamic effects and wholly different hit it gives. It's also not an herb to be using while driving or performing other dangerous tasks, at least until you get used to the effects of natural tobacco.

Making Rolling Tobacco

First take several well-cured leaves, and seat yourself at a comfortable working area. Working with a sharp blade--we've found that single-edge razor blades work well - cut out the mid-rib of each leaf. If the leaves you're working with have not been previously moistened with a flavoring spray, they are going to be stiff and brittle, and will require that you mist them several times over the course of a day or two before you can begin cutting.

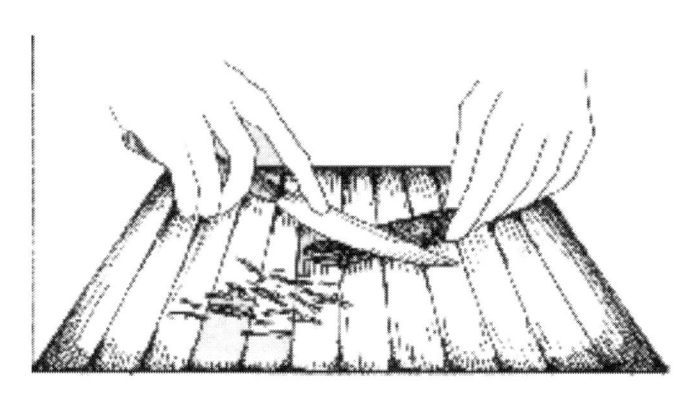

First, split each leaf along the fibrous mid-rib, and then remove both halves of the vein. Next, split each of the secondary veins, or ribs, and remove both halves of each of them. You'll be left with a little pile of beautiful golden wedges of deveined tobacco leaf.

Take a small stack of wedges and roll them into a compact tube, and holding the tube firm with the fingers of one hand, shave off a little pile of tobacco curls from the end. As you can see (left) some growers use scissors. If you use a sharp blade you can control the thickness of the curls that you shave off this roll of tobacco leaf and wind up with a perfect thickness for either rolling into cigarettes (shavings on the thin side) or for pipe tobacco (shavings somewhat thicker.)

Some people advocate using a food processor but I'm not that good at controlling the cut with this machine and generally wind up with a pile of tiny flakes. If you want to use a cutting machine, there are several types of tobacco cutting machines available on the internet.

Two familiar brands are the Teck 1 and the Cuthof Shredder, both of which work best with a compressed brick of tobacco rather than a rolled tube. If you are making smoking tobacco primarily for yourself the handheld methods works just fine; if you are going into business you might want to invest in a professional small-scale machine.

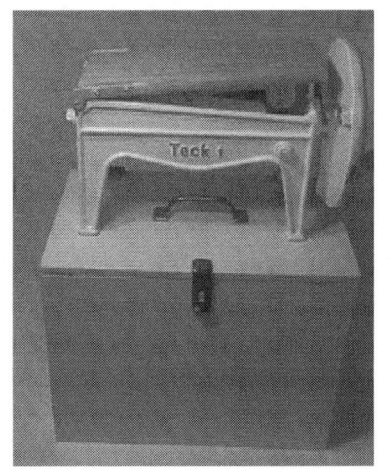

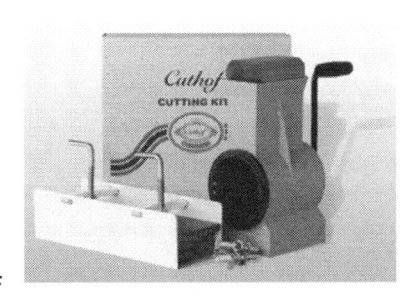

Now, if you want a more flavorful rolling smoke, flavor the cured leaf by misting it with extract for several weeks before cutting it up. But in wetting a flavored leaf, you'll notice several things.

The flavored and aired leaf is more flexible than the unflavored, natural, air-cured leaf. When you're cutting a flavored leaf with a knife, it's easier to remove the ribs, but harder to chop it finely.

Now, let's say that you've been priming your plant for a couple of weeks, and you take one of the first- cured leaves and prepare it for smoking. But on the first puff you discover that the smoke is terribly harsh and hot. It can happen with natural tobacco, which is not the domesticated, uniform plant of commerce but the wild, dark magical herb of ten thousand years of Indian experience. You'll find a lot of variation between tobacco plants that you believe you've raised in the same way. That's because tobacco is highly mobile in a genetic sense, and responds individually to soil, climate and culture conditions.

If you find that the first leaf or two off a plant are too harsh, the easiest approach I've found to reduce harshness is to soak the other, cured leaves for 24 hours in strong red wine--any of the bulk process red wines does the job, although the traditional European cure for harshness calls for strong red wine. Some people like to add sugar to the wine, but my experience is that this makes hot smoke. After soaking the leaves, allow them to air-dry in a well-ventilated, semi-dark environment, then proceed to prepare them for rolling tobacco by shaving and chopping them until they are very fine. Or, you can use a food processor quite easily on wine-soaked tobacco after it has dried almost completely.

Another traditional approach to reducing the harshness of tobacco and mellowing out the smoke is, essentially, composting, the leaves not quite to the point of disintegration, aiding the process by pressure and heavy, usually sugary soakings. The simplest fermenting method is one of the oldest - simply fine-chop a quantity of your already air-cured tobacco, soak it in a rum and molasses solution or simply spray some on the chopped tobacco, and roll the tobacco inside a plastic bag. Poke a dozen or so air-holes in the bag, put it somewhere that's not in direct sunlight for a few days. Every couple of days open up the bag, stir the tobacco around, and re-roll. The key to success in this process is to control any mold that begins to show by immediately airing and drying out the tobacco before re-rolling it. Continue opening the bag, stirring the tobacco around, and re-rolling it every couple of days for a week or two. Then the tobacco out and air-dry it on a screen in a shady area, then proceed with whatever preparation you care to use. The slow fermentation processes in the tightly rolled, moist, warm tobacco will have reduced the harshness of the smoke and the nicotine levels significantly.

Making Pipe Tobacco

Here is an area where you can really let your imagination soar. There is no single best cut for pipe tobacco, no best flavor or aroma, no best combination or leaf. You can do what you want to make pipe tobacco. Here, generally, is how to proceed.

Using either flavored, air-cured leaf or natural, air-cured leaf: If you're not using flavored leaf, you'll have to mist it with water until some flexibility can be restored.

Carefully remove the central and side ribs with a sharp blade, and then secure a cutting board and long, thick-bladed, very sharp knife. Compress the leaf tissue into as solid a mass as possible--we found making a roll, or twist, works well.

With the point of the knife held down on the board, operating the knife handle up and down, carefully shave off very fine little curlicues, or shavings of tobacco from the side, or end of the little compact mass you have. We find it easy to hold the tobacco twist with the thumb, index and middle fingers, and feed it into the knife by pushing with all three fingers.

After you have a pile of little tobacco curls, using the same large-bladed knife, cut across the pile several times, but don't chop up the curls so much that they become little tiny pieces. If most of them wind up about 1/4" long, you're just about right on.

Place your little pile of chopped shavings in an airtight container--along with any sort of flavoring device you might like, such as a citrus peel, or some raisins soaked in rum, or a brandied vanilla bean--and you'll have a fine supply of pipe tobacco to enjoy and share.

Making Natural Tobacco Snuff

Snuffing and smoking are equally ancient forms of tobacco use. While early explorers were struck first by the amazing New World practice of smoking, it didn't take them long to notice, with equal interest, that the Caribs and Mayas with whom they first came in contact also made a practice of vigorously inhaling little piles of brown dust through elaborately carved bird bones. And, as with smoking, the art of snuffing was soon being practiced and mastered, first by the explorers in the New World, and soon by the entire home continent of Europe.

The Indians made snuff without great elaboration. Most often, the cured leaf of tobacco was simply ground to a powder, perhaps with the addition of one or two other powdered psychoactive herbs or mushrooms, and taken in natural form. As the popularity of snuff grew in Europe, manufacturers competed with each other to produce ever-different varieties for the market; and, of course, manufacturers also worked hard at increasing their profit by adding cheap adulterants to snuff, many of which were toxic and even lethal. Snuff was not even remotely a sacred experience for Europeans; it was a worldly pleasure, and a source of profit, exclusively.

Thus, the European tradition of snuff-making is a complex history of use of perfumes, oils, flavoring ingredients, dyes and coloring agents, powders and extenders, and all other sorts of snuff stuff which has nothing at all to do with the authentic experience of natural tobacco.

There are today several hundred commercial varieties of snuff. None of them that we've tried are even close to natural snuff in potency or pleasure. In fact, very few people who use snuff today do so by taking a nose-hit; most snuff is dipped--that is, a pinch of it is placed between cheek and gum, and used very much like chewing tobacco, without the chew. What a pity. Of course, it makes sense that few people would find pleasure in tooting commercial snuff, which even today is filled with as much crap, and as little valuable tobacco as possible.

Adulteration aside for a moment, another reason that snorting has gone out of style is that it's often difficult to come up with a clean sneeze, and nobody likes to wind up with nose twinkle on the shirtfront as the result of a ferocious aachoo! It's ironic that the potentially unsanitary aspects of snuffing have obscured its psychedelic properties.

As the ancients observed, there is in every sneeze, at the instant before the explosion of breath, a momentary release from consciousness, a small window in time. This is the source of the blessing we automatically bestow on every sneezing soul, a relic from the days when early European churchmen observed this lapse in world-centeredness, and feared that it provided a pathway by which the devil might enter. This was also the fear that the church had with regard to orgasm--that moment when the world dissolves and our mind floats free was considered a fearfully open door for the devil.

Daring the devil was, and is, an extremely popular sport, and no matter that the pious did, and do their best, much of mankind will still open their minds to realms beyond this world, apparently not terribly fearful of the consequences dolefully predicted by the churches.

With this brief background in mind, let's now go into the making of natural snuff. While there are hundreds if not thousands of different approaches to snuff making, there are really only eight kinds of snuff. There is coarse and fine snuff, dry and moist snuff, dark and light, and scented or plain snuff. Here's how to go about making tobacco into the basis for each of these kinds, which originate from a single process.

Step 1: Take one or more fully cured tobacco leaves. Remove the veins as described elsewhere, after moistening the leaves with a plain or scented spray to restore flexibility.

Step 2: Arrange the leaf parts in an even pile, and then apply pressure to them. This can be done by putting a board on top of the pile and weighing it down with a heavy rock, a pile of magazines or books, or however you choose to do it. You can also build a press quite easily with two boards that fit top & bottom into a pressing box, and four C-clamps or fit the assembly into a bench vise and tighten as much as possible..

Step 3: After three days, remove the pressure and take out the compressed leaf, break it up, moisten with a light water spray or with a scented spray, and reapply the pressure.

Step 4: Repeat the previous step every 3 days for two weeks.

Step 5:   After the two weeks, you are ready to hand-process your tobacco for either smoking or snuff.

Step 6   If you are making smoking tobacco, hold the 'brick' firmly and proceed to slice the leaf into small strands by shaving off the end of the brick with a very sharp knife..

Step 7:   If you are making snuff, break apart the 'brick' and lay the pierces out on an absorbent paper in a cool, dry place until the tobacco is dry to the touch. Now it's time to grind it into a very fine powder. There are several methods that can be used. Several folks have found that if they make a mortar out of a block of aromatic wood, an extremely pleasant aroma is imparted to the snuff as it is ground. I can recommend several types of wood for this purpose. Rosewood is an excellent, hard wood, as is walnut, hickory, or olive. To make a mortar, simply take a small block of wood, maybe 4"x4"x2" thick, and hollow out a space in the center of the block 3/4 to 1" deep. This cup should be sanded very smooth to provide a uniform grinding surface. I don't recommend treating the wood in any way, simply sanding until a glass-like polish is achieved.

If, in the beginning, you don't want to go to the trouble of making your own mortar, go ahead and buy one if your kitchen isn't already equipped. Use a smooth mortar, like one of glass or ceramic, rather than a rough one, such as those made of pumice stone for Mexican cooking – called a molcahete.

Step 8: When your tobacco is fully reduced to a fine powder, you have pure, unadulterated natural snuff. No soot, no sawdust, no ground tobacco stalk, no ash, no heavy metal oxides, no arsenic--none of the past or present additives to commercial snuff.

One of the main problems of commercial snuff is that it comes in compressed little cakes, and if you want to snort a line you have to go through a process of shaving and grinding to reduce the snuff to powder. The manufacturers pack the stuff in blocks, but as a home producer of fine tobacco toot, there's no need for you to add this complication. Simply store your fine powdered snuff in an airtight, moisture-proof container, and dip out small amounts as you want them. If you're going out for a while, even a small container will handle more than enough for an evening's social supply.

If the aroma of your powdered snuff doesn't quite suit you, or if you want to add some additional savory smells after you've already ground the tobacco, it's a simple matter to spread the snuff out on some absorbent paper (like brown grocery store bags) and mist it lightly with the desired extract. Be sure to stir the snuff thoroughly as you spray to get even distribution of the essence. After the snuff has thoroughly dried, run the whole batch through a food processor, or a flour sifter if a processor isn't available, and store again in the tight container.

An Online Forum of Tobacco Growers

As I mentioned earlier, tobacco growers are a lot like bakers in that a hundred growers will have a hundred different ways to do things. Perhaps the best resource for you to explore the many different ways that people grow their own is www.howtogrowtobacco.com. There are excellent and very helpful forums and lots of great information, and joining is free.

A Few Words On Chewing Natural Tobacco

The words: it is a bad idea. Most of those who have tried chewing natural tobacco have found it unpleasant, and I think it's probably outright dangerous.

There's the real possibility that a person might make chewing tobacco of a plant which is incredibly potent without realizing it, and swallow a toxic dose of nicotine-laced saliva before realizing they were being poisoned.

Do not make chewing tobacco out of any tobacco that you grow. **It can easily make you sick and even kill you. Keep in mind also that home-grown heirloom varieties of tobacco must be used with care and moderation no matter how you use them because of their much greater nicotine content, compared with commercial tobacco products.**

Growing Natural Tobacco Hydroponically

This section of the Cultivators Handbook has been devoted largely to an exploration of traditional methods of growing tobacco in an outdoors garden, adapted for the home gardener and based on Native American techniques, as well as to some historical and contemporary themes that are intended to place native, natural tobacco in context.

Fortunately for those living in an urban environment, or in any situation where there isn't an option of planting a small crop of natural tobacco outdoors, T. A. James has written an extraordinarily well-researched and thorough book detailing his work with growing native strains of tobacco indoors using simple but effective potted and hydroponic methods. "The Heirloom Tobacco Garden" also covers outdoor gardening in substantial detail, but for tobacco lovers who want to grow an indoor crop for themselves and friends there is no better reference than Tim James' book.

In the following pages you'll find some samples of Tim's documentary photos (his originals are in brilliant color) of a hydroponic crop of N. shirazi – with a few container-grown plants thrown in for good measure. As I mentioned earlier, this is one of my favorite strains of tobacco and is an excellent choice for both indoor and outdoor growing.

If you want to order Tim's book you can do so by going to www.Xlibris.com and asking for The Heirloom Tobacco Garden by T. A. James ISBN 978-1-4363-2508-0

I would also like to thank Tim for his kind permission to use several of his photos elsewhere in the Cultivators Handbook of Natural Tobacco. I hope that they have added to your reading pleasure and helped to make my points more clear and understandable.

After starting his seedlings in seed trays and thinning them at 3 and then again at 5 weeks, Tim James then transplants his strongest seedlings to their final destination at the ripe old age of 6 weeks. As you can see here with N. Shirazi seedlings at about 5 weeks, they have been thinned down from an original density of perhaps 50-100 sprouts per tray to 5-10 per tray at this point, and they are ready to be transplanted to either their new indoor or outdoor home.

From this point on it is simply a matter of making sure that your plants have enough (but not too much) water, light, circulating air, warmth, and nutrients.

Tim's N. Shirazi crop at 9 weeks (below) is beginning to look more like tobacco and less like spinach. While not yet pointed the leaves are losing their rounded shape. The pots are still clustered tightly to take maximum advantage of the High Intensity Discharge lighting.

For indoor growing you want to begin with a lot of seedlings and then winnow out the weakest until you finally get the number of plants you want to raise to maturity depending upon the amount of space you have.

By the way, in addition to pulling some obviously weak plants – those that have been shaded by the leaves of their faster-growing buddies – you'll also be pulling some that you just hate to lose. Since these are castaways anyway, you might try re-potting them with the idea that you can give them to friends if they survive the transplanting process.

As delicate as tobacco plants may seem to be at this stage, nature has given them remarkable recuperative properties and you'll be pleasantly surprised how many survive being pulled and transplanted.

By week 10 (below) Tim's N. Shirazi plants are elongating and leaf definition is improving, so it's time get the plants spread out a little. The strongest plants are selected and their pots are inserted into square holes in a tabletop covered with reflective foil.

This same kind of calculation applies to outdoor gardening – you want to produce about twice as many transplants as you will actually set out into your garden.

By the way – foil is a good idea when growing indoor under lights, but not when growing outdoors in the sun because the underside of the leaves are much more sensitive than the upper, and can burn easily even in reflected sunlight.

Week 11 is the beginning of the sustained growth in height and leaf mass that will mark the plant's maturing cycle.

Week 12 (left) continues the strong growth period

Once the rapidly growing plants are receiving a full ration of light their leaves begin to put on weight, building the sugars and proteins that make up so much of their complex biochemistry. All the leaves will still be green, and the plants can gain an inch or two a day at this vegetative stage of their life cycle.

Week 13 is shown here (right) as the plants gain height and the leaves continue to fill out. This is still the vegetative stage

Week 14 – Note the plants (left) in ten gallon pots alongside the table. All are gaining height at about the same rate. Tim grows some of his plants indoors for the full cycle, and moves some of his plants outdoors on nice days. This is a good approach when you live in an area where the weather is variable and you need the option of 100% indoor growing combined with the option of taking advantage of nice days.

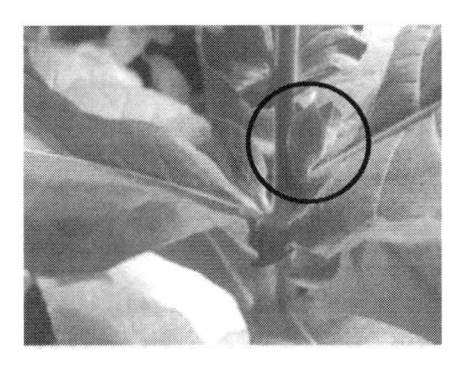

Time to begin watching out for and removing suckers – see circled area in photo. Looks innocent – but it will sap your prize plant's energy quicker then you can imagine.

Week 15 is getting close to the end of the most rapid vegetative growth – from this point the plant will begin to develop the flowering spike and the leaves will begin to die progressively from the bottom up.

Week 16 (right) marks full maturity for this hydroponic crop. From this point onwards the lower leaves will begin showing signs of turning the yellow-brown that they will ultimately become when fully cured. You will have to be especially watchful for both suckers and the emergence of flowering spikes. As the ripening process continues up the plant over the coming weeks, growers begin picking (called 'priming') these leaves and putting them through the ripening and curing processes.

Since we've covered the processes of priming and curing elsewhere I won't repeat it here – there are no differences between a hydroponic crop and a soil-grown crop with regard to priming and curing the leaves.

For additional detailed information on all kinds of cultivation techniques for heirloom tobaccos please consider acquiring Tim James' excellent book "The Heirloom Tobacco Garden" published by www.Xlibris.com.

Section Two: Advice From Old-Time Master Tobacco Growers

In Section One I discussed my own experiences in growing the great and powerful Native American Tobacco, N. Rustica, in the high desert environments of New Mexico, California and Oregon. While most of my experiences and lessons-learned with N. Rustica apply equally well with most other kinds of Tobacco, every grower has their own approach and their own 'tricks of the trade". Growing Tobacco is a lot like baking bread – a hundred bakers will all wind up with a loaf of bread, but they will each use a slightly different means of getting there, and of course, each will be absolutely convinced that their way is the best, and that their bread has superior taste.

In this section you'll find some of the best advice available from several dozen books by small Tobacco farmers writing in the $17^{th} - 20^{th}$ centuries. I've had to be quite selective – many of these books run hundreds of pages – but every excerpt was chosen to offer a unique hint, perspective, technique, observation, or opinion on one or more key elements of producing a successful tobacco crop from a wide range of the traditional tobaccos.

Of course these writers were commercial tobacco growers over 100 or more years ago and they are discussing their methods for growing, harvesting, curing and preparing hundreds of acres of Tobacco, unlike most of the readers of this book, who will probably be interested in growing a few dozen or maybe a few hundred plants. However, all of the advice on selecting a growing site, preparing the soil, starting your seedlings, fertilizing and cultivating the crop, destroying the dreaded Tobacco hawk moth, harbinger of the destructive Tobacco Hornworm as this green slimy menace is often called – all this advice is eminently scalable. And although you might want to ignore such advice as putting a little dab of arsenic in the flower of some Jimson weed you've inter-planted with your tobacco because the Tobacco Hawk moth will go to the Jimson Weed first and then die before laying its eggs on your tobacco – these growers also suggest some other less toxic possibilities for control of this pest in a small garden where you don't have to patrol acres of plants. In other words, taking into account the scale of your probable efforts, and the differences between these growers resources and our own in the 21st century – almost all of their advice is at least interesting and useful.

So if after browsing this section you are especially interested in reading all of what one or more of these often highly literate, practical-minded growers has to say, you'll find a list of the books cited at the end of this section, along with a web site where you can go to download any or all of these books in any of several different formats. If you have a Kindle reader, most of them are available in that format. If you would like to print a copy for yourself, all are available in PDF format. And there are several other formats, such as

Epub and plain text, for most of the books – and all are available without charge, all are public domain, and all are downright fascinating both as instruction in the art of tobacco growing and as history.

General Advice

In the 1700-1900's there was a genre of Tobacco book in which the author, an experienced and prosperous grower, aimed to share his knowledge with poor farmers struggling to make a living growing conventional crops. These books invariably compared the herculean efforts required to scratch out a living on conventional farms with the comparatively easy way to make a fortune with this miraculous crop. And this wasn't all hype – a good crop of Tobacco could indeed raise a farm family out of poverty and give them hope for the future. Here are a few select quotes along these lines.

A TOBACCO CHAT—TO THE POOR MAN.

Before entering upon the subject proper of this treatise — the cultivation and curing of Tobacco—I will say a few words to those who for the first time contemplate engaging in the cultivation of this plant. In the first place do you own a piece of land, say one, two or three acres, more or less? If you do not, can you lease a tract of that number of acres at, say, $15 or $20 per acre, such land as will hereafter be shown containing the necessary elements for successfully growing the weed? Are you a married man and have you several half-grown children, all of which are necessary adjuncts to the work. Have you a horse, plough and cultivator, (by cultivator I mean a single or double shovel plow). I am addressing myself now to the poor man, the cropper or tenant of very moderate means. Do you keep a cow? With one or two horses and a cow, quite a large amount of good fertilizer can be produced from season to season. The soil required for cultivating tobacco is of no small importance as regards its selection, as I shall show more in detail in another chapter. If you own a nice dry and warm tract of sandy, loamy soil, rather rolling, not too flat and not so hilly as to wash by excessive rains, either old land or that which has been recently cleared and worked for a season or two, you may make your first attempt at raising a crop of tobacco. If you do not own such a piece of land it will pay you to rent a piece, and pay from $15 to $30, or in case of its being exceptionally fine land $50 per acre tor it as lessee. You will encounter difficulties and will often meet with obstacles calculated to discourage, but a good crop will pay for all of these and soon dissipate your troubles. You will meet with rains when there has been too much of it, hot sun when you want rain or cloudy weather on your young and tender plants. When you set out your plants it may be just at the beginning of a week or two of dry hot weather. Then like cabbage plants you will have to water, water, water, and in spite of all, see numbers of your plants pine away and die.

You will have to replant and replant again. You will find cut worms ravaging the young plants, and in the season for them the tobacco worm will come down on you like the frogs and locusts in the land of Egypt. You must fight them. Raise turkeys, turn them into your patch, they will aid you well and nobly. Here too, the half-grown children will be found to be of great service, with their willing feet, pliant backs and nimble fingers they skip along, bend down, examine, pick, kill and pass on to the next, and few of the destructive and ugly creatures escape their acute optics. The mother is attending to home duties, the children are with you in the patch daily. They look after the worms, you after the cultivating, hoeing, weeding, topping and suckering the plants. All this I will tell you fully in another chapter. Then as the time draws on you will soon begin to cut and house your crop. To do this you must have prepared for yourself a Tobacco knife, four or five hundred plastering lath and a few roofing lath. At each end of your field or patch make a small platform for piling on the green plants which you intend impaling on the lath. Have a long rail or two fastened to posts, about five feet from the ground, and just near enough to a fence so as to allow of your hanging up each lath when filled with plants. You will have to utilize all the spare room in the attic of your house, in your stable or the eaves of your barn, or under the roof of your wagon shed. All this prepare beforehand, so that you have store room to hang your laths of Tobacco where it can cure. All these seemingly trivial matters I mention here to the poor man, the beginner, so that when he has raised a crop he may not lose it by finding no place to house it. Look out for frost, your crop may be late and you be taking advantage of every possible day to give it larger growth. See to it that old "Jack" does not catch you napping, for if he does, your whole crop may be ruined in a night. One energetic and industrious man may handle successfully and well, two acres of tobacco. This, if of fine quality, may yield him from $250 to $400 per acre, if the weed be commanding a fair price in market. In the county of Lancaster, in the State of Pennsylvania, this is not by any means an uncommon yield, indeed I am informed that figures much beyond these have been obtained from a single acre.

Let the poor man try it.

A Practical Handbook for the Tobacco Planter (by) B. Rush Sensensy, M.D. 1875

Contribute to your land liberally from your barnyard. Forget not that. Remember that no fertilizer can take its place. You may find plenty of valuable adjuncts to use, but none "in the long run " to bear comparison with it. Keep plenty of stock. Use up all the food material you raise on your farm, converting hay, straw, fodder, &c., into manure. Have all the tobacco stalks and stems saved and ground up, and spread upon your patch.

Have a care that you do not put out too much tobacco, because you may have to apply manure on it to the detriment of the balance of your land. Remember tobacco is a luxury, not food. Your first duty is to supply food for yourself and your stock. You must not lose sight of this fact. Therefore do not neglect your grasses and potatoes, and the cereals, in your eager haste to reap gold from a tobacco crop. Cultivate just what you can well manage, and without interfering with the ordinary products of your farm. Do not think you can buy food and manure. This some farmers have followed to their sorrow. Make all the manure you can. Raise your usual crops of corn, wheat, oats, rye and potatoes, together with hay and fodder. Keep good thrifty young cattle. They will fatten, grow into money for you, and every season fill your barnyard with well rotted manure and thus you will not see your soil run down and yourself become impoverished. Keep these things in view, and if you do so well and wisely, tobacco will make you rich.

A Practical Handbook for the Tobacco Planter (by) B. Rush Sensensy, M.D. 1875

It is at once apparent that the successful cultivation of tobacco requires the greatest care and attention, from the preparation of the seed bed to the final fermentation and baling of the ripened leaves. While anyone unfamiliar with tobacco culture can probably produce a crop, it is to be doubted if it will be of such a character as to command a good price. Judgment, only to be gained through experience in growing the crop, is necessary at so many stages of the growth of the plant that it is doubtful if it is profitable for the planter to undertake its cultivation unless he can engage the services of some one who has had such experience. And yet it is possible for the careful planter, who persistently studies the requirements of the crop, in a very few years to produce tobacco of a quality superior to that grown in regions where its' cultivation has been practiced for scores of years. When the Department of Agriculture attempted growing Sumatra tobacco under shade in the Connecticut Valley, the idea was greatly ridiculed by conservative New England planters, who scoffed at the idea of trying to grow a new kind of tobacco. They maintained they had grown tobacco for years, and knew the limitations of the soils and climate and the kind of tobacco best suited to the conditions. It took only one year to convince them that a new type of tobacco could be grown and sold for prices many times in advance of the best prices ever obtained for the finest of the old standard crop. And this has been the experience of tobacco cultivation the world over. Experiments have been tried in tobacco growing in new areas and in a few years, in many cases, have entirely revolutionized the agriculture in certain districts. New areas are constantly being opened up, with results that are very gratifying, even to the most sanguine experimenters.

Cultivation of Tobacco (by) Clarence Dorsey, 1903

The following epitome comprehends the species and varieties of Nicotiana possessing interest for the cultivator:

I. N. Tabacum macrophylla (latifolia, lattissima, gigantean) - Maryland tobacco.

Of this, there are two sub-species - (1) Stalkless Maryland, of the following varieties: (a) N. macrophylla ovata—short-leaved Maryland, producing a good smoking-tobacco, (b) N. macrophylla longifolia—long-leaved Maryland, yielding a good smoking-tobacco, and excellent wrappers for cigars, (c) N. macrophylla pandurata - broad-leaved, or Amersfort, much, cultivated in Germany and Holland, a heavy cropper, and especially adapted for the manufacture of good snuff; (2) Stalked Maryland, of the following varieties : (a) N. macrophylla alata, (b) N. macrophylla cordata - heart-shaped Maryland, producing a very fine leaf, from which probably the finest Turkish is obtained, Cuban and Manila are now attributed to this group.

II. N. Tabacum angustifolia - Virginian tobacco.

Of this, there are two sub-species - (1) Stalkless Virginian of the following varieties : (a) N. angustifolia acuminata, grown in Germany for snuff, seldom for smoking, (b) N. angustifolia lanceolata, affords snuff, (c) N. angustifolia pendulifolia, another snuff" tobacco, (d) N. angustifolia latifolia - broad-leaved Virginian, used chiefly for snuff, (e) N. angustifolia undulata—wave-like Virginian, matures quickly, (f) N. angustifolia pandurata, furnishes good leaves for smoking, produces heavily, and is much grown in Germany, and said to be grown at the Pruth as " tempyki," and highly esteemed there; (2) Stalked Virginian, of the following varieties: (a) N. angustifolia alata, (b) N. angustifolia lanceolata (N. fructiosa), growing to a height of 8 ft.,(c) N. angustifolia ohlonga, (d) N. angustifolia cordata - East Indian, producing heavily in good soil, and well adapted for snuff, but not for smoking. Latakia and Turkish are now accredited to N. Tabacum.

III. N. rustica - Common, Hungarian, or Turkish tobacco.

Of this, there are two varieties: (a) N. rustica cordata - large-leaved Hungarian, Brazilian, Turkish, Asiatic, furnishing leaves for smoking; (b) N. rustica ovata - small-leaved Hungarian, affords fine aromatic leaves for smoking, but the yield is small. Until quite recently, Latakia, Turkish, and Manila tobaccos were referred to this species; Latakia is now proved to belong to N. Tobacum, and Manila is said to be absolutely identical with Cuban, which latter is now ascribed to N. Tabacum macrophylla.

IV. N. crispa - This species is much grown in Syria, Calabria, and Central Asia, and furnishes leaves for the celebrated cigars of the Levant.

V. N. persica - Hitherto supposed to be a distinct species, affording the Shiraz tobacco, but now proved to be only a form of N. Tabacum.

VI. N. rapanda.—A Mexican plant, with small foliage. Long thought to be a distinct species peculiar to Cuba, but none such is now to be found in Cuba, whether wild or cultivated, and all the Cuban tobacco is now obtained from N. Tabacum macrophijllum.

Among the many other forms interesting only to the botanist or horticulturist, the principal are N. paniculata, N. glutinosa, N. glauca, attaining a height of 18 ft., and N. clevelandii, exceedingly strong, quite recently discovered in California, and supposed to have been used by the early natives of that country. Thus the bulk of the best tobaccos of the world is afforded by the old well-known species Nicotiana Tabacum.

Tobacco: A Handbook For Planters (by) C. G. Warnford Lock 1886

ENVIRONMENT

Tobacco And The Growing Environment
It is possible to grow a fine crop of Tobacco in almost any location now that we have 21st Century indoor/outdoor growing technology, but in the early centuries the grower had to choose where they were going to plant their crop very carefully. Certain kinds of land had been found to be superior growing environments, and other kinds of land (like river bottomlands) proved invariably disastrous.

The weed is grown to some extent throughout a wide range of latitude, and most excellent varieties are produced in the equatorial regions. As an article of traffic, however, bearing heavily upon the trade, and tobacco revenue of the different countries of the world, Cuba is perhaps the most noted hot climate in which it is produced. Scientific men assert that the high flavor and delicate aroma of the Cuban plant is produced by the influences of its climate, the sun's warm rays by day, warm moonlight nights, the frequent and heavy dews and air at all times heavily laden with the perfumes of spices, flowers and tropical fruits.

Tobacco is a great absorbent, and it is not at all improbable that, to a combination of these influences, we may ascribe much of the piquant and spicy aroma of the plant produced in the "ever faithful Isle."

A Practical Handbook for the Tobacco Planter (by) B. Rush Sensensy, M.D. 1875

Few, if any, plants are so easily modified as tobacco by climate, soil, elevation, nearness to the sea, and different methods of cultivation. This is plainly demonstrated by the rapid changes which take place in the character of the leaf, flavor, aroma, and special fitness for the varied uses and for different markets in introducing seed of well marked varieties into new districts. Each new class of soil, materially aided by climatic conditions, gives peculiar qualities to the cured leaf as to its flavor, texture, color, etc. It has long been recognized that tobacco grown near the sea or large bodies of salt water has poor combustibility and, while the taste may be sweet, it commands a low price for the manufacture of cigars on account of its poor burning qualities.

Cultivation of Tobacco (by) Clarence Dorsey, 1903

The aromatic principles, on the presence of which the value of a tobacco chiefly depends, can only be properly developed in the plant by the agency of high temperature and moisture. The fame that Cuban and Manila tobaccos enjoy is mostly due to the climate. The article produced in Cuba is most highly esteemed; up to this time, no other country has been able to compete successfully with it. However it cannot be doubted that there are many places whose climate justifies the assumption that a tobacco could be grown there, not inferior to that produced in the West Indies.

The more closely the climate of a place corresponds with that of Cuba, the greater chance is there that a Havana variety will preserve its peculiar aroma. In such places, a fine and valuable tobacco may be grown with less expenditure on labour, &c., than it is necessary to bestow in raising an inferior article in less suitable climes. In countries where a low temperature rules, the plants must be raised in hot-beds, and there is also a great risk that the young plants may be destroyed by frost, or afterwards by hailstones. When damp weather prevails during the tobacco harvest, it is often injured; and to give the required flavour, &c., to make the article marketable, macerating has often to be resorted to, thus involving great risk and expenditure. But in spite of these drawbacks, tobacco cultivation is often very remuneratively carried out in countries possessing an unfavourable climate. The deficient climatic conditions are here partly compensated for by making the other conditions affecting the quality of tobacco, and which can be controlled by the cultivator, the most favourable possible.

Tobacco: A Handbook For Planters (by) C. G. Warnford Lock 1886

Take the case of the yellow tobaccos of Carolina, Georgia and Tennessee. About 1850 some planters sowed their tobacco in poor soil, and as a result of the poverty of the ground it grew up a light-coloured, sapless plant. Cured with charcoal-fires, the leaves became a lemon colour and very sweet. Considerable difficulty was found in disposing of this poor, weak crop, but as no better soil was obtainable it continued to be grown. To the surprise of planters, manufacturers and retailers, the light weed caught the taste of the public, who preferred it to the rich, full-flavoured, dark, matured tobacco.

The Soverane Herbe (by) W. A. Penn 1902

Lorin Blodget, author of an able essay, in the Patent Office Report, on climatology, has these remarks " Wherever the growth of corn is completely successful, as in districts of a temperature for July above 68°, tobacco is and may be freely grown. Connecticut, Central New York, Ohio, and parts of Michigan, Indiana, Illinois, and part of Iowa, are all scarcely less adapted to tobacco culture than Kentucky and Virginia. The chief difference is a slight limitation of its period in time, and experience has fully shown that, to this extent, this may be very safely effected by a little care in selection of varieties. Southward, its range is, also, like that of maize, with perhaps the exception of producing more desirable varieties in tropical climates. Cuba is the favorite of all known districts indeed, and there seem to be no dangers to this plant from tropical excesses either of heat or humidity during the period of growth alone."

(in) Tobacco Culture: being a complete Manual or Practical Guide (by) C. M. Saxton 1868

But the English tobacco hath small credit, as being too dull and earthy ; nay, the Virginian tobacco, though that be in a hotter climate, can get no credit for the same cause: so that a trial to make tobacco more aromatical, and better concocted, here in England, were a thing of great profit. Some have gone about to do it by drenching the English tobacco in a decoction or infusion of Indian tobacco; but those are but sophistications and toys; for nothing that is once perfect, and hath run his race, can receive much amendment. You must ever resort to the beginnings of things for melioration."

"Sylva Sylvarum: or, a Natural History" Francis Bacon

Few, if any, plants are so much affected by the peculiarities of the soil on which it is grown, by circumstances of fertilization and mode of curing, as tobacco. For example, the Broad Leaf Orinoco, when cultivated on the rich and highly manured lands of Kentucky, produces the dark, strong-flavored " shipping tobacco" and when grown on the light gray soil of Virginia or North Carolina, with but little or no manure, and cured in a close barn with artificial heat, will produce the bright " wrappers" for which these States are so famous.

The variety known as Connecticut Seed Leaf is grown principally in Massachusetts, Connecticut, New York, Pennsylvania and Ohio, and is used in the manufacture of cigars, both for fillers and wrappers. Florida, portions of Ohio, Pennsylvania and other States, produce the Cuba, which is also used in the manufacture of cigars. Maryland, Virginia, North Carolina, Kentucky, Tennessee, Missouri and other States, cultivate many varieties, prominent among which are the Big and Little Orinoco (or Broad and Narrow Leaf Orinoco), Big and Little Frederick, Blue and Yellow Pryor, Big Stem, White Stem, Gooch, and numerous other kinds that bear different names in different localities ; and though mostly hybrids, they each possess some good qualities which recommend them to the growers.

The Planters Guide for Curing and Cultivating Tobacco (by) Shelton Tobacco Curing Company 1871

Types of Soil Favorable for Tobacco Growing
Not only the location of the field, but the type of soil, were found to affect the growth as well as the flavor and 'smokability' of the final product, Since Tobacco is grown is literally hundreds of different soil environments around the world, it is useful to see what the early growers discovered along these lines.

To be brief, the soil required should be deep, of a sandy or loamy nature, rich, mellow and warm. Virgin soil is better than old land. It should be of a rolling nature, and with an eastern or southern exposure if upon a hill. Lowlands, river bottom lands, will do well if not subjected to overflow. Land which produces heavy crops of clover, timothy and blue grass will, in general, if well conditioned, yield fair returns in tobacco.

A Practical Handbook for the Tobacco Planter (by) B. Rush Sensensy, M.D. 1875

The best soil is a light, mellow and deep sandy loam, if sufficiently enriched. New land will require less manure. A good black loam I consider next best, if sufficiently drained. Lime soil is not good. Heavy loams produce large crops of tobacco, but not so fine a quality. Choose a location that is not exposed to early frosts; low swamp holes are bad on this account. First rate corn land is good tobacco land. Good drainage, sufficiently manured, well aired and pulverized, is the necessary preparation of the soil for an abundant crop. Locations, subject to hail storms late in the season, are very destructive to the tobacco crop.

The Tobacco Growers Guide (by) James Mossman 1863

The cultivation of tobacco is a matter of great care, requiring constant and experienced attention. The best soil is alluvial, or a light loam with plenty of potash. New land gives a large crop of coarse, strong leaves, and old soil a smaller but better and sweeter tobacco, provided it has been well dressed with potash. The rich, moist soil is exhausted of its mineral constituents by the plant in a remarkable degree, more so, in fact, than by any other plant. It is these minerals which form the ash of burning tobacco. On an average four pounds of smoked tobacco yield one pound of ash or mineral matter. Careful manuring of the ground and alternation of crops is therefore necessary, as a single crop of tobacco robs the ground of all its mineral constituents. Lime yields a large but rather poor crop. The best manure is naturally tobacco-ash, for it is simply the restoration to the earth of the minerals the plant absorbed from it. Just as four pounds of tobacco yield one pound of ash, so will one pound of ash yield four pounds to tobacco again. It is almost surprising that steps have not been taken to collect smokers' ashes for dressing the growing crops. But the practical difficulties in thus raising tobacco. Phoenix-like, from its own ashes, are insurmountable.

The Soverane Herbe (by) W. A. Penn 1902

"Thaer, in his Principles of Practical Agriculture, says: "Tobacco prefers a light soil; it thrives better on a sandy, than on an argillaceous soil. Sandy clays agree with it best; but it is also successful on soft clays, which contain a large quantity of humus. But to produce a perfect and plentiful crop, the land must be rich in ancient humus; and must, besides, have been recently fertilized with some sort of manure. The best tobacco is that which grows on clearings, especially if the turf which covered the surface has been burned upon them; and still better if the wood which grew upon them, or wood brought for the purpose, has also been consumed on the spot and reduced to ashes. It is certainly, to this treatment, rather than to difference of climate, that we must attribute the great superiority of the American tobacco.."

(in) Tobacco Culture: being a complete Manual or Practical Guide (by) C. M. Saxton 1868

The soil affects to a great extent the quality of a tobacco. The plant thrives best in a soil rich in vegetable mould; this, however, is not so much required to supply the necessary plant food, as to keep the soil in a good physical condition. No other plant requires the soil in such a friable state. A light soil, sand or sandy loam, containing an average amount of organic matter, and well drained, is considered best adapted for raising smoking-tobacco; such a soil produces the finest leaves.

The more organic matter a soil contains, the heavier is the outturn; but the leaves grow thicker, and the aroma becomes less. As, in tropical climates, the physical properties of the soil play a prominent part in its productive capabilities generally, and the presence of organic matter in the soil tends to improve these properties, it will rarely occur that in such places a soil will contain too much humus. The more clay in a soil, the less is it adapted to the production of fine smoking-tobacco, on account of its physical properties being less favourable to the development of the aromatic principles; the leaf becomes also generally thick and coarse, but the outturn on such soils is commonly heavier than on a more sandy one. A clay soil possessing a great amount of humus may, if properly tilled, produce an ordinary smoking tobacco, and may even, if great attention be paid to the selection of the variety, &c,, produce leaves for cigar wrappers.

An experienced Ohio planter, Judson Popenoe, speaking of soil, says " A rich, sandy, second bottom, I believe to be the best for raising tobacco, although our chocolate coloured uplands, when very rich and highly manured, will grow an excellent quality of tobacco, but will not yield as much to the acre. Black river-bottoms will yield more to the acre than any other kind of land, but the tobacco is not of so fine a quality ; it grows larger, has coarser stems, and heavier body, and consequently, in my opinion, is not so good for wrappers or fine cut as the second bottom or upland tobacco."

On the same subject, an Illinois grower observes, " for us in the West, and for all the localities that have not an over-amount of heat, experience has proved, that a dry, warm soil (loam or sandy loam), rich, deep, and containing lime, is most suitable for tobacco. The more sandy, to a certain degree, the soil is, the better will be the quality of the tobacco; the nearer the soil is to clay, the poorer will be the crop under similar circumstances, although the yield may yet be satisfactory. Clayey soil will hardly produce tobacco suitable for cigars. Wet and tough clay soils are under no circumstances suitable to tobacco,"

Tobacco: A Handbook For Planters (by) C. G. Warnford Lock 1886

Judge Adam Beatty, Vice-President of the Kentucky- State Agricultural Society, at the time of writing the treatise on tobacco culture, from which we quote, said " Tobacco requires a rich soil, and that which is new, or nearly so, answers best. Next to ground which has been recently cleared, lands which have been long in grass, especially if pastured by sheep, answer best for tobacco. In preparing ground for tobacco, great care should be taken to plow it deep, and pulverize it completely. Grass land intended for tobacco, should always be plowed the previous fall. And it is better that all kinds of land intended for that purpose, should be plowed in time to have the benefit of the previous winter frosts. It should be kept light and free from weeds, by repeated plowings, till near the time of planting."

(in) Tobacco Culture: being a complete Manual or Practical Guide (by) C. M. Saxton 1868

Allen's American Agriculture says " The soil may be a light, loamy sand or alluvial earth, well drained and fertile. New land, free from weeds, and full of saline matters, is best for it; and next to this, is a rich grass sod which has long remained untilled. The seed should be sown in beds which must be kept clean, as the plant is small and slow of growth in the early stages of its existence, and easily smothered by weeds. If not newly cleared, the beds ought to be burned with a heavy coating of brush."

(in) Tobacco Culture: being a complete Manual or Practical Guide (by) C. M. Saxton 1868

In the Prairie Farmer of December 21, 1862, -we find the following by Jonathan Periam, we presume a practical Tobacco Cultivator : " Tobacco, being so much affected by soil and climatic influences, cannot be raised in all situations, even where it will mature. In rank soils, it will be strong and acid, and the price obtained for it will not be sufficient to pay the cost and trouble of raising. In exposed situations, subject to strong winds, it will sometimes be entirely ruined, by being broken and bruised. Indeed, in some situations, good wrappers can scarcely be obtained at all. In lands highly manured with nitrogenous manures, it will consist so much of nitre, that it will spit and fume in burning, which can only be tempered by age; therefore, after making the land sufficiently rich, some other crop should precede it. The best soil is thought to be a deep sandy loam, rich in potash, lime, soda, and carbonaceous matter."

(in) Tobacco Culture: being a complete Manual or Practical Guide (by) C. M. Saxton 1868

Professor J. T. Rothrock is of the opinion that the early natives of California smoked the leaves of Nicotiana clevelandii - a species only quite recently described by Professor Asa Gray. It is a small plant with small flowers, and it was found by Professor Rothrock only in association with the shell heaps which occur so abundantly on the coasts of Southern and Central California. He states that perhaps of all the remains of extinct races so richly furnished by that region, none were so common as the pipes, usually made of stone resembling serpentine. The tobacco of N. clevelandii Professor Rothrock found by experience to be excessively strong.

Tobacco: A Handbook For Planters (by) C. G. Warnford Lock 1886

The kind of a leaf a person wishes to grow will have to be determined, to a great extent, by the nature of the soil and the different locations. Many are deterred from trying to grow tobacco because of their lack of knowledge of the right kind of soil, believing that only a certain kind of soil will produce this plant, not realizing that tobacco is pre-eminently a weed, and a native of America. We have never found a soil that failed to grow tobacco, and a leaf that could be used commercially; but here comes in the benefit of good judgment and care in the selection of extra favorable locations for the production of the finer grades which command the greatest values; nevertheless, most any kind of soil will be found to produce a quality that will pay.

In certain clays that are heavy and strong, it will be difficult at first to get the plants to live when transplanted from the seed bed ; but after getting well started, or, in the common parlance getting a " stand,'* such soils will often produce the very best crops, the growth being strong, heavy, and of fine quality.

The nature of the soil, method of culture, etc., makes a great difference in the quality, and texture of the leaf. It would be well in commencing to grow tobacco in different localities, to try several of the varieties observing carefully their growth, when, by hybridizing, better cultivation, together with a perfect adaptation of soil, new varieties may be produced, and the old kinds improved, forming new types, the same as with all other plants. There is no crop that has a wider diversity of quality than tobacco, and none that will respond more quickly to extra skill, labor and management in its cultivation.

As in others kinds of farming, the culture of tobacco will vary in different localities, and every cultivator must modify the hints here given, to suit his own particular soil and location. Especially is this the condition in California. Take most any location in this end of the state, and we will find, that the nature of the soil, even on adjoining ranches, is almost entirely different in its elements, the very climate having different conditions of temperature on opposite sides of an avenue. The principle thing is to understand the nature of the plant, that is, the necessary requirements of the soil, climate, and culture, and the variety that is found best adapted to the particular locality^

As has been remarked before, tobacco will grow in almost any soil that is fit to grow anything else ; the variety that best suits the locality is the kind to grow, and that can only be learned by experiment.

Tobacco from the Seedbed to the Packing Case (by) W. T. Sim 1897

PREPARATION OF SOIL

Methods of Treating, Fertilizing & Tilling The Land
As mentioned earlier, growing Tobacco is a lot like baking bread, in that each grower has his own recipe for successfully working the land to produce a bumper crop. Even though most readers of this book will probably be more interested in growing a small, personal crop of a few dozen or perhaps a few hundred plants, the methods described by the early growers for working a farm of hundreds of acres apply just as well to a backyard garden except in the matter of scale.

After the race the rest of the society came up to the site, where the Mixers spread a blanket on one side of the garden and put all the medicines on it. Then anciently members as well as outsiders got axes, hoes, and other implements to remove all the grass from the ground, making it bare and smooth. Some men and women went off to fetch dry grass and small dry twigs, which were spread over the site. Next a man having the eagle for his medicine (even though he might not be a member) was chosen to sing to the ground. He sang four songs, at the close of which the people set fire to the dry grass. The singer held two feather fans in his hands and fanned the fire. When the grass had been consumed, the people took leafy branches and brushed the site with them. The Mixers gave pemmican to all who had helped. Nowadays the ground is not burnt over but merely undergoes a preparatory ploughing.

The Tobacco Society of the Crow Indians (Robert Lowie) 1919

In selecting a place for plant-beds, remember that you wish to obtain early and vigorous plants; therefore, take a rich, warm hillside, protected by timber or otherwise. Red lands are usually unsuited for this purpose. Never use wet or cold land. After finding a suitable place, select a dry time during the month of December or January - the sooner the better

- rake off the leaves, lay down skids (about three inches in diameter), three feet apart, across which lay a bed of wood five or six feet wide, and high enough to burn for about an hour and a half and a half and leave a sufficient quantity to remove and kindle in another place. After the fire has burned the length of time specified, move it the width of the first layer, then throw on brush, a good bed of wood, and continue as before. Every farmer ought to provide himself with iron hooks for pulling plant-bed fires. If it is possible to injure land by hard burning, we have never experienced it; and think that where one bed is injured by burning, ten are injured for the want of it.

For every ten thousand plants required, there ought to be at least ten yards square of plant-bed. A bed of this size will supply more than the number mentioned, but it is much better to have some for your neighbor than to be under the necessity of begging plants. After burning, the land should remain untouched a few weeks, that the rains and frosts may assist in pulverizing the soil; then with a mattock, dig up the bed without turning it over, and pulverize thoroughly with a hoe and rake. Remove all the roots, spread a light coating of stable manure, chop it in, rake again, and the bed is ready for sowing.

The Planters Guide for Curing and Cultivating Tobacco (by) Shelton Tobacco Curing Company 1871

In all sections, where tobacco is now grown, clover seems to be a most favorite soiler. It seems, more than any other grass, to carry with it most abundantly all the chemical constituents required for tobacco. It is a ready, rich and cheap manure, and in combination with stable manure, in many tobacco growing regions, is displacing all other fertilizers, planters finding in it all the requisites for keeping the land in a condition of fertility necessary to produce the greatest possible yield. I speak now, of course, of those sections of country where clover is a common and a favorite crop. Where it is not, then dependence is to be had upon other grasses and stable manure with artificial fertilizers.

A Practical Handbook for the Tobacco Planter (by) B. Rush Sensensy, M.D. 1875

I get my land in order by the first of May, have it well ploughed, and by well ploughed I mean deeply ploughed, cleanly ploughed, and ploughed when the ground is in the best possible order. If it be ground that was in tobacco the previous year I have it well manured with stable manure, generally putting on twenty-five two horse loads of the same to the acre, and from seventy-five to one hundred bushels of leached ashes. I say if it was in tobacco the year previous because it is better to rotate the crop, if one season in tobacco, sow it in the fall in wheat and you will, without fertilizing, secure an exceptionally large yield of that cereal, the former crop not having required or taken from the soil the elements which are needed in order to produce a good crop of wheat. If the ground which I intend for the plant is a clover sod, I plow it down and have it harrowed until well smoothed. All clods are broken and smoothed out, and the field made as nice as "a garden patch."

On this patch, I will mention, I put about ten two horse loads of stable manure to the acre, but you may readily add ten more per acre, if you have it, with profit to your land, your crop and your purse, always bearing in mind your pocket. I then score out with shovel plow, drawing my furrows straight, and for large variety of tobacco, three and a-half feet apart, for small or Havana seed leaf three feet between furrows will be right. Some planters prefer to score out each way, thus checker boarding the patch, and allowing of passing the cultivator each way during the season. It is also claimed that in this way water accumulates around each square, and forms a minute reservoir for each and every plant. I however have tried both plans and cannot say that I find any decided advantage in this last plan, hence I run my furrows but one way, three and a-half feet apart.

A Practical Handbook for the Tobacco Planter (by) B. Rush Sensensy, M.D. 1875

Prior to the work of transplanting, the ground should be thoroughly plowed or spaded to a considerable depth. Deep cultivation is advisable on any character of soils, as it readily allows the free percolation of rain and air through the soil, and increases the amount of available plant food contained in the soil, and helps to conserve the moisture, especially in times of drought. If only small amounts of manures are to be applied, it can be spread broadcast after the first plowing; but, if large quantities of stable or straw manures are used, it is best to plow them in several weeks before the time of setting out the plants. After plowing, the land should be harrowed with a disk harrow, and then with a smoothing harrow.

Cultivation of Tobacco (by) Clarence Dorsey, 1903

After seeding, the land should be rolled or trodden until it is smooth. Now is the time to manure. We consider horse manure collected under cover (and free from litter or grass seed) to be the best for this purpose. Chop it fine, and spread a coating (say half an inch or more) evenly over the bed. This should be the last manuring unless the spring is very dry, when a light top-dressing occasionally will be beneficial. As to the use of guano on plant-beds, we are not prepared to recommend it as highly as stable manure. We will add, that in the absence of this manure, a light dressing of plaster will be of service ; but if you have good stable manure, "let well enough alone " for if these directions as to land and management are followed, there is about as much chance to fail in plants as to fail of going to sleep at night after a hard day's work burning land.

The Planters Guide for Curing and Cultivating Tobacco (by) Shelton Tobacco Curing Company 1871

In preparing the ground for the seed, spade it up deep and fork it up perfectly mellow, and remove all roots and all undecomposed objects; then throw it up in beds four feet wide, with paths at the sides, so as to enable the hand to weed the Plants from both sides of the bed, and keep them perfectly clean. After the bed is forked up perfectly mellow and loose, lay on some dry brush and litter and burn them. The object of this is, to destroy insects, grass and weed seed. The ashes add fertility to the soil, the charcoal gives it a dark, warm color, and makes a most friendly preparation for the fine seeds. If the bed is stirred any after it is burned, fork it up so as not to turn the top soil under.

The Tobacco Growers Guide (by) James Mossman 1863

In preparing the soil, it can be manured to most any extent; apply your coarsest manure before plowing the first time and your finest at the second. Early in the spring plow your ground deep, harrow fine and smooth, and if lumpy, roll so that the soil will keep moist and give the weed seed a better chance to germinate. Let it remain in this condition until the plants have attained about half their size for transplanting, or when the leaves are the size of the thumb nail. Then where sub-soil has been turned up, apply from fifteen to twenty bushels of hard wood ashes to the acre, and as much more fine manure as you like ; then plow and harrow again, letting it remain until the time to prepare it for the plants about the first of June, then plow and harrow the third time ; after that take a two horse plow, throw your ground up in beds four feet wide; then if you want to plow your tobacco both ways, make it crosswise with a light sled, three and a half feet apart.

The Tobacco Growers Guide (by) James Mossman 1863

The best soil for the seed bed is a rich, friable, dark, virgin loam or sandy loam. A deep, well-drained soil is greatly to be preferred. The necessary operations of tilling and stirring the soil should precede sowing the seed by several weeks. It is usually customary to thoroughly plow or spade the land and mark the land off into a number of beds surrounded by boards. In the famous Deli district in Sumatra the beds are built up about 30 centimeters high and surrounded by ditches. The size and number of the beds varies, but they are usually rectangular in size, with suitable walks or passageways between them. The beds are highly fertilized with rich manures or with any complete, specially prepared commercial fertilizer. Stable manure, or any complete guano, may be used. Care should be taken to thoroughly mix the fertilizers with the soil, so that the greatest amount of plant food may be available for the young plants. In the case of old lands, it is always advisable to burn the land over, to insure safety against grass and weeds. With new land the trouble from such sources is slight; but burning is sometimes practiced, to increase the richness of the soil by adding the fertilizing properties of the burned wood. The burning is usually done one week before planting the seed. After burning, the soil is well spaded and all roots and tufts arc carefully removed, and the surface made loose and smooth.

Cultivation of Tobacco (by) Clarence Dorsey, 1903

The following preparation for a hot bed we have found to answer the purpose perfectly: Select the ground for the desired bed, say sixteen feet square with a path through the centre about two feet wide, and dig the bed two feet deep, removing the soil to sides and ends of bed. As a foundation, put in about six inches of leaves, and tramp as solid as possible; then on top of leaves, fill in with about twelve inches of fresh barnyard manure, which ought to be well packed; then give it all the water it will take up ; then cover with about three inches of fine soil which rake smooth, removing all stones and lumps; after getting in fine tilth, cover with boards and let it remain for eight or ten days to allow it to ferment and the rank heat to pass off. At the end of the time specified, remove the boards and rake the soil again, which will kill any weeds that may have germinated. The bed is now in condition to be sown. One tablespoonful of seed will be ample to sow the bed. Sow the seed evenly, on the surface, and press by walking on a board. Place boards around the beds, with edges up three inches above the surface, and bank the soil taken from the bed against the outside of these boards ; the boards are necessary to lay cloth or boards on to protect against heavy rains and frost.

The soil, when the seed is sown, should neither be too wet nor too dry ; the Seed-bed must be kept damp but not wet, and is better to be a little higher on the north than on the south, to insure drainage.

It is absolutely necessary that the bed does not get dry; it must be sprinkled every day, and, if necessary, twice a day. The most critical time is when the plants are beginning to show. Keep the beds covered with muslin cloth from ten a. m. to four p. m., unless there is likely to be frost or heavy rain, then it will be found necessary to cover with boards, also. We wish to impress upon the minds of those who intend raising tobacco, that the Seed-bed will require careful attention; as neglect in exposing the seed bud to very hot sunshine for one hour may prevent the seeds from germinating ; there is also constant danger from allowing the bed to get too dry after the plants come up.

If it is shown, by small holes in the leaves, that bugs are working in the plants, a simple remedy is found in unleached wood ashes; sprinkle the bed in the morning while there is dew, and, if necessary, give the plants another sprinkle of ashes in a' few days; and also give the bed a little more sunshine.

The Seed-bed should be kept free from weeds; the weeding should begin as soon as the weeds are large enough to pull. This is a laborious process, especially when the seed-bed has not previously received the attention requisite for destroying the seed of weeds in the soil. The weeding should not be slighted, but attended to thoroughly, as often as necessary.

Should the foregoing directions be carefully followed, the plants will be ready for transplanting in from six to eight weeks after sowing.

Tobacco from the Seedbed to the Packing Case (by) W. T. Sim 1897

In its natural state, the soil will rarely possess the elements of plant food in such a form as is most conducive to the production of a fine tobacco-leaf. Any deficiency must be supplied in the shape of suitable manure. Schlosing found that a bad burning tobacco was produced on a soil containing little potash, on unmanured soil, on soil manured with flesh, humus, calcium chloride, magnesium chloride, and potassium chloride. A good burning tobacco was produced on a soil manured with potassium carbonate, saltpetre, and potassium sulphate.

More recent experiments carried out by other investigators tend to corroborate these conclusions. It is generally assumed that a soil rich in nitrogenous organic matter produces a strong tobacco that burns badly. The results of Nessler's experiments clearly show that it is not sufficient to apply the element most needed by the plant – potash - in any form, but that, to produce a good tobacco, it is necessary to apply it in a particular combination. It was found that potash carbonate applied as manure produced the best tobacco: it burned for the longest time, and its ash contained most potash carbonate; whereas potash chloride produced a much inferior tobacco. The assertion of other experimenters that chlorides produce a bad tobacco is thus confirmed. Potash sulphate and lime sulphate produced a good tobacco.

It may be noticed here that tobacco which was manured with gypsum contained a great amount of potash carbonate in the ash, probably due to the fact that gypsum is a solvent for the inert potash salts. From the foregoing, it may be concluded that in tobacco cultivation, the elements potassium and calcium should be restored to the soil in the form of carbonate, sulphate, or nitrate, but not as chlorides. Poudrette, or prepared night-soil, generally contains a considerable amount of chlorides, and is not well suited as manure for fine tobacco. It has been found that fields manured with chlorides produced heavily; a small proportion of chlorides may therefore be applied in this form, whenever quality is of less importance than quantity.

Farmyard manure may suffice when tobacco is cultivated in proper rotation, but here also, unless the soil be very rich in potassium and calcium, the application of some special manure will greatly enhance the value of the outturn. Wood-ashes are a valuable supplement to stable dung. Gypsum is an excellent dressing for soils in a good manurial condition: it supplies the lime needed by the tobacco, and acts as a solvent on the inert potash salts. Gypsum applied on poor land, however, hastens the exhaustion of the soil. It is said that crops manured with gypsum suffer less from the effects of drought, and require less irrigation, than when manured otherwise the leaves of plants that had been manured with gypsum exhaling less water than when manured with other substances.

Tobacco: A Handbook For Planters (by) C. G. Warnford Lock 1886

E. E. Burton, in the *Sugar Cane*, translating from Mitjen's essay on tobacco growing in the most renowned district of Cuba, has the following sensible remarks on the all-important subject of manuring: " Each veguero or farmer should make a hole or rotting bin in which he should deposit as much muck and leaves as he may be able to accumulate, and, before giving the last ploughing to prepare his field for planting the tobacco, he should spread over it all the prepared rotten manure he can procure. Manure that is not thoroughly rotten injures the plants more than benefits them. A piece of land, well manured and thoroughly worked up, will produce four times more tobacco than one badly prepared would. Consequently no expense or labour is so remunerative as that which is applied to the soil. This is a very important point which should fix the attention of every agriculturist who desires to prosper.

" Agriculturists acknowledge the advantage of manuring. In tobacco cultivation it produces the most brilliant results, but in Vuelta-Abajo it is very difficult to procure sufficient country manure. Yagues (i.e. strips of palm bark used as screens, and for baling) and all the refuse from palm trees are excellent; grass from the savannahs and all kinds of vegetables in a thoroughly putrid state are very good, but it requires a great quantity, and the immense labour to collect and prepare these, frightens the greater number of vegueros, and few have sufficient constancy to enable them to collect enough properly prepared manure for their fields.

Tobacco: A Handbook For Planters (by) C. G. Warnford Lock 1886

To be applied shortly before planting, and in equal quantities, for all kinds of tobacco: 1. Guano, 200 to 300 pounds on the acre; 2. Poultry-droppings, 400 to 500 pounds ; 3. Green manure in any quantity ; 4. Sheep-dung, six two-horse loads ; 5. Cattle manure, ten two-horse loads.

For chewing-tobacco and snuff: 1. Sheep-dung, 10 to 12 loads per acre; 2. Cattle manure, 20 to 30 loads; 3. Horse-dung, 1.5 to 2.5 loads; 4. Hog manure, 20 to 30 loads. The last two are useless for smoking tobacco, or for that to be used for segars.

Tobacco Culture: Practical Details (by) Orange Judd Company 1884

Tobacco is an exhausting crop, and for the best results, requires a rich, warm, soil. In fact there is no plant that is so largely influenced by the character of the soil as tobacco. A deep, mellow, soil will always secure the best results, one that is naturally rich, or made so, by the application of the proper kind of fertilizers. A light loamy, sand, is one of the very best adapted to it; alluvial lands that are well drained and fertile are also good. It will not thrive on soil containing a surplus of water, however rich or whatever their character, and such lands should never be devoted to this crop, until they have been thoroughly under- drained. Soils containing a large amount of potash and lime, either naturally or by application, are the best suited to it. It will not thrive upon such lands as are denominated "sour," unless the quality be first remedied by the application of salt, or lime, and previous cultivation. On such lands it will generally attain about one-fourth of its growth and then seem to remain stationery for a time the leaves assuming meanwhile a yellowish tinge. The crop, in such cases, will prove almost worthless - what there is of it - the stalks being hard and the quality of the leaf poor.

If the land is fresh and of good quality, manure will not be necessary although tobacco is a gross feeder and grows rapidly when once started; therefore it requires plenty of food to make it grow well. There is nothing better that we know of than well rotted barn yard manure. Any green crop plowed under is also good, adding humus to the soil, but may be the cause of bringing more worms. Excellent results have been attained an old alfalfa land, that has been well pastured; such is calculated to make strong tobacco. Our ordinary mesa land will be found to produce a fine quality of tobacco of light weight and fine texture; the more fertilizer being used the heavier the product.

Tobacco from the Seedbed to the Packing Case (by) W. T. Sim 1897

The following, from the pen of the lamented Peter Minor, of Albemarle County, Virginia, may better meet the wants of sections where land is yet new and plenty. Mr. Minor is characterized by Col. Skinner, who published it, in The Plough, the Loom, and the Anvil, in 1852, as " a good farmer and a better man." He says: "The best tobacco is made upon new or fresh land. It is rare to make more than three successive crops upon the same ground, of which the second is the best, a the first and third being about equal. But it is more common to make only two. The new land, after all the timber and brush is removed, and the surface very cleanly raked, is twice closely coultered as deep as two horses or oxen can pull. After this, hands with grubbing hoes pass regularly over the whole ground, and take up all the loose roots that have been broken by the coulter, which are heaped and burnt, or removed. One, and sometimes two more coulterings are then given, and the same operation repeated with the grubbing hoes."

(in) Tobacco Culture: being a complete Manual or Practical Guide (by) C. M. Saxton 1868

From the Prairie Farmer of January 3, 1863, by J. Periam :

" About the 1st of April, the hot-beds should be prepared thus: Having previously drawn sufficient fresh heating horse manure into a conical pile, and turned it at intervals of three days, to get the rank heat out of it, mixing the dry and wet together, a space should be cleared fifty feet long and eight feet wide, upon which proceed to lay up the manure about sixteen inches high; spread it evenly, long and short, patting it down from time to time with the fork, to discover the soft places and make it pretty firm. To heat properly, the manure should be uniformly moist; if too dry, it should have been moistened while in the heap.

" The most thorough preparation of the soil is required to the successful cultivation of tobacco. If not previously done, it should be thoroughly sub-soiled in the fall, to the depth of at least twelve or fourteen inches, by following after the turning plow with a subsoil lifter. As soon in the spring as the land is in condition to work, cart on twenty-five loads per acre of well-rotted manure, spread evenly, harrow and plow about six inches deep. As soon as the weeds start, harrow again. About the 20th of May, give it a final plowing, and harrow again thoroughly, and if not sufficiently fine, roll.

(in) Tobacco Culture: being a complete Manual or Practical Guide (by) C. M. Saxton 1868

The necessity for manuring is well understood by the Turks. They dress the seed-beds with goat and sheep dung, and manure the fields during winter with horse and cattle-dung. In the spring, sheep and goats are folded on the land. The soil of tobacco lands will be found quite impregnated with ammonia and nitrate of potash, both absorbed by the plant; the former is thought to influence the aroma, and the latter may be seen in crystals on the surface of the dried leaf. In order to keep the leaves small and delicate, the planting is performed very close, the usual distances being 5 inches apart, and 9 inches between the rows.

Tobacco: A Handbook For Planters (by) C. G. Warnford Lock 1886

I usually haul out and broadcast uniformly over the land intended for tobacco, all the farm, pen and other coarse home made manures that I have been able to save during the season, as early in the spring as possible, after the land gets dry enough for the teams to enter without poaching, and thus turn these under with a moderately shallow plowing, and harrow over until the soil is well pulverized. I have found the early application of all coarse manures to be the best, as giving them more time to decompose and become incorporated with the soil. About the 1st of May I lay the rows off, 3 ½ feet apart, with a one horse turning plow. In the furrows thus made I apply from four hundred to six hundred pounds of some standard fertilizer, (I find none superior to Gilliam's), then lap the dirt on this with a two horse turning plow, and chop and pat the lists thus thrown up every three feet with hoes, in order to make a place for the plant to be set. The planting season with us on the south side generally commences about the 20th of May, and continues till about the 20th of June, by which time with proper diligence, most planters can succeed in getting a good "stand," As soon as the young plants show signs of growth they should receive a light working, with the plow and hoe, to keep down the growth of weeds and grass, and this should be kept up at intervals until, the tobacco having well covered the land, it is no longer necessary.

A Practical Handbook for the Tobacco Planter (by) B. Rush Sensensy, M.D. 1875

Barn-yard manure will answer all purposes of farming. No other would be necessary, if any prescription could be found whereby the farmer could obtain it in sufficient quantities. The droppings of well-fed animals are all he needs, if so preserved as to retain all their original constituents, with no loss and no change of their relative proportions of soluble and insoluble matter; that is, if both the liquid and the solid portions, combined with a little dried clay, or charcoal dust, or dry swamp soil, be preserved with no deterioration till applied to the soil they afford all that plants require. But as no one has yet been able to prescribe how they can be obtained in sufficient quantity, and as not one farmer in a thousand has yet learned to preserve them in full value, it is well to inquire, what other fertilizers are suited to tobacco? Guano is good for this crop beyond question. Superphosphate of lime is good. In soils pretty well supplied with barn manure, we think that superphosphate plays a more important part in making out the tobacco crop than guano. We would apply both, say from 1 to 2 cwt. of guano, and from 2 to 3 cwt. of phosphate, depending somewhat upon how much other manure is to be applied.

Our idea is that barn manure, composted largely with leaf-mold, hedge-scrapings, swamp-muck, or something of the kind, should be used plentifully, and, then, to supply deficiencies in quantity with some of the' more portable manures, as Peruvian guano, superphosphate, castorbean pomace, butchers' scraps, etc., etc. With reference to the tobacco, as well as to the wheat, which is now pretty generally made to follow it, we would certainly apply more or less of both guano and of superphosphate, not mixed, but separate, because the guano requires to be covered deeply and diffused throughout the soil, while the superphosphate should be left on or very near the surface, the tendency of guano being to rise into the air, that of superphosphate to dissolve and flow downwards.

But the cultivator of tobacco may safely conclude that almost any thing which has been found favorable to general cultivation, will hardly fail to be favorable to this crop, and so may be guided very much by circumstances. The wastes from cities, villages, and manufactories may all be made to supply the wants of the farm; and the grower of tobacco will, naturally, look around him, and see whence he can purchase, with the least expense for transportation. Unleached wood-ashes, the spent ashes of soap-boilers, the refuse of alkali works, the flocks from woolen factories, poudrette, night-soil, the horn and bone dust from comb-makers, ground bones, almost any of the wastes offered for agricultural purposes, may be profitably used by cultivators near the places where they are produced and sold cheaply as wastes. Gas lime would be good, if spread on the ground the previous autumn and left exposed till the time for spring plowing; and green sand marl would be profitable on most soils, so situated that the transportation would be light. The latter is better adapted to sandy or slightly loamy soils ; but is good for any soils not already abounding in potash. As tobacco requires much alkali, the soil should be supplied with this in the form of lime, potash, soda, and ammonia. All those are contained in well-preserved barn manure. Ammonia, as all know, abounds in Peruvian guano and in all barn manure not half spoiled by mismanagement. Lime may be most cheaply supplied from the gas-house, only it must not be applied in a fresh or hot state immediately before planting tobacco or any other crop. A small dressing of common salt, not more at one time than five or six bushels to the acre, will supply all the soda required. That a soil for tobacco should contain lime is important; and the spent ashes from the soap boilers are perhaps, the next cheapest way of supplying it, after that before named - the waste lime from the gas-house.

In virgin soils, and in all limestone regions, that have not been long cultivated, it is safe to presume that there is lime enough already in the soil. But, in all other cases, the farmer cannot safely presume upon there being lime enough in his soil for a large crop of tobacco and then a large crop of wheat to follow, unless he has put it there; and will do well to apply it in some form, as gas lime, leached ashes, or a pretty large dressing of the superphosphate.

Tobacco Culture: being a complete Manual or Practical Guide (by) C. M. Saxton 1868

" Peruvian guano is the most compact fertilizer known, and a very small quantity suffices to manure a tobacco field ; its cost is not excessive, and is very frequently less than the carriage of other manures to the spot where they are to be used. Its most active results are shown on light and sandy soil; it quickens vegetation, and experience has shown that it increases prodigiously the quantity and value of crops; we therefore recommend the use of guano as a fertilizer of the first order for tobacco cultivation, and as light and sandy soils possess in themselves the substances most suitable for the development of the tobacco plant, on such soils guano acts as a stimulant to the plant.

" Before using Peruvian guano, it should be sifted; all the stones and lumps remaining should be broken up, and again sifted, so that nothing may be lost. After this, three or four times its weight of dry sandy soil should be thoroughly mixed with it, and it should remain thus 6-8 days before being used. This preparation should be made under cover, to avoid the possibility of rain falling on the mixture, and the heap should be covered with the empty guano bags, or anything else, to prevent the evaporation of the volatile alkali which it contains.

" It is better to prepare this mixture in detail, each heap containing one bag of guano, whose weight is 150-160 lb., so as to facilitate the calculation of the quantity that should be applied, and prevent mistakes. We will start, therefore, on this calculation.

" On lands of good quality, but which, nevertheless, require manure, from having been overworked, one pound of guano should be applied to each 15-20 superficial yards, or, say one heap of compost for each 2500-3000 yards, or, otherwise said, one heap of manure will suffice for a surface that contains 5000-6000 plants. In sandy unproductive soil, and on sterile savannah lands, 1 lb. of guano to 9-12 yards ; or a heap of compost guano to 1500-2000 yards; or one heap for 3000-4000 plants. These are the proportions to be used for the first year for the second, and forward, two-thirds of that employed the first year will he sufficient.

" When crops of tobacco and com are grown on the same lands, half the guano should be applied to the corn and the other half to the tobacco; but then a somewhat larger quantity will be required. The manure should be applied shortly before transplanting, and after the ground has been well cross-ploughed and prepared, and the ground should be plotted out into squares or beds of 50 yards square. The manure should then be spread and ploughed in, and the land should at once be furrowed and planted.

" Under this system of applying Peruvian guano as manure for tobacco the best results have been obtained, and, of all the various trials made, this is the most simple and the easiest to execute."

Tobacco: A Handbook For Planters (by) C. G. Warnford Lock 1886

PREPARATION OF NEW LAND.

First take up every growth not too large to grub, and throw them into heaps. Then cut the small trees, the brush of which throw on the grub heaps; then cut and remove the larger timber. After the ground has been cleaned off it should be coultered at least three times; then harrow and rake it to pulverize the soil and remove the roots. It should now be laid off at a distance of three feet each way and hilled. The hilling is very important, as a plow in new land will not prepare it right, and "whatever is worth doing is worth doing well." Thin ridge land will produce a beautiful crop with a tablespoonful of guano to the hill. The second year it may be manured as other land; for if the first year's work is well done, it will be prepared to receive manure broadcast. New land should be hilled at least three weeks before transplanting, and while the land is moist, so that the soil will become compact enough to retain moisture, that the plant may thrive without rain after being set out.

The Planters Guide for Curing and Cultivating Tobacco (by) Shelton Tobacco Curing Company 1871

SEED-BED

Growing & Preparing Tobacco Seed

In Section One I gave you the address of the National Plant Germplasm System, where you can order top quality Tobacco seeds from any of hundreds of varieties, so getting the seed for your initial garden will not be a problem. However after your first crop you'll probably want to produce your own seed from the strongest, most beautiful plants in your garden. Since the early growers were not only skillful but also financially conservative, most of them chose to produce their own seed rather than buy commercially for each planting.

The proper season for the mixing is in May, "when the chokecherries are ready" (blossoming). Later in the spring the man who invited the Mixers for a discussion of their dreams announces, "I am going to move near the site." He moves and the other people follow, the whole tribe camping near the site.

The Mixers prepare pemmican and on the same day all of them mix Tobacco seed, each in a separate tipi. The most circumstantial account was given by Pretty-tail. As stated elsewhere the details of the mixing vary slightly. In former times they gathered elk, deer, or buffalo dung to mix with the Tobacco, also different kinds of flowers, roots, and wild onions, according to their dreams Now cow dung and eight different roots and flowers are used. The Tobacco seeds are mixed in a wooden bowl with a red ring painted on the inside. Formerly a dipper of buffalo horn was used, at present one of cow horn is substituted.

Pretty-tail shakes his rattle and begins to sing while his wife, Strikes-in-the-house, sits by him. At the close of each song she makes a motion above a bucket of water as if about to dip in her ladle until after the fourth song she actually dips the horn into the vessel and pours water into the bowl up to the red ring, when she lays down her spoon. There are several miniature bags with Tobacco seeds which she opens. Her husband sings four songs. At the fourth she empties the entire contents of one bag into the bowl, next she adds other ingredients of the mixture, and when these are well soaked the cow dung is put in. By this time peeled cow paunches representing buffalo manifolds of old days have been prepared and the contents of the bowl are emptied into one paunch.

A big pipe with cloth over the mouthpiece is taken and the smoke from it is blown into the paunch, which in order to retain the smoke is quickly tied with sinew looped at one end. A stick of cherry wood, hooked at one end and sharpened at the other, is painted red, then the filled paunch is tied to the hooked part. Other paunches are treated in the same way. Then they go to a big tipi, and the sharp ends of the sticks are driven into the ground.

A rope is stretched between two poles of the lodge and to this rope they tie the cherry sticks. These labors consume the entire day. In the evening they begin to dance in the Mixer's lodge and continue all night, then they go home. In this way each member in every chapter turns over his Tobacco seeds to the Mixer, who receives a fee for mixing them.

The Tobacco Society of the Crow Indians (Robert Lowie) 1919

The foundation of the tobacco plant is the seed. A good seed may produce a poor tobacco if the conditions are favorable but a poor seed will never produce a good tobacco even if the conditions are ideal. The method commonly used of gathering the seed from left over suckers is ruinous, and if kept up for a number of years, the grade of the tobacco will deteriorate in spite of all other precautions taken. In the West Indies where usually only one variety is grown there need be no fear of intermixing with other varieties and it is not the purity about which there is any question, but the seeds from an inferior plant will produce an inferior plant hence nothing should be used but seeds from the very choicest plants.

An ideal method is to go through the field before the plants are topped and mark those with. the most desirable leaves which should be left untopped. After the flower buds appear and before the flowers expand paper sacks should be tied over these untopped plants to prevent insects from entering the flowers. The paper sacks should be adjusted every few days to allow room for the flowers to develop. Besides the difference in the seed from the different plants there is also a difference in the seed from the same plant. Those from the largest and well ripened pods are very superior and when separating the seeds from the capsules two grades may be had by shaking out all of the seeds that fall out readily, which .are always larger and better ripened than those that 'adhere closely.

It is also well to cut off and throw away all the smaller pods and the imperfectly developed ones of the lower cluster. A good clean seed will run about five million to the pound and it will take from forty to fifty plants to produce that amount. A clean seed can be kept without deteriorating as well as one containing chaff, by drying it thoroughly and filling into tin cans which should then be soldered up and kept in a cool place until seeding time.

Tobacco Culture in the West Indies (by) The German Kali Works, Havana, Cuba c. 1920

The best and strongest plants are selected for affording seed. These are not "topped" like the remainder of the crop, and are left standing when the crop is gathered. All suckers are carefully removed from the stems, and sometimes from the leaves also. When the crop is cut, the seed-stalks should be staked, to prevent their destruction by the wind. As soon as the seed-pods blacken, the seed is ripe; the heads are then cut off below the forks of the plant, and are hung in a dry and safe place to cure. Care must be taken to gather them before frost has impaired their vitality. During leisure time, the pods are stripped from the stalks, and the seed is rubbed out by hand, and winnowed. Its vitality is proved by its crackling when thrown upon a hot stove.

Tobacco: A Handbook For Planters (by) C. G. Warnford Lock 1886

A very important matter to be considered in the culture of tobacco is the selection of seed, both as regards quality and variety or kind. It must not be too old, but fresh, full in the grain and well ripened, I have used seed two and three years old which yielded me as good results as that which was but one year old, but it had been fully matured before gathering, well kept and was clean, and bright. If seed be harvested immaturely it will not germinate, and if it be kept from one season to another in a damp compartment it will absorb moisture, mould, and when planted prove worthless.

A Practical Handbook for the Tobacco Planter (by) B. Rush Sensensy, M.D. 1875

Go over your patch and select a sufficient number of large, vigorous and symmetrical plants, which you must allow to stand untopped, that their seed buds may ripen for your future supply of seed. The number of plants which you will let stand must depend upon how much ground you may wish to plant in tobacco the following year. Always select the largest and most fully matured plants for seed.

Two stalks will generally be found ample for the seed necessary for an acre of ground, if well ripened, and much of that will be to spare. It is safe, however, to allow two stalks of your finest, most fully matured, brightest, heaviest and largest leaved plants to remain un-topped for next year's seed. If the plant runs up very high, put a stake along side and tie it, so that in case of a heavy storm it be not blown over and broken. Do this to all those intended for seed, which have shot up to any considerable height, for if they be blown down and broken before the seed is ripe, it will be worthless.

A Practical Handbook for the Tobacco Planter (by) B. Rush Sensensy, M.D. 1875

At the time of topping, or when the buds have made their appearance, a few plants are usually left for seed. Only the best, finest, and healthiest looking plants are selected for this purpose. These are allowed to grow and blossom at their full height. Sometimes all of the leaves are removed; but, usually, only the bottom leaves are taken off. When ripe, the little balls containing the seed are carefully cut off with a knife or other sharp instrument. The cutting must be done carefully, so that the seed will not fall out. The seed pods are then spread out in the sun and, when thoroughly dried, the seeds can be removed. The seed should be cleaned, preferably in a small seed mill, and only the heaviest seed preserved for the next planting.

Cultivation of Tobacco (by) Clarence Dorsey, 1903

SOWING

Methods of Sowing & Starting a Tobacco Crop

Very few of the early growers sowed seed directly into the field, since the tiny sprouts are vulnerable to all kinds of weather and critter disasters. Instead they used seedbeds to start their little plants, and there were all kinds of designs for these protective environments. Today, a home gardener intending to grow only a few plants might not need a seedbed because the little plants can be sheltered where they lie with little plastic or cheesecloth tents, or they can be started in peat pots in a protected environment and then set out when they are ready – as described in Section One. However, there is lots of excellent information on the care and handling of infant Tobacco plants in this early seedbed literature, and even a home-grower might want to consider building a seedbed, depending upon weather and predator conditions where you are growing.

I make ready my frames in the fall of the year, generally about the latter part of October. A hole is digged, in a southern, south-eastern or eastern exposure, twelve feet long, five feet wide and about twelve inches deep. On this, on the edges, I place a frame, supported at each corner by a strong stake driven into the ground. In the fall, before the ground freezes I secure two cart loads of leaf mould which I place along side of my frame, and cover up closely with straw and bundles of corn fodder, ready to be unearthed in February or March.

When the proper time arrives, say about the last of February to the middle of March, when the sun has acquired good power, when the ice breaks up and the ground begins to thaw, then I begin my first Spring operations for tobacco. This, in our latitude is ordinarily a month sooner than you would be enabled to seed in the open ground, unless it be an exceptionally early Spring. I then have the hole filled to the top with a lively, half rotted stable manure, that produced from the horse stable, a straw manure, hot and in an active stage of decomposition. I never use old or fully rotted manure, as it would not generate the heat necessary for the purpose required. This manure, is packed well into the hole by being firmly trod upon. Then I unhouse my pile of leaf mould by removing straw and fodder. It is in fine condition, not having been frozen, or if so, only a few inches in depth. This is turned over and thoroughly pulverized. Then my frame, which is about the same size as the hole in length and breadth, and fifteen inches high at the back and ten inches in front, giving a slope of five inches to the sun, being all ready is placed over the hole and secured on the stakes. I then mix with the leaf mould about one bushel of leached ashes, and two bushels of finely pulverized horse droppings.

The soil being then prepared, is placed upon the manure inside the frame, to the depth of about eight inches, moderately pressed down, and evenly and smoothly raked over its entire extent. Then I take my seed, which I am most careful to assure myself is of first-rate quality, not more than a heaped teaspoonful, I then mix this seed intimately with a quart of ground plaster or dry leached ashes, and sow it evenly over the surface of the bed, I never rake the bed but take a light, inch thick, pine board and use it to press the earth down lightly over the whole surface. Then my sowing is completed, and I place on the frame four sashes containing window glass, each frame being three feet wide by about five feet long, sufficient to effectually cover the frame, and made close enough to exclude cold and to retain all heat generated within. I then bank up the earth all around against the sides of the frame. If the sun lie bright and warm, in the course of four or five days I open the frame by lifting one of the sash, and I find it quite warm within and a gentle vapor arising. I run my hand down into the earth, and I find it has become quite warm, and in case the soil be a little dry I take a can or two of tepid water and sprinkle it all over. I then leave it, and in the course of eight or ten days I find the seed germinating nicely, coming up thick enough, all over the bed. From this time on, as often as the weather will allow of it I open the frame about noon of each day, for an hour or two, and give the young plants an airing.

A Practical Handbook for the Tobacco Planter (by) B. Rush Sensensy, M.D. 1875

No step in the cultivation of tobacco is more important than proper care in the preparation and sowing of the seed beds. This work can not be neglected without running the risk of a partial or total failure of the crop. To make good seed beds is a laborious task and requires good judgment in the selection of the location, soil and in the preparation of the land. To have plenty of good, strong, healthy plants is the surest foundation for a good crop of tobacco, provided they are from seed true to the desired standard. It is very important that in the preparation of the seed bed an abundant supply of seed should be sown, and provisions made for a succession of plants; so that, when the planting season comes, the supply of plants suitable for transplanting will be ample for the purpose, and the supply will be maintained throughout the period in which the planting is to be done.

Cultivation of Tobacco (by) Clarence Dorsey, 1903

The following is the direction of Hon. George Geddes: " To raise the plants, the fall before pulverize the bed fine, and mix with the soil hog or some other manure that has no foul seeds in it. Sow seeds on the well-raked bed, as soon as the ground can be properly prepared in the spring, about one ounce to a square rod, equally distributed all over the bed. Roll hard with a handroller, but do not cover the seed. Glass should be kept over the bed until the plants appear, which will be in two or three weeks; after they are up and started, the glass will be required only at night, and in cold days. The bed should be kept moist and free from .weeds. When the plants are three inches high they are large enough to set."

The following are Mr. Minor's directions for the seedbed " A rich virgin loam with a slight mixture of sand is ascertained to be the best soil for raising tobacco plants. Such spots are indicated by the growth of alder and hazel bushes in bottoms, and on the margin of small streams, and if the situation has the command of water, for irrigation, it is on that account to be preferred - the spot being selected, the first operation is to burn it with a strong fire. For this purpose the growth of ever kind is cut off (not grubbed up), and the whole surface raked very clean; the burning should be done before Christmas, or as soon after as the weather will permit - and if done thus early it cannot be well too heavy, even bringing the soil to a hard cake.

"The wonderful fertility imparted to soil by fire, has of late years been clearly proved and developed by various experiments in this and other countries, but judging from long-established practice, we suppose it is a fact that has been long known to tobacco planters, that this fertility is imparted by the fire, and no ways dependent upon the ashes left by the process, is clearly proved from the fact, that the same results will ensue if the ashes are swept off clean. Or take another piece of ground of equal quality, cover it with as much or more ashes, and prepare it in every respect similar, except burning, and plants cannot be raised in it. Hence the necessity and propriety of regular and uniform burning, the want of which is always manifested by a diminutive, yellow, and sickly growth of plants in those spots not sufficiently acted on by the fire.

" After the ground becomes cool from burning, the whole surface should be swept with a coarse twig broom to take out the coals. In this operation some of the ashes will be removed, but that is of no consequence; it should then be broken up about two inches deep, with grubbing hoes, in which operation and in repeated choppings afterwards, with hilling hoes, all roots will be cut, and finally got out with a fine iron-tooth rake, which leaves the ground in proper order to receive the seed.

" The most approved time for sowing is about the 1st of February, the beds previously prepared being suffered to lie and mellow by the frost and snows to that time. But it will do very well to burn and sow after that time, as late as the first of March, taking care not to have the heat so great. The quantity of seed is as much as can be taken up in a common table spoon for 100 Square yards, and in that proportion. This quantity of seed should be mixed with about one gallon of clean ashes, and half that quantity of plaster of Paris, and the whole well incorporated, and then strewed uniformly over the bed at two operations, crossing at right angles to ensure regularity. Cabbage seed, for early planting. Tomato, Celery, and Lettuce seed may be sowed in small quantities with the Tobacco seed, without injury to the growth of the plants.

"After sowing the seed the ground is immediately. This quantity of plant bed is generally considered, under good circumstances, as sufficient to set ten thousand hills in good time. But the prudent planter, taking into consideration the casualties of fly, drought, &c., will do well to make a large allowance. We know of no certain remedy or antidote against the fly which destroys the early plants.   trodden over closely with the feet, and covered thick with naked brush. If the frost is severe from this time it is common to take off the brush some time in the month of March, before the plants appear, and tread the bed again, and at the same time give the ground a slight dressing of manure. The dung of fowls of all sorts, is sought after for this purpose, which being beaten, is sifted over the bed through a coarse basket or riddle. The brush is then restored, and not finally removed until the leaves of the plants are half an inch in diameter; when the dressing of manure is again applied taking care to wait the approach of rain for that purpose. Any grass or weeds that may have sprung up in the mean time are carefully picked out. In dry seasons, if the situation admits of it, the bed must be irrigated by draining a small stream of water around the edge of it. If not it should be watered every evening with a common watering pot, or pine bushes dipped in water and shook over the bed until sufficient moisture is obtained. Under a careful observance of this management, the plants, according as the seasons have been favorable or not, will be fit to transplant from the 15th of May to the 10th of June. A planter thinks himself lucky if he can get his crop pitched by the 10th of June. After that, the seasons are uncertain from the heat of the weather, and the chances of success for a crop are precarious ; though it has been known to succeed when planted in the middle of July."

(in) Tobacco Culture: being a complete Manual or Practical Guide (by) C. M. Saxton 1868

The following, by Judge Beatty gives, no doubt, what the author regards as the best practice for Kentucky :

" The first step in the process of tobacco culture is to make provision for an abundant supply of plants. Tobacco seed are very small, and the plants, when they spring from the ground, grow very slowly, and would soon be smothered by weeds if not carefully guarded against. The places selected for plant beds, should be such as would not be likely to produce many weeds. New ground or that which has been long set in grass, would be best for this purpose. To guard still further against weeds, and to insure a thrifty growth of plants, it is essential that the place in which the seed are to be sown, should be burnt. A light burning with straw or other light material will not be sufficient. A good coat of brush laid upon the ground intended to be used for a plant bed, and arranged so closely as to make it burn readily, serves best for the purpose. Care must be taken also, before laying on the brush, to take all trash from the ground, so that the heat may readily destroy the seeds of any weeds which may have been deposited there. New ground is always to be preferred for plant beds, and brush as the material for burning the ground. But if the tobacco planter have no new ground, then he must substitute grass land in its stead, and this should be well burned by having a range of logs (those which are seasoned are best) laid along one edge of the ground, intended for plant bed, and heaped up sufficiently to make them burn readily These must be set on fire, and after burning the ground which they cover sufficiently, they must be moved by means of hooks, to the adjacent ground not yet burnt ; and so on, in succession, until the entire space, intended for a plant bed is burnt. If one set of logs is not sufficient to burn a space as large as will be necessary, others must be added so as to enlarge the space, or they may be burnt at different places as may be most convenient.

" Where sod ground is intended to be used, it would be advantageous to have the sod slightly skinned off with sharp hoes, before the space is burnt over, After the ground is burnt it must stand sufficiently long to cool, and then the ashes should be carefully removed. The ground should now be dug up with hoes, to the depth of two or three inches, and so as to pulverize it as much as possible, and should be well raked with an iron tooth rake, so as to break up the soil into the most minute parts. It will now be ready for sowing the seed. It is important that this operation should be as regular as possible, and care should be taken to put the proper quantity of seed upon the ground. If sowed too thick, the plants will be so much crowded as to injure their growth. If sowed too thin, a deficiency of plants may be the consequence. A common silver table spoonful of seed will be sufficient for fifty square yards. More than that quantity should not be sowed on that space of ground. But if the ground prepared be abundant, the plants would grow more thrifty by sowing a spoonful of seed on seventy or eighty square yards. The seed allotted for a particular bed should be put into a vessel half filled with fine mould or earth, and stirred so thoroughly as to cause the seed to be equally distributed in all parts. It should now be separated into two equal divisions. And the plant bed having been divided into convenient lands for sowing, one portion should be sowed as equally as possible in one direction, and the other portion in the same bed, in the opposite direction. The plant bed should now be well raked with an iron tooth rake, both ways, and should then be well trodden by the feet of men or boys, so as to render the loose soil firm and compact. The bed should be thinly covered over with brush to keep it moist, and to protect the plants from frost. Plant beds should be prepared and sown as early in February as the weather will admit, though it will be in good time if sown any time in that month."

(in) Tobacco Culture: being a complete Manual or Practical Guide (by) C. M. Saxton 1868

For every thimble full of seed mix it with one pint of ashes or fine soil that will crumble in the hand, and sow it broad-cast. After the seed has been thus sown, rake the surface of the bed over very slightly; then tread it down with the feet, or spat it down with the spade ; or, a better way is, to take a piece of plank, twelve or fourteen inches square, put a handle in it like a churn-dasher, then walk backward, spatting the bed down evenly, in order that the ground may at once adhere closely to the seed.

The Tobacco Growers Guide (by) James Mossman 1863

Mr. Schneider, whose success as an Illinois planter has already been mentioned, expresses himself thus : "Raising tobacco-plants from seed is somewhat similar to raising cabbage-plants, but is different in two important things : It takes considerably more time for the seed to sprout (six weeks), and, on account of disturbing the roots, cannot well stand weeding. Therefore the principal care in providing the seed-bed is, to prepare for the early starting of the seed, and to have the bed free from all weed-seeds.

In the West we prepare the seed-bed in the following manner : we take a plot of land - newly cleared land is preferred - sloping southward, and protected against winds. The bed should be 4 feet broad and 8 feet long; on this we pile brush, wood, and heavy logs, sufficient to keep up a strong fire for at least one hour, and burn it. When the coals begin to die out, or before the soil is cold, the bed is cleared off, and only the fine ashes are left; then it is hoed thoroughly and as deep as the strongest heat has penetrated, after which it is raked cross and lengthwise, until the soil is entirely pulverized. Everything that might hinder the growing of the plants, and their taking out afterwards, is carefully removed.

On this bed a thimbleful of seed, well mixed with a few handfuls of ashes or earth, is sown broadcast, and tramped in with the feet, or slapped with the under side of the spade or any other suitable instrument. After this, the bed is thoroughly wetted with a weak manure water, 12 lb. of hen-droppings, or 1 lb. of soot in 10 gallons of water, and lightly covered with straw. The seed-bed does not need much attention at first, if the weather remains mild ; but if there is danger of night frosts, a layer of brush must be made, and on this a layer of straw 2 to 4 inches thick, according to the degree of frost. The straw is removed in the morning, and put on again at evening, leaving it off entirely when the nights are mild. Although the seed-bed is ready now, it must not be left to itself, and requires some care. The plants must always have sufficient moisture, and if timely rains do not fall, they must be watered with weak liquid manure as often as needed. Should weeds appear, notwithstanding all precautions, they must be removed with the utmost care. The above-mentioned quantity of seed is sufficient to raise plants for one acre.

Tobacco: A Handbook For Planters (by) C. G. Warnford Lock 1886

In preparing my seed bed I am always careful to select a warm and sheltered locality, looking to the south or east. Select, if you can, a piece of new ground, protected at the north and west by a copse, piece of a woodland or a large building or close board fence. Then rake all the dead leaves, old brush, corn stalks and old limbs of trees, into small heaps about twenty feet from each other and then set afire. When they are thoroughly consumed have the ashes raked cleverly over the surface which is intended for your seed bed. Then have the ground well spaded to the depth of at least twelve inches. While it is being spaded work into the furrows a plentiful supply of well rotted horse manure. After spading the ground have every clod broken, all stone and stubble removed and rake it clean and smooth. Then top dress the surface with a compost made up of horse droppings two parts, leached ashes two parts, and one part Peruvian guano or chicken manure. This must be well raked and thoroughly incorporated in the surface soil. When this is done the ground is in readiness for the seed. The ground must not be too wet neither too dry, when the seed is sown, but select a day when there is an appearance of approaching rain, or one or two days after a light rain. Do not sow the seed on a windy day, as the light grain will be blown and fall unevenly over the surface of the bed, but choose a mild and calm morning.

For every twenty-five yards of surface square, take one tablespoonful of seed and mix thoroughly in about one peck of ground plaster or finely sifted ashes. Then sow it broadcast over the bed, endeavoring to secure as even an application to the whole surface as possible. Secure from the slaughter yard about one bushel of hog hair and spread it evenly over the bed. This answers several purposes. It secures warmth and protection to the delicate young plants and in addition seems to supply to them some chemical ingredients which tend to promote their rapid growth. When this is done get a few bundles of small branches of pine or cedar and place them over the surface of the bed. These also furnish heat and protection and may be removed when the plants have grown to the size of a silver dollar. During the growth of the plants great attention must be given to weeds, taking them out as soon as large enough to be distinguished from the young plants and this must be done by hand. In a case of a drought, sprinkle the plants in the evening from a watering pot, giving them a thorough soaking. This will be all that will be found necessary to mature the plants for use when wanted to set out in the patch.

A Practical Handbook for the Tobacco Planter (by) B. Rush Sensensy, M.D. 1875

After the assignment of space within the garden the women stand just inside the site facing away from it, with digging-sticks in one hand and the Tobacco seed in the other. The men sit facing the women. The women dance, pointing their sticks at the ground. After the singing of four songs each woman punches a hole in the ground, then each walks backward along the space allotted to her. The husbands follow in their wake, walking forward and dropping the seeds into the holes.

The Tobacco Society of the Crow Indians (Robert Lowie) 1919

The best way and manner of planting and curing it would be easily obtained by experience: many attempting it, some would be sure to discover the right way of ordering of it, and what ground or places it best affects. But that which hath been observed is, that it affects a rich, deep and warm soil well dressed in the spring before planting time: The young plants raised from seed in February or March, on a hot bed, and then planted abroad in your prepared ground, from whence you may expect a very good crop, and sometimes two crops in a year. The leaves, when gathered, are first laid together on heaps for some time, and then hanged up (by threads run through them) in the shade, until they are through dry, and then put up and kept, the longer the better. In this, experience is the best master."

The Introduction of Tobacco into Europe (Berthold Laufer) 1924

The growing of crops under shade is not a new idea, but was practiced perhaps hundreds of years ago; but the cultivation of fields of tobacco under a light cloth shelter of some character is comparatively recent. The idea of using shade started in the United States in Florida, where in the last few years tobacco cultivation has made enormous advances. It was noticed that in new land, only partially cleared of the forest growth, the plants grown under the scattered trees were far superior to plants not so shaded. From this the idea of artificial shade had its birth and now large fields, nearly 5 hectares in size, are grown under shade with great success.

Cultivation of Tobacco (by) Clarence Dorsey, 1903

TRANSPLANTING

Transplanting or Setting Out The Young Plants

Here again, gardeners in the 21st century have innovations like peat pots to help them grow their seedlings to the point where they can be set out after the last frost has come and gone. Planters in earlier times had to develop techniques for pulling their tiny plants from the seedbeds in which they were started and transplanting them successfully, often by the tens of thousands at a time. While modern gardeners have it a lot easier (and so do their little plants) there is still a lot we can learn about handling our tiny charges from these master growers of earlier centuries.

From the Report of Hon. Geo. Geddes, of New York.

" Mark the land one way for rows, three feet four inches. Make hills by hauling up a few hoes full of dirt and press it well with the hoe. In taking the plants from the bed take care to keep the roots wet. Unless the ground is quite damp, put a pint of water on each hill half an hour before setting. Make a hole, put in the root, and press the dirt close to it, all the way to the lower end. If any plant does not live, take care to set another. Unless the earth is wet, or at least moist, water the plants as soon after setting as may be necessary. In about one week, cultivate and hoe."

(in) Tobacco Culture: being a complete Manual or Practical Guide (by) C. M. Saxton 1868

The best size for setting is when the leaves are from an inch and a half, to two inches in length, or something like the size of a silver dollar. The plant bed, several hours before being ready to transplant, should be well watered to allow the young plants to be easily drawn out, they may be pulled by taking hold and gently doubling up the several large leaves of the plant at once. Should they not come up easily, then, if necessary, use a knife or fork.

No careless person should be allowed to perform this work, for much injury to the crop might result from mutilating the plants in any way.

The practice of crowding a large number of plants into a basket, to be taken to the field, is a poor one, resulting in the bruising and breaking of the roots and leaves. The young plants should be kept straight, after being taken from the Seed-bed, with their roots together, and placed in shallow boxes, or pans, to be taken to the fields; and not a sufficient number placed together to admit of crushing, keeping what little soil that adheres to their roots from being loosened. They should also be protected from the hot sun, on the way to the field. Many plants will sometimes become wilted before setting, through carelessness in this respect. One person should drop the plants ahead in the row, one plant to each hill, and the 'setter' follow; in setting, the plant should be taken in the right hand and a hole made in the center of the hill with the left forefinger for the roots, and should be deep enough to take them in, without bending, to the same level they occupied in the seed-bed. The earth should then be pressed firmly around the roots with both hands ; the pressure should be sufficient to close the hole in the soil at the bottom as well as at the top.

Care should be used not to get the plants too deep, or press the bud of unopened leaves, in making the soil compact. They should, however, be well covered and have a sufficient depth of soil.

It is also a good plan to set an extra plant about every rod or two, which may be used to fill vacancies that will be found in the after cultivation; such plants may be taken up, with a small quantity of soil attached to the roots, and reset without injury. As the Cut Worm will destroy some of the young plants, and others will wither, the ground should be carefully examined and reset, every few days, until a good stand is secured. It is important that the setting of the plants should be well done.

When a hot sun succeeds the transplanting, shading the plants with a handful of grass, or straw, for a few days, will prevent them wilting as badly, as they otherwise might. The reason for using grass or straw, is, that it soon dries up, and the winds will remove it from the settings, saving the trouble of removing by hand.

Tobacco from the Seedbed to the Packing Case (by) W. T. Sim 1897

When the plants are four or five inches high in the beds they are ready to set out in the hills. As a rule we prefer a medium-sized plant, because the larger the plant the more moisture and sustenance it requires, and the small plant is safer, but not so far advanced as the medium or larger one. After giving that part of the bed from which you wish to remove plants a thorough soaking with water, for the purpose of softening the soil to prevent the breaking off of the finer roots, remove the plants carefully and wash or shake off all the plant-bed soil in order to give them a fresh free start in the new soil. Take great care of them, and do not place so many together that they all be crushed or bruised, nor keep them out of the ground until the tender roots dry up, but take them at once to the field and drop one on each hill, to be followed immediately by the planter, who should take hold of it near the roots with the thumb and forefinger of the left hand and with the right hand smooth down, or in other words, straighten out, the roots. Then, with a peg about six inches long, make a hole in the centre of the hill large enough to admit the roots without their touching on the sides ; also make it deep enough to take in the longest roots without bending them. Put in the plant carefully as deep as the bud; then, with the peg and thumb of the left hand, press the soil firmly to the roots, and draw the earth around the plant so as to fill the entire hole. The best time to transfer the plants from the bed to the hills is when the soil is moist, but not so wet as to cause it to bake around the roots and kill them, or prevent their getting an early start. If the season is very dry, before setting out, take the dry earth from the tops of the hills, set the plants late in the day, giving them the benefit of the night dew, and before the dew has dried off in the morning, cover them with straw, brush, leaves, or anything suitable.

The Planters Guide for Curing and Cultivating Tobacco (by) Shelton Tobacco Curing Company 1871

In Sumatra, where all necessary operations are carried on by hand, the coolie is provided with a plant string, the same length as the field. Each end of the string is securely attached to a stick of the same length that it is intended the rows shall be separated. This string is divided into intervals by means of colored string to show the proper distance of the plants in the row. By means of a sharp stick, holes are made at the proper distance, about 10 centimeters deep and 7 centimeters in width. The holes are watered immediately before the plants are put in. The plants are pulled from the bed when the dew is still on them, and set out late in the afternoon, when the rays of the sun are not very strong. During the daytime the pulled plants are kept in a basket and carefully watered, and covered with cloth. About 4 o'clock in the afternoon, the coolie drops from the basket a plant beside each hole and, when all of the plants are dropped, commences to plant. He holds the plant in the center of the hole with his left hand and, with his right hand, presses the soil around the roots carefully but firmly, and gives the plant a slight pull without removing it.

Cultivation of Tobacco (by) Clarence Dorsey, 1903

From an Essay of Peter Minor, Esq., of Virginia.

" It is most common to wait for rain, or season as we call it, to perform this operation, in which case the hills must be previously cut off" about four inches above their base ; but in early planting it is quite safe to proceed without a season, provided it is done in the evening, and the hills cut off at the same time. It is universally admitted that a moderate season is better than a very wet one ; and that is considered the best, in which the earth does not entirely lose its friability, but at the same time will bear to be compressed closely about the roots of the plant without danger of becoming hard or baked. Under the most favorable circumstances, however, some plants will fail or perish, and therefore the ground must be gone over after every rain until the last of June to replant the missing hills."

(in) Tobacco Culture: being a complete Manual or Practical Guide (by) C. M. Saxton 1868

From the Prairie Farmer of January 10, 1863.

" Mark out in ridges, three feet four inches apart, which may be done with a winged shovel plow. Then cross at right angles at the distance of thirty inches, and the land will have been divided into hills three feet, four inches one way, by thirty inches the other. The hills may now be dressed up with a hoe, if necessary, and patted down, so that they shall be somewhat rounding, and about twenty inches broad near the base. The ground may be left until a proper day comes for planting - cloudy weather, with indications of rain is the best; if not, as soon after the rain as the ground is in suitable working order. As good a plan as any, if the weather is dry, is to make a hole in each hill, and pour therein about a pint of water, and set the plant as soon as it has soaked away, drawing the dryer earth about it, which may be done very quickly by having one hand to water, while another sets the plants. If the hills have become weedy between the fitting and the planting of the land, they should be scraped before planting, by making quick, shallow cuts with a hoe, just beneath the surface. In extensive cultivation, a division of labor of this kind will save a large expense, in the crop.

If the weather continues dry and hot, they should be slightly watered about nine o'clock in the morning, and again about three P. M., if they show a disposition to wilt. Reset immediately if the plants are destroyed by worms. Considerable care is sometimes necessary in order to get a good stand. Setting the plants is performed, by thrusting the left hand deep into the soil, and placing the plant properly with the right, and pressing the dirt pretty firmly about it."

(in) Tobacco Culture: being a complete Manual or Practical Guide (by) C. M. Saxton 1868

Cultivating The Growing Crop

A grower with acres of Tobacco faced serious challenges from weeds until the plants got tall enough to crowd out the weeds growing between the plants. This required labor-intensive cultivation either by mechanical plow or, more often, by hand with a hoe. Today's growers will face the same problem of destroying the weeds without damaging the root systems of their precious tobacco plants, but the prospect of weeding a small garden is far less daunting than the need to manage dozens or hundreds of acres. Nevertheless, the weeding skills remain the same, and a modern Tobacco grower can benefit from the lessons of the past.

In a week or ten days after the plants have been set out, or as soon as they secure a good "stand," that is a good " send off" "or "start," have taken root and started growth in their new quarters, then I begin cultivating the soil. About this time grass and weeds will put in their appearance and require close attention. I first send my cultivator through the patch, twice through the same row, not too near the plants, but well off so as not to throw the soil over them. This being done my men go carefully along every row with their hoes, breaking clods, smoothing the soil where inequalities exist and stirring the soil between the plants, carefully digging out all grass and weeds, and uncovering any plants that may have had soil thrown upon them. Where there is a small or sickly looking plant, place alongside of it another and a more vigorous one. Do not pull out the first one but allow both to grow together for a time, and then remove the least vigorous of the two.

My first cultivation I generally consider the most important, and hence exercise more than ordinary care. I keep the soil immediately under each plant and around it fine and loose, and draw a little fine, moist earth, well up around each stalk. Great care must be exercised in plowing and hoeing that the roots are not disturbed. Everything depends on your plants getting a good hearty "send-off," or in other words a good stand. When you secure this, when you look over your patch and see long straight lines of delicate green, each plant standing up, vigorous and meaning to grow, then half the battle is won.

The cultivator I prefer to the shovel plow, as it better reduces the soil, and as before stated I pass once up and once down through the same row. Never neglect this first cultivation and attention to your plants, for if you do your crop will be lost. A warm rain and hot sun will so stimulate weeds and grass that what at an early day could be easily eradicated, soon becomes a deep seated enemy to destroy which will surely also uproot, tear out, break down and ruin your young and tender plants. If you are careless and dilatory at this time you will surely suffer by having a poor and perhaps a worthless crop.

Failures, particularly in new growers, most often result from lack of attention at this critical infantile period of the crop

A Practical Handbook for the Tobacco Planter (by) B. Rush Sensensy, M.D. 1875

As it is always desirable to get a uniform growth, great care should be exercised to have each plant live. Replanting should be done as quickly as it is possible to determine where fresh plants are needed. If the soil is moist and showers are frequent, watering the plants is unnecessary; but, if the ground is dry, they should be watered immediately after setting and each day thereafter, as long as the plants require it. The quantity of water used is in all cases governed by the condition and nature of the soil. Usually, after setting, the plants are undisturbed for a period of several days, during which time they are taking root. After this time cultivation should be begun and continued rapidly and frequently, until further cultivation is liable to injure the growing leaves. Cultivation at first can be done by a light plow or hoe; but, after the plants have reached a considerable height, only the hoe should be used, and this very lightly. At this period the leaves furnish sufficient shade to prevent the soil from baking and hindering the growth of the surface roots.

Cultivation of Tobacco (by) Clarence Dorsey, 1903

Early and frequent cultivation are beneficial for several reasons - First : exposing the soil to atmospheric action is good for the soil itself, and indirectly to the plant. Secondly: It breaks up the hardened and sun-baked surface soil, thus favoring the early rooting of the young plant. Thirdly: It destroys grass and weeds which would otherwise soon crowd and smother the young plants. To sum up, then, always see that your plants have a good, fair start. You may cultivate between the rows as often as once a week, and keep at it until the tobacco becomes too large to allow of horse and plow passing up and down the furrows. As the leaves increase in size, you must see to it that they be not covered by the soil, those lowest down, which is thrown towards them by the plow.

A Practical Handbook for the Tobacco Planter (by) B. Rush Sensensy, M.D. 1875

Transplanting should be done, if possible, when the ground is damp, otherwise it will be necessary to water while transplanting. Three feet apart both ways is a safe rule in setting the plants, and the earth should be pressed firmly about the roots. Great attention is necessary to the newly set plants. Some cover them during the heat of mid-day, others water them morning and evening until they get established. Many will fail, and should be at once replaced. If the ground is very dry, a little hole should be made for the plant and a pint of water turned in. (By selecting a damp day, or just after a rain you escape this trouble. Never set out in dry weather if you can avoid it). As soon as it has disappeared, set the plant. In a week or ten days after setting cultivate and hoe. Repeat the operation as often as once in ten days, and keep the ground loose and clean until the crop is too large to be worked among.

A Practical Handbook for the Tobacco Planter (by) B. Rush Sensensy, M.D. 1875

INSECTS

Insects That Damage Tobacco & How To Control Them
The 'Tobacco Hawk' moth is without question the most costly predator known to the Tobacco grower, and the old-time growers had to develop ingenious, effective ways to keep this insect from destroying their crop. Not just the Tobacco Hawk but other predators also threatened their crop, and thus their livelihood. Some used poisons; some used biological control; and some used their thumb and forefinger and the heel of their boot. Again, managing this insect and its hungry little grub is a daunting challenge if you have to inspect each plant in a crop of hundreds of thousands of plants, every day for weeks during the moth's season. In contrast, a garden with a few plants, or even a few hundred, makes for a far less strenuous task – but one that is essential nonetheless!

Soon after the plant is set, the cut worm makes his appearance, cutting off the stems of the young plants. Go through the field every morning, and where a plant has been cut off dig open the hill and destroy the worm. This is the only method we know of as being effectual.

A Practical Handbook for the Tobacco Planter (by) B. Rush Sensensy, M.D. 1875

The plants are liable to be cut by the cut worms until they get well to growing. These worms generally cease their work in June, when the warm, showery and growing weather sets in; it is best therefore to watch when they quit working on the young sprouts, as the most proper time to commence setting the plants. You must look over your fields every morning, for some days, to look after the worms, carrying a few plants with you to reset, if any have been destroyed by the worms or failed to grow. You will often find the worms close by the injured plants, under ground, which should be destroyed.

The Tobacco Growers Guide (by) James Mossman 1863

Soon after setting out the plants, look sharp for long black or brown worms, which burrow in the hills and destroy the plants. Unearth and kill them every morning as long as they can be found. They seldom trouble new land to any great extent. The best time and method we know of for destroying them is to plow up the land during the winter and freeze them.

If the worms are numerous, the plants should be thoroughly examined at least twice a week. Destroy not only the worms, but all the eggs that can be found; or, what is still better, seek out and destroy the flies which deposit these eggs. These flies are gray in color, with yellow spots on each side of the body, and may be found about sunset flitting about the weeds and flowers, extracting their juices by means of their peculiar tongue, which is four or five inches in length. The Jamestown weed, or "Jimson" weed, as it is commonly called, which bears a white, bell-shaped blossom, is very attractive to these flies. Many of them may be destroyed by dropping a little of the following mixture into these blossoms: One ounce of cobalt, dissolved in one pint of water and sweetened with some kind of syrup. But this is equally as fatal to the blossoms as to the flies; therefore we give you the following instructions for making an artificial substitute, which will prove to be more durable than the natural flower, and quite as effective. The ladies can best perform this work, as they happily possess more taste and skill in such matters.

Procure for their use a quire of white paper and a bottle of mucilage. Then make a small block of suitable size and shape, on which to form the cone, and furnish them with a natural flower to imitate. If you have no blossom of the Jamestown weed, let them try their powers of imitation in making a "morning-glory." After forming the cone, clip it around the rim and curl slightly, to make it look as much like a flower as possible. Attach them to branches or bushes, and place them in your thickest growth of tobacco. They should be supplied with a few drops of the poison every evening, and it may be necessary to replace the flowers after a heavy rain. By following the above instructions you will save much trouble in worming. A flock of turkeys will also be found very useful in catching and destroying worms, and can only be equalled by children to whom premiums have been offered.

The Planters Guide for Curing and Cultivating Tobacco (by) Shelton Tobacco Curing Company 1871

Mr. J. Pcriam in the Prairie Farmer for January l7, 1863, says :

" After the first of July look out for worms upon the leaf, and from this time until harvested, great care will be necessary, in keeping them down, and removing the suckers as fast as they appear. When the plant has begun to form buds, it should be topped leaving from nine to fifteen leaves, according to the strength of plant—the latter number is not too many for strong healthy plants. From this time until the crop is ready to cut, it will be necessary to go over it as often as once a week, and remove suckers, as they appear, keeping a sharp look out all the time for worms, killing them as fast as they appear, by throwing them on the ground and scraping them with the foot. They are a large green worm such as often appear on tomato plants, and are more destructive to the crop than anything else. If the directions have been properly attended to, by the middle of August the crop will have entirely covered the ground ; hereafter the utmost care must be used not to break the leaves in passing among the plants, and in consequence, some people neglect the suckering and worming, to do which would be fatal to the crop. Turkeys are sometimes used for picking off the worms by calling them to the field with corn, but think the better way is to keep help enough in the field to get over the crop about once a week, which will enable them to look for worms constantly

(in) Tobacco Culture: being a complete Manual or Practical Guide (by) C. M. Saxton 1868

From the *Country Gentleman*, a letter from John C. Roberts, of Tariffville, Conn.:

"Messrs. Editors - As my communication on the culture of tobacco, was so favorably received, I thought I might venture to write again. We have had a very large amount of wet, cold weather this spring. On the 12th (of June, 1859) we have a severe frost, which killed corn, potatoes, beans, and other garden vegetables to a great extent, though it did no injury to the tobacco. We are just setting out the tobacco plants, 5,500 or 6,000 to the acre, but the cut-worm keeps us busy; we have to go over the lot every day, early in the morning; and we find 200 or 300 worms to the acre. Is there no remedy for the ravages of these pests? We have tried every thing we know of, but have not found any thing to answer the purpose, but the thumb and finger.

"When the tobacco is set previous to the 15th of June, the cut-worm works at it more than when set later. Some of the best tobacco we had last year, was set on July 5th. After the cut-worm leaves, the greenworm appears. You will find the eggs from which they are produced on the under side of the leaf; they are a pea-green color and the size of the head of a large pin. The worm grows so rapidly that they are from three to four inches long in a week, if not sooner destroyed. They require close watching, for they will frequently destroy a large plant in a single night. The insect which lays the egg is a large moth, about two inches in length; when the wings are spread, they measure from tip to tip from three to five inches. They fly mostly at night, and hence are rarely caught; they are a brownish color, with a head very much like an owl.

(in) Tobacco Culture: being a complete Manual or Practical Guide (by) C. M. Saxton 1868

Insects which attack the tobacco must be carefully sought for and killed at once. They can easily be discovered in the mornings ; if not killed, they may destroy the whole crop in a few days. Turkeys are invaluable for their grub-eating propensities.

Worms, in the American phraseology, here generally known as caterpillars, are the bete noire of the tobacco grower. The most common is highly destructive also to the potato and tomato foliage. The worm as it comes from the egg is so small as to be unobserved, but having an enormous appetite, it devours rapidly, and soon grows to a great size. When not feeding, it lifts up the head and fore-part of the body, and remains apparently lifeless. From its resemblance in this position to the Egyptian Sphinx, Linnaeus gave the name Sphinx to the genus. The larva is of a light green colour, with whitish oblique stripes, and has a horn upon the rear end of the body. Though it is repulsive in appearance, it is perfectly harmless to touch, and may be picked off with the hands without fear.

After it has reached its full size, it leaves the scene of its ravages and goes into the earth, where it throws off its skin and becomes a brown-coloured chrysalis. The curious projection, like a handle, at the end of the chrysalis, is a sheath which holds the tongue of the future moth. The moth or perfect insect is fully 2 in. long in the body and the spread of its wings reaches 5 in. It is of a grey colour, with orange-coloured spots on each side of the body. As there are five of these spots on each side, it is called Sphinx quinque-maculatus, or Fivespotted Sphinx. The moths may be seen towards night flitting about the flowers, from which they suck the juices by means of their remarkable tongue, which is 5-6 inches long. When the tongue is not in use, it is closely coiled up and hidden between the two feelers. From the manner of their flight and feeding, they are frequently mistaken for humming-birds, and are called " hummingbird moths," and "horn-blowers." The moths should always be destroyed if possible; by so doing we prevent the production of several hundreds of most destructive worms. Naturalists make one or two other species, which closely resemble the Five-spotted Moth, and are only distinguished by characters which would not be noticed except by the entomologist.

Tobacco: A Handbook For Planters (by) C. G. Warnford Lock 1886

"Hardly is the cut-worm out of the way, and sometimes the tobacco grower, soon after transplanting, has to hunt up, pursue, and slaughter two or three hundred of these per acre, day after day, before the horn-worm, green-worm, or tobacco-worm, as variously called, makes his appearance. Scarcely ten days in succession, from first to last, can the field be left to take care of itself. Three months of constant care and frequent toil attend the growth, and about as many more the harvesting, curing, and marketing.

"We know of no short way of dealing with the cut worm. It is possible that the piercing of the ground with a crow bar, in two, three, or half a dozen places, near the plant, might entrap some of them ; and though laborious, this process might, in some extreme cases, where these worms are very numerous, be worth resorting to, inasmuch as it would, in some degree operate as a preventive of mischief, while the cultivator sleeps, or is absent for other reasons. If the depredator falls into the hole, he will be pretty sure to be hindered awhile from his mischief, and if the cultivator drops his bar into same holes, at his next round, the hindrance would become permanent. But we doubt whether there is any way less laborious, than to crush them under the heel, or more than half as sure. Some would say^ instead of using the heel, use a stick of wood, say six feet long, an inch and a half through at the lower end, and enlarging slightly upwards, on the ground that this, brought down heavily upon the depredator, would not only put a stop to his mischief, but, when withdrawn, would leave a trap for his fellows. Where the cut-worms are very numerous and destructive, we think the suggestion may be worth heeding, as the killing of each worm would virtually be the setting of a trap for more.

"Plowing late in the fall, and then again early in the spring, tends much to diminish these pests; but it cannot be relied upon to kill them all; the survivors must be met promptly and annihilated ; or a full crop of tobacco, uniform in the time of ripening, and all of a superior quality, cannot be expected. Replanting in the spaces should be attended to promptly, but it cannot wholly repair the mischief, as the replanted hills will rarely show precisely the same forwardness as the first planted.

Tobacco Culture: being a complete Manual or Practical Guide (by) C. M. Saxton 1868

When plants are found with a portion, or all, of their leaves gone, it is another sure indication of the cut worm's presence. Should the weather be clear, and the sun hot, stirring the soil around the plant will make them go deeper into the ground as they cannot stand a loose soil or a hot sun. Ashes m the hill will sometimes destroy these pests, but they are difficult to eradicate. It will often pay to search for them in the hill, and kill them, when they are very troublesome. Plants that have been destroyed, should be replaced, and the hill searched for the worms.

When the plants are about half grown, the tobacco worm is hatched from an egg deposited by a. moth. The egg is generally laid upon the under side of the leaf, and when first hatched - which is in about six days - the worm is so small that it would scarcely be noticed by one unfamiliar with its habits. It grows very rapidly, and proves one of the most destructive of enemies. It begins to eat the leaf on the under side, and is not at first easily detected. A small hole through the leaf is the first indication of its depredations. They increase in size so rapidly, and are so destructive, that if left unmolested for a few days the entire leaf would be destroyed. When full grown, the worm will eat nearly an entire leaf of large size in a single day. Their size and length at this period is nearly that of the forefinger of a man. There are two sets, or broods, of these worms during the season, the first appearing when the plants are about half grown, and the other when the tobacco is almost ripe. It is particularly important that the first brood be destroyed for if they are not they become transformed into the moths which lay the eggs for the second brood, each moth laying about two hundred eggs. Unless the worms that feed upon the leaves of the tobacco are destroyed, the crop will be liable to be lost, or at least rendered so worthless as not to pay for the labor bestowed on its cultivation. The surest remedy is hand picking, and this must be sufficiently frequent to prevent injury to the leaves. The field should be gone over every few days, if possible, during the period of worming, as many will escape notice, and the eggs will continue to hatch ; by a careful examination of the under side of the leaves, the eggs may often be seen and destroyed before the worms are hatched. They are about the size of a mustard seed, of a light greenish cast and seem transparent.

Tobacco from the Seedbed to the Packing Case (by) W. T. Sim 1897

Mr. Thomas describes tobacco worms as "hatched from eggs deposited by what is called the ' tobacco fly.' It is a large, dusky-brown, winged miller, nearly as large as a humming-bird. It lays its eggs on fair evenings and moonlight nights in July and August. It can be seen almost any clear evening, among what are called 'Jimsonweeds,' sucking the flowers. The eggs will hatch out in 24 hours, and the worms commence eating when less than ½ inch long, and continue to eat till they attain the length of 4-5 inches. One worm, in 6 weeks, will destroy a plant so completely as to render it utterly valueless. This pest is vastly more numerous in some seasons than in others. Four years ago there were scarcely any; but for the last three years they have been destructively numerous. The worming of the crop, when they are numerous, is, by far, the most disagreeable and tedious labour attending it. Much of the value of the crop depends upon the care or inattention of performing this part of the work. The crop may have been planted in good time—ploughed, hoed, primed, suckered, topped, cut, and cured well; yet it may have been so riddled by worms as to be comparatively good for nothing.

Tobacco: A Handbook For Planters (by) C. G. Warnford Lock 1886

Worms ought to be picked off and killed as fast they appear, or they will destroy the crop. Turkeys are of great assistance in destroying these insects; they eat them and kill thousands which they do not eat, for it seems to be a cherished amusement to them to kill worms on tobacco; they grow passionately fond of it - they kill for the love of killing.

There are every year two "gluts," as they are called bv planters; the first attacking the plants about the time that they are about one third or half grown, the other comes on when the tobacco is ready for cutting. The first can be easily subdued by a good supply of turkeys, and if they they are effectually destroyed the second glut will be very easy to manage, for it is the opinion of many intelligent and experienced planters that the greater portion of the first glut reappears the same year, as horn-blowers, and breed myriads. When the second army of worms makes its appearance, the tobacco is so large that the turkeys do but little good. The only method, then, to destroy them, is to begin in time. Start when they are being hatched, and keep up a strict watch upon them, going over the whole field, plant by plant, and breaking the eggs, killing such as may be seen, and by constant attention during each morning and evening to this business alone, with the whole force of the farm, they may be prevented from doing much harm. When they disappear the second time, there is no more cause of trouble.

Tobacco Culture: Practical Details (by) Orange Judd Company 1884

The late Peter Minor, of Albemarle County, Va. concludes his treatise, in the following words:

" Tobacco is subject to some diseases, and liable to be injured by more casualties and accidents than any other crop. That growing upon new or fresh high land is seldom injured by any other disease than the spot or firing, which is the effect of very moist, succeeded by very hot weather. For this we know of no remedy or antidote. Tobacco growing upon old land, particularly upon low flats, besides being more subject to spot, is liable to a disease we call the hollow stalk, which is an entire decay and rottenness of the inside or pith, terminating gradually in the decay, and final dropping off of the leaves. This disease is sometimes produced by the wounds caused by pulling off overgrown suckers, thereby admitting too great an absorption of water into the stalk through the wound.

" In land not completely drained, the plants are sometimes apt to take a diminutive growth, sending forth numerous long, narrow leaves, very thickly set on the stalk. This is called walloon tobacco, and is good for nothing. As there is no cure for these diseases when they exist, we can only attend to their prevention. This will at once be pointed out by a knowledge of the cause, which is too much wet, and indicates the necessity of complete and thorough draining before the crop is planted. It may not be amiss here to mention, that tobacco is more injured than any other crop by plowing or hoeing the ground when it is too wet, and to express a general caution on that head.

" The accidents by which tobacco is often injured and destroyed, are high winds, heavy beating rains, hailstorms, and two kinds of worm, the ground or cut-worm, and the large green horn-worm. High winds, besides breaking off the leaves and thereby occasioning a great loss, are apt to turn them over.

" The plant, unlike most others, possesses no power to restore the leaves to their proper position, which must shortly and carefully be done by hand, otherwise the part inverted will gradually perish and moulder away. Those who have studied the anatomy of plants can tell us the cause of this, as well as why nature has denied to tobacco the faculty of restoring its leaves to their proper position.

"The ground-worm, the same which is sometimes so fatal to corn, is ascertained to be the larvae of the common black bug found in great numbers under wheat shocks, &c. This worm is seldom or never found in new land, but abounds in old or manured ground ; and in some years I have seen them so numerous, as to have from forty to fifty taken out of one hill in a morning. The alternatives are either to abandon the crop, or to go over the ground every morning, when they can be found at or near the surface, and destroy them. The missing hills to be regularly replanted.

" The horn-worm is produced from a large, clumsy, gray colored fly, commonly seen late in the evening sucking the flowers of the Stramoniun or Thornapple, or commonly called here the Jamestown Weed. The flies deposit their eggs in the night on the tobacco, and all other narcotic plants indiscriminately, as Irish potatoes, tomatoes, &c. In twenty-four or thirty-six hours the eggs hatch a small worm, which immediately begins to feed on the leaf, and grows rapidly. Great care should be taken to destroy them while young. Turkeys and Guinea fowls are great auxiliaries in this business, but the evil might be greatly lessened if the flies where destroyed, which can easily be done in the night by a person walking over the ground with a torch and a light paddle. They will approach the light and can easily be killed. In this way I have known a hundred killed in one field in the course of an hour.

(in) Tobacco Culture: being a complete Manual or Practical Guide (by) C. M. Saxton 1868

Judson Popenoe gives the following advice with regard to these pests. "As soon as worms appear, which is generally when the leaves are as big as a man's hand, go over the tobacco, looking carefully at every plant. The worms usually stay on the under side of the leaf; if you see a hole in the leaf, no matter how small, raise it up and you will generally find a worm under it. Worming can not be done too carefully. Miss one or two worms on a plant, and before you are aware of it the plant is nearly eaten up. When you find a worm, take hold of it with the thumb and forefinger, giving your thumb that peculiar twist which none but those who are practised in it know how to do, and put the proper amount of pressure on, and my word for it you will render his wormship harmless. Worming has to be continued until the tobacco is cut; the last worming to immediately precede cutting and housing."

Tobacco: A Handbook For Planters (by) C. G. Warnford Lock 1886

This destructive enemy is known by the several names of "Tobacco worm," and "tobacco hawk moth," or " horn blower." Its ravages are not confined to any one section of country or climate, but it invades the tobacco patch wherever the weed is grown, and if not strenuously combated, will certainly ruin the crop. Its ravages are also extended to tomato plants, which, however, are but comparatively little damaged by their incursions. It first appears as a moth, tobacco hawk-moth, and deposits its larvae or eggs on the leaves of the plants. In May and June, and sometimes July, this large moth may be seen during the early summer twilight, hovering over flowers and honeysuckle and Jamestown weed. It is often mistaken for a humming bird, which in its quick and humming flight it much resembles, with its long and flexible tongue it sucks nectar from the flowers, and when at rest it folds its tongue up into a coil. This insect is much like the northern so-called potato worm, and is often mistaken for it in all its stages of larvae, pupa and insect, and can scarcely be distinguished from it by young entomologists. In the tobacco worm, however, the tail horn is (in the insect) reddish instead of bluish, as is the case with the potato worm in the insect stage. It also has no longitudinal white stripe, the pectoral feet are ringed with black, the body is more hirsute, and the insect itself is more indistinctly marked, and always has a white mark at the base of its wings and partly on the thorax, which the moth of the potato worm has not.

There are several parasites, and one in particular, that is very useful in destroying the potato and Tobacco worm. It is a minute, four winged fly (microgaster congregata) which deposits its eggs in the caterpillar and eventually kills it. The eggs of this parasite, to the number of one hundred or more, are deposited on the hack and sides of the caterpillar, in small punctures made by the ovipositor of the fly. The larvae, when hatched, feed upon the fatty substance, and when fully grown eat a hole in the skin, and each maggot spins for itself a small, white, oval cocoon, one end of which is fastened to the skin of the worm, and the caterpillar appears as if covered with small, white eggs.

The parasite, however, is said to he itself destroyed by another hymenopterous insect, (Pteromalus tabacum), which deposits its eggs in the cocoons of the microgaster. Another species, forming an immense mass of loose, woolly cocoons, is also said to kill the caterpillar of the potato sphinx, and most probably attacks also that of the tobacco worm in a similar manner. It is, therefore, of great consequence, when destroying the caterpillars by hand-picking to avoid crushing or injuring any caterpillars which appear to have either white floss or egg-like cases on their backs or sides, as these are the cocoons of a very useful insect, which if left undisturbed, would produce multitudes of flies, which would destroy an immense number of these injurious worms. This is an important item and will well bear remembering - not to kill a worm with little, white, egg like substances all over his back. These are the cocoons which in time will turn into flies and help you destroy your enemies.

The best remedy against these insects is to poison the fly which produces either the potato or tomato worm by dropping a mixture of " blue stone " of the druggists, or crude black arsenic into the flower of the Jamestown weed, or Stramonium, in the evening, when the fly will come and insert its long proboscis into the flowers, sip up the poisonous mixture, and die before depositing its eggs. A correspondent finds it advantageous to cultivate a few plants of the Jamestown weed among his tobacco, and then to poison the blossoms as they appear, with the above mentioned liquid, every evening, and has thereby saved a great, part of his crop uninjured. In Maryland some growers utilize young turkeys by driving them into the tobacco field, where they pick the worms from the leaves. Some planters also pay a small premium to children for the dead millers or flies, which are readily killed with a piece of shingle or board, as they hover over the flowers in the twilight of evening.

A Practical Handbook for the Tobacco Planter (by) B. Rush Sensensy, M.D. 1875

Mr. White recommends the planter "on the next, or at farthest, the second morning after having set your plants, go over to see that the worms do not eat up one-half of them. You can tell where they are and have been, by seeing a plant with a single leaf, and sometimes the whole plant eaten off and drawn down into the hole occupied by a large brown or black worm; you will see little ant-hills like, and round holes in the ground; by poking around a little in the dirt, you will find a worm very near the mouth of these little holes. Destroy it, and all you can find, and thus save your crop, This searching for worms must be kept up till they cease to do mischief. All plants missing in the field should be renewed from the bed at the first opportunity. The morning is the best time to find the worms, as they are near the surface of the ground; later, they retire into the ground to appear again near sundown, and work during the night and early morning."

Tobacco: A Handbook For Planters (by) C. G. Warnford Lock 1886

SUCKERING

Suckering & Topping – Critical Practices for a Quality Crop
Modern commercial growers use a chemical – Maleic Hydrazide – to perform the tedious but essential task of suckering their Tobacco. And a conscientious gardener you no doubt seek to limit the amount of chemicals you use, and with a small crop of personal Tobacco there's no need to resort to MH – a slow stroll through your plants every couple of days as they reach the point in their cycle where suckers begin appearing, along with a practiced eye and a good nail on your thumb is really all you will need for sucker control – which is exactly how the early master growers did it.

Suckering is by no means an unimportant matter to be looked after, as upon its being well done depends, to a great extent, the size and weight of the valuable leaves. Suckers are small leaves or sprouts which shoot out from the stalk just above and at the junction of every leaf with the parent stem. These shoots are not alone valueless, they are an absolute injury to the balance of the plant, as they grow rapidly and if allowed to remain they draw to themselves nutriment from the plant which ought to go to the commercial leaves. They also tend to crowd the valuable leaves. They must he taken off.

To do this go over your patch when they are about an inch or two in length. Do not use a knife but pinch them out with your thumb and fore-finger. Go over the ground as often as once or twice in a week. You will always find more or less of them springing out, and if the season be wet they will grow very rapidly. By pinching out the suckers and topping low you will secure large, fine and heavy leaves as the balance resulting on the stalk. In pinching off these suckers, commence at the top of the plant and go down to the lowermost leaves, being very careful to break none of the large leaves, as they are quite brittle and break easily under careless handling. Any leaves which you may turn over in your efforts, or which may have blown over by the wind, you must turn back again to their proper position. The sun shining upon the under side of the leaf will burn it in a few hours and injure both the texture and the color of the leaf.

A Practical Handbook for the Tobacco Planter (by) B. Rush Sensensy, M.D. 1875

The great object the planter has in view is the production of well-developed leaves, and to this end his constant care is to concentrate all the energies of the plant in their production by the ruthless nipping in the bud of all its superfluous attempts to flower, to grow to a great height, or to propagate itself. In the old days of Virginia a custom sprang up of resetting fields with these suckers ; the tobacco thus grown was naturally poor in quality, as the soil could not produce a first-class double crop. In order to preserve and maintain the high standard of their tobacco the planters prohibited the practice, enacting that crops from suckers should be destroyed by the officers of the law. Its enforcement was rarely necessary, for the good name of their tobacco—the word ' Virginian ' being a warrant for quality—was too valuable to be tampered with.

The Soverane Herbe (by) W. A. Penn 1902

The young growing leaf has an intense green color, showing that it is quite rich in the nitrogenous constituents which go to make up the living or vital part of the leaf and which are active in building up the food supply of the plant. At about the time the leaves of the plant as a whole have reached their maximum power of elaborating the food supply the flower head begins to develop. This food supply, consisting of starch and other similar substances, is carried from the leaf into the seed head to furnish the necessary food for the development of the seed. This accomplished, the leaves have completed their full task and they now pass into a period of gradual decay. In practice, however, the plant is topped, so that the seeds are not allowed to develop. Making a last effort to reproduce itself, the plant now sends out secondary shoots or suckers, but these, too, are removed by the grower. Under these circumstances, the food built up by the leaves is not carried away to other parts of the plant but accumulates in the leaves themselves. The result is that both the size and body of the leaf are increased.

Principles and Practical Methods of Curing Tobacco (by) W. W. Garner 1909

From the Farmers Encyclopedia, on Priming, Topping, Suckering, and Worming :

" As the tobacco plant grows and develops, a blossom bud puts out from the top, which is termed buttoning. This top must be pulled off along with such of the upper leaves as are too small to be of any value. The plants are thus left usually about two or three feet high. The plants also shoot out suckers from every leaf, which must be broken off, care being taken not to break the leaf from the main stem. This causes the leaves to spread. The most regular topping is performed by measure.

The topper carries in his hand a measure six inches long, by occasionally applying which, he can regulate the priming with great accuracy ; and as the remaining leaves are numbered, this governs the operation, and gains the object of even topping. The topper should always carry this measure in his hand, as it serves to prevent excuses for negligence and uneven topping. Prime six inches, and top to eight leaves. We have found by experience, that this is the best average height. We sometimes, but seldom, vary from this general rule. If the land is poorer than common, or if, from the backwardness of the plant, and the advanced state of the season, we apprehend frost, we do not prime as high (say four inches) . If we have an uncommonly rich spot, and there is danger that the top leaves will come to the ground, we should rise in the same proportion. The crop should be wormed and suckered, at least once a week."

(in) Tobacco Culture: being a complete Manual or Practical Guide (by) C. M. Saxton 1868

In the words of Judson Popenoe, "tobacco is ready to top when the button (as the blossom or top of the stalk is called) has put out sufficiently to be taken hold of, without injury to the top leaves. As tobacco is not regular in coming into blossom, it is the usual practice to let those stalks that blossom first, run a little beyond their time of topping, and then top all that is in button as you go. There is no particular height to top at, but as a general thing 16 to 18 leaves are left. Judgment is necessary to determine where to top; if topped too high, 2 or 3 of the top leaves are so small as not to amount to much; if topped low, the tobacco spreads better; if just coming out in top, reach down among the top leaves, and with thumb and forefinger pinch the top or button off below 2 or 3 leaves; if well out in top, break off several inches down from the button and 4 or 5 leaves below it.

As soon as the tobacco is topped, the suckers begin to grow; one shoots out from the stalk at the root of each leaf, on the upper side. When the top suckers are 3-4 inches long, the suckering should be done; with the right hand take hold of the top sucker, with the left take hold of the next, close to the stalk, and break them off, and so proceed, using both hands, stooping over the stalk, taking care not to injure the leaf. Break the suckers about half-way down the stalk, the balance being too short to need removing until the second suckering. In about 2 weeks from topping, the tobacco is ready to cut; now give it the last worming and suckering, breaking all suckers off down to the ground, and remove every worm, if you don't want your tobacco eaten in the sheds."

Another process, called "priming" by Mr. Schneider, is thus described by him. " The object of priming is to break off the leaves that come out too near the ground, which, when large, lie fiat on it, and therefore rot or get dirty. This work should be done early, the sooner the better, so that the plant does not lose much strength by their growing. These leaves must not be torn off, especially not downward, because the plant would be injured, and instead of throwing the strength gained into the other leaves, it would be thrown away to heal the wound. The distance from the ground at which this priming should be done, depends upon the variety grown and upon the time at which the work is done: 4-6 inches is the right distance.

This priming is not done by every one. One farmer may practise it, while his neighbour does not; but sorts the lower leaves separately, and sells them as so-called ' lugs,' for which he gets a little over half the price of the good upper leaves. Those who do not prime, must generally top lower, or they must risk that the whole plant, or at least the upper leaves, will not mature fully.

Tobacco: A Handbook For Planters (by) C. G. Warnford Lock 1886

Early or low topping is not desirable, as it throws too much growth into the leaves, making them coarse and large. If the plants are thrifty and the weather favorable for growth, it is frequently advisable, if thin, fine-textured leaves are desired, not to top the plants at all, but let them produce their flowers and seed pods. If, however, the plants seem weak and it appears that they can not mature the full number of leaves, they should be topped by pinching out the "buttons," allowing to remain as many leaves as the plant will be able to mature. When plants have been topped too low and the leaves thicken and curl, a few suckers may be permitted to grow, which will remedy any thickening and curling. By using good judgment in the matter of topping and suckering, and making proper allowance as to the soil and climatic conditions, the leaves can be grown to almost any thickness that is desired.

Cultivation of Tobacco (by) Clarence Dorsey, 1903

I think there is no harm in letting the earliest plants bloom before being topped, but after once beginning, they should be broken off as soon as the buds begin to look yellow, and the latest plants as soon as the buds appear. A new beginner will be apt to top the plants too high. The object is to ripen and develop as many leaves as the plant can support; if topped too high, the top leaves are small, and when cured are nearly worthless, and the other leaves are not as large or heavy, whereas, if topped too low, then you lose one, two, or three leaves, which the plant might have supported. As a general rule, a plant just in blossom should be topped down to where the leaves are full seven inches wide, leaving on the stalk from fifteen to eighteen leaves. This will leave the stalks about two and a half feet high in good tobacco.

Later in the season top the plants sooner and lower. Let as many of the earliest plants as will be wanted remain for seed. One plant will furnish seed enough to put out five acres, at least. These should be wormed and suckered like the rest, only leaving the suckers above where you would ordinarily break it off, were you to top it. The piece should now be looked over every other day, to break off the suckers and catch the worm. This should be done as soon as the dew is off in the morning, and towards night, as the worms are eating then, and can be found more readily, while in the heat of the day they remain hid. Great care should be taken not to break off the leaves while going through it, as they are nearly all wasted before the crop is ripe.

TOPPING

Tobacco Culture: Practical Details (by) Orange Judd Company 1884

At the top of the plant a plume comes up which is called the seed bud. It generally comes into view in the middle States about the last of July or first of August. As soon as it is fairly out from the parent stem, so that you can lay hold of it, pinch it out—do not cut it off, as in that case it may bleed—the stalk will waste some of its substance. Pinch it out with thumb and fore-finger. If the grower intends growing twenty leaves to the stalk, then he must top so as to leave that number on the stalk, but if he wishes to grow but twelve or fourteen leaves then he must top low enough down so as to secure this result.

Time of topping depends first upon climate and locality; that is, the grower may be in a locality where his crop will mature rapidly and come to seed bud early, say in July, first part, instead of August. In this case he must top when the seed buds appear and are of sufficient size.

The grower must top early or late, high or low, as the kind of tobacco demands which he is endeavoring to produce. For instance, is it tobacco for chewing or pipe smoking purposes, then he must top accordingly, taking off not the seed bud alone, but such of the upper leaves as will allow of the proper number below fully ripening. If the tobacco be for cigar purposes, then in that case the top, and leaves enough with it, must come away to allow of the proper number on the plant which are intended to be forced to their utmost.

.When, where and how often to top depends much upon the soil and vigor which the growing crop displays. I have said that from twelve to twenty leaves may be desirable on a stalk, but the soil may not be sufficiently rich nor the crop far enough advanced to allow of maturing even the minimum number of leaves. You cannot top all at once. You must go through your patch two or three times a week, or daily if the crop be working rapidly ahead, and top all plants which are ready for beheading. They do not nearly all come to seed bud at one time.

A Practical Handbook for the Tobacco Planter (by) B. Rush Sensensy, M.D. 1875

If the soil is rich and the season favorable, a second profitable crop can be produced from the suckers. The first suckers, of course, should be broken off from time to time; otherwise, they will sap, hinder, and check the growth of the leaves. When all of the leaves have been primed from the original stalk except four or six leaves at the top, two suckers should be allowed to grow from the bottom of the stalk. These will be well started by the time the top leaves of the original stalk are ripe. The stalk should then be cut just above where the suckers sprout, and cultivation should begin' at once, by carefully placing soil up around the old stubble. The suckers should not be allowed to have more than six or seven leaves each. The growth of these will be rapid, and they will mature early. Usually these are not primed, but the stalks should be cut. In northern Luzon these mature in about three weeks and, in years of great humidity, a second crop of suckers is allowed to grow.

Cultivation of Tobacco (by) Clarence Dorsey, 1903

The leaf being matured, it should be harvested only after the dew is off the plants, and not on a rainy day. There are two modes of harvesting - gathering the leaves singly, and cutting down the whole plant. Gathering single leaves admits of removing them from the plant as they ripen; the bottom leaves are removed first, and the top ones are left some time longer, until they have attained full maturity. The cultivator is thereby enabled to gather his crop when it possesses the greatest value. This plan necessitates, however, a great amount of labour, and, in a hot climate, the single leaves are apt to dry so rapidly as not to attain a proper colour, unless stacked early in heaps. But stacking in heaps involves great risk of the leaves heating too much, and developing a bad flavour, whereby the tobacco loses more or less in value. For Indian circumstances generally, cutting the whole plants is better than gathering the leaves singly.

Tobacco: A Handbook For Planters (by) C. G. Warnford Lock 1886

TOPPING

This operation consists in taking off the top of the plant, and must be done for the purpose of concentrating the strength of the land in such number of leaves as will best mature. It should be performed as soon as the seed-buds show themselves. No rule can be given which will apply to all cases, as much depends on the variety grown, the condition of the soil, and whether your crop is well advanced or otherwise. With an early crop on rich soil, do not take off more than one or two of the top leaves, if any at all while on the contrary, if your soil is poor and crop late, top down to that number of leaves which, according to your judgment, will fully ripen. The number of leaves to be left on the plant varies, in different sections and under different circumstances, from eight to twenty.

PRIMING.

This consists in removing the lower leaves of the plant to the height of five or six inches from the ground ; these are removed for two reasons. First, if allowed to remain, they will be made worthless by coming in contact with the soil. Second, to improve the quality of the remaining leaves, - as in topping. Do not commence priming until the principal part of your topping is done; then continue it regularly, and save every leaf with as much care as if it were gold. Though light in weight, you will get some as fine tobacco from these primings as any in your crop, and it is simply folly to throw them away.

SUCKERING.

The suckers are small leaves that start from the base of the larger ones after the plant has been topped. They make their appearance at the top first, and should be continually nipped off as fast as they become large enough to get hold of; otherwise they will retard the growth and prevent the early maturing of the plant.

REMARKS.

We have described the operations of worming, topping, priming and suckering, separately and in the regular order which they first appear; but they cannot be wholly performed and finally disposed of in the same manner. Soon after you commence worming, the buds make their appearance and claim their share of your attention: then follows the priming and suckering. The first suckers will appear in about a week after topping, and will afterwards require plucking two or three times in the same number of weeks.

The worming must still be attended to. Thus it will be seen that two or more of these are continued operations and can be performed in connection with each other. To the experienced Tobacco Grower, much that we have written in the way of explanation may seem altogether needless ; but our intention is to embody, in this pamphlet, all the practical information needed by new beginners, together with valuable hints to all Tobacco Growers.

The Planters Guide for Curing and Cultivating Tobacco (by) Shelton Tobacco Curing Company 1871

No explicit directions can be given for topping, because not all plants should be topped at the same height. A strong vigorous plant may be able to develop from two to three pairs of leaves more than one less vigorous, but in all cases plants should be topped before flower buds expand because the formation of flowers and seeds is detrimental to leaf growth. The flower bud should preferably be removed as soon as discernible by pinching it off without impairing the terminal bud of the plant.

Tobacco Culture in the West Indies (by) The German Kali Works, Havana, Cuba c. 1920

CUTTING

Harvesting and Drying Ripe Tobacco Leaves
The early Tobacco growers faced problems of managing scale in every phase of the process but nowhere is the scale of effort required so different between the early growers and contemporary gardeners than in harvesting, drying, curing and flavoring your crop of natural tobacco. Whereas commercial growers need a crop of hundreds of thousands – even millions – of plants to be able to make a living, a gardener growing a personal crop must only think in terms of dozens, perhaps hundreds of plants. Thus where a commercial grower may need multiple barns and other buildings to process their crop, a modern gardener will need little more than a spare room, or a garage, of a garden shed. Still, the considerations for harvesting your plants and managing the drying/curing process are very mush the same, and much can be learned from these early writers.

When gathering Tobacco the members take the very best food to the garden and give it to other people. After picking the Tobacco they take it to an adoption lodge on the following day and dance with it there. Then they clean their hands by rubbing them on the ground, for otherwise if they touched their faces with their hands pimples and sores would break out on them.

The Tobacco Society of the Crow Indians (Robert Lowie) 1919

Tobacco must be cut when fully ripe, and the point is to determine just when it is ripe. When the leaves begin to assume a mottled and yellow appearance, with reddish or brown spots, when they feel thick and sticky to the touch, and break easily when bent, then the tobacco is ripe and may be cut. In passing over your patch you may find that "here and there" plants have matured and are ripe, but the majority are not. Then, in this case, cut only the ripe plants and house them for the time.

Another thing, you may find some plants which have leaves, both ripe and immature ones. Cut the lower ripe ones and allow the others to remain on the stalk. This only applies to the small farmer, he who has but a small patch, and can take the time to cut and string such leaves as may ripen thus early. The lower leaves ordinarily ripen before the upper ones, hence they are the first which will demand cutting and housing. These individual leaves, when cut, must be strung with a needle on pieces of twine, and then carefully hung in the dry house. They require much care when thus handled, as they are very brittle and break quite easily.

Cut no more leaves than you can string and properly put away in the dry house the same day, as they spoil if allowed to lie in the field. When the tobacco has been well topped, and topped low down, not too many leaves having been left on the stock, if the ground he in very fertile condition, the upper leaves should attain to or nearly the size of the lower ones, when the crop is ripe and ready to be cut.

A Practical Handbook for the Tobacco Planter (by) B. Rush Sensensy, M.D. 1875

Mr. Minor, late a distinguished .farmer of Albemarle County, Va., remarks on the same point as follows : "We have now arrived at the most difficult and critical stages of the whole process; every operation, from this time until the plant is cured, requiring great attention and care, as well as skill and nicety of judgment in the execution. And hence a great contrariety of practice in some of the smaller prevails, according to the superior skill and ability of different planters.

" It is difficult to convey an idea of ripe tobacco by description. It can only be learned by observation and experience. In general, its maturity is indicated by the top leaves of the plant turning down and often touching the ground, becoming curdled with yellow spots interspersed on their surface, looking glossy and shining, with an entire loss of fur, a manifest increase of thickness in the substance of the leaves, which, when pinched in a fold between the finger and thumb, will crack or split with ease. But the most experienced planters acknowledge that they are more apt to err in cutting their tobacco too soon, than in deferring it too long. As a proof of this, take two plants growing side by side, of equal size and appearance in every respect, and both apparently ripe ; cut one and weigh it both green and when cured; let the other stand a week longer, and when weighed like the first, the difference in favor of the latter will be astonishing.

" If it be asked, why we do not avail ourselves of he advantage to be derived from thus deferring the operation; it may be answered, as I have before observed, that tobacco, while standing", is liable to be injured and destroyed by more, accidents than any other plant, such as hail-storms, heavy rains, high winds, the depredations of worms, the growth of suckers from the root, which abstract greatly from the weight and thickness of the leaves if suffered to grow, and which it is not always convenient to pull off. Besides this, the season of cutting tobacco is a very busy one to the planter, and too much work would accumulate on his hands by deferring it to the last moment.

" For these reasons it is considered most prudent to cull out the plants as soon as they will make good tobacco, in which case the loss in the aggregate amount of crop is balanced by avoiding the risk of accidents, and being able to bestow more care and attention to what remains."

(in) Tobacco Culture: being a complete Manual or Practical Guide (by) C. M. Saxton 1868

As a general rule, Judson Popenoe thinks " tobacco should be cut in about 2 weeks from topping, at which time the leaves assume a spotted appearance and appear to have fulled up thicker; double up the leaf and press it together with thumb and finger, and, if ready to cut, the leaf where pressed will break crisp and short. Do not let your tobacco get over-ripe, or it will cure up yellow and spotted; it is better to cut too soon than too late. Take a hatchet or short corn-knife, grasp the stalk with the left hand, bend it well to the left, so as to expose the lower part of the stalk, strike with the knife just at the surface of the ground, let the stalk drop over on the ground without doubling the leaves under, and leave it to wilt.

The usual practice is to worm and sucker while the dew is on in the morning, and as soon as the dew is off to commence cutting. There are some who advocate cutting in the afternoon, say 3 o'clock; let it wilt and lie out until the dew is off next day, and take it in before the sun gets hot enough to burn it. I prefer the first plan, because a heavy dew may fall on the tobacco, and next day be cloudy, leaving the tobacco wet and unpleasant to handle. After cutting, allow the tobacco to wilt long enough to make the leaves tough, so that they can be handled without tearing. Great care is now necessary to keep the tobacco from sun-burning; cutting should be commenced as soon as the dew is off, and all that is cut should be housed by 11 o'clock, unless it is cloudy; from 11 to 2 o'clock the direct rays of the sun on the tobacco, after it is cut, will burn the leaves in 20 minutes;

after 2 p. m., as a general thing, there is no danger of such burning, the sun's rays not striking direct on the tobacco.

Tobacco: A Handbook For Planters (by) C. G. Warnford Lock 1888

More satisfactory results are obtained when the leaves are "primed" than when the entire stalk is cut. By cutting the entire stalk, much green tobacco is carried to the shed, since all the leaves never ripen on the plant at the same time. By the system of priming the leaves are taken off the stalk as soon as they ripen, and carried to the drying sheds in baskets. Sometimes half of the leaves are removed and the balance of the stalk cut, and the leaves cured on the stalk. Tobacco should never be cut or primed when wet with rain or dew, as this causes the leaves to sunburn and little holes to form, which lowers the value of the leaf. The different primings should be kept separate in the shed, so that they can be fermented separately, as each set of leaves from different parts of the plant requires different treatment in the subsequent fermentation.

Cultivation of Tobacco (by) Clarence Dorsey, 1903

All the leaves of the tobacco plant do not ripen at the same time. The lower leaves ripen first and the younger leaves towards the top last, necessitating from three to four cuttings in order to get all the leaves of the same degree of ripeness. This method of cutting the leaves one by one is employed where the tobacco is grown for wrapper but seldom for filler. The usual method for filler is to either cut the whole plant with all the leaves attached, close to the ground, or to cut the plant stalk off in sections, each section having one pair of leaves attached. The method best adapted will depend upon local conditions as well as the class of tobacco produced. A wrapper leaf must be of a uniform ripeness in order to attain the standard of perfection. It must of course be free from blemishes, such as worm holes and rents, and must therefore be handled very carefully all through the process of growing and harvesting. A filler leaf is very much improved also if cut and handled in the same manner.

Tobacco Culture in the West Indies (by) The German Kali Works, Havana, Cuba c. 1920

The leaves of the tobacco plant naturally grow in three grades. Those nearest the roots are the strongest, since they have the first call upon the sap of the plant; leaves half way up the stem are of medium strength, while the topmost are the mildest. Hence the planter obtains a strong, medium or mild crop, as he requires, by pruning the plant at any part. To obtain strong and full-flavoured tobacco he snips off the upper leaves; the removal of the lower ones gives him a crop of medium strength. When leaves of a uniform quality and strength are required the plant is allowed to grow untouched. First the lowest leaves are gathered, and for eight or ten days the whole strength of the plant is directed to the improvement of the remaining higher leaves. When the planter judges that the middle ones are of equal strength to those already gathered they are stripped, and the upmost leaves left to strengthen, in this way obtaining a crop of uniform quality.

HANGING

The Soverane Herbe (by) W. A. Penn 1902

Having housed the whole of your crop, give it all the air you can, by opening doors, shutters, etc. Let them remain open during pleasant weather, remembering to close them in wet, damp weather, as well as nights ; and also shading the crop so far as may be from the direct rays of the sun, to prevent blanching. When it has nearly cured, shut it up and let it remain till perfectly cured. This may be known by the stem of the leaves being dried up, so that no green sap will show itself. If you have hung in your stables and other places that you wish to use, it will be necessary to take it down and strip it at the first favorable opportunity, which is described farther along.

The separate building elsewhere described is to be preferred, as it does not necessitate any immediate hurry in getting it down. In such it can be allowed to hang and freeze and thaw two or three times, which improves the color and weight, and will give more leisure in stripping, etc. Watch a favorable time, when it rains and is damp, to open your buildings, and let in the damp air till the tobacco is damped, so that it can be handled without any danger of breaking the leaves. It need not get too damp, as in that case it is liable to injure in the pile before you can get it stripped. It will gain dampness from the stalk.

You may now commence where you hung the last plant on the pole, and you can very readily unwind and take down the whole. (It is best to save the twine, at present prices, as it will answer to use again.)

Tobacco Culture: Practical Details (by) Orange Judd Company 1884

When the reserve food supply of the mature leaf is no longer required for the nourishment of other parts of the plant it is deposited in the leaf tissue in the form of starch granules, while the green coloring matters are dissolved and carried to the younger, growing parts. This interchange causes the appearance of the light-tinted flecks so characteristic of the ripe leaf. Moreover, the accumulation of the starch granules in the leaf causes it to become brittle, so that it snaps when folded between the fingers, another characteristic sign of ripeness. Now the replacement of the complex nitrogenous constituents, including the green coloring matter, by the starchy matter has a most important effect on the color, flavor, elasticity, and finish of the leaf. Indeed, much of the success in curing tobacco depends on harvesting it just at the right time, when it is neither too ripe nor too green.

Thus, in the case of cigar tobacco, the brightest, clearest, brown colors are obtained when the leaves are harvested just before they would be called fully ripe. If harvested before this period the colors will be dull or "muddy" and too dark, because they still contain too much of the green coloring matters with which the brown coloring substances are closely associated. On the other hand, if the leaves are allowed to become too ripe, the colors will be uneven and mottled and lacking in freshness because of a deficiency of the green coloring matters. For the same reasons a green leaf after curing will be tough and leathery, while an overripe one will be " strawy " and lifeless to the touch. Finally, since the materials which develop the flavor and aroma are derived from the green nitrogenous compounds. the fully ripe leaf will be deficient in these qualities, while the green leaf will possess them much more highly developed.

It is evident, then, that the lower, fully mature leaves of the plant when moderately ripe will be best suited for the production of cigar wrappers bright in color and having the necessary elasticity but neutral in flavor, while the upper leaves harvested before they have fully matured will give the best fillers, having the required flavor and aroma but being much darker in color than the wrappers. In curing the bright yellow tobacco it is necessary that the leaf be fully ripe, for the content of the green coloring matter must be reduced to the minimum consistent with the required toughness in order to obtain the cured leaf free from green or brown discoloration.

Principles and Practical Methods of Curing Tobacco (by) W. W. Garner 1909

About the beginning of September the crop is gathered. As they ripen the leaves become rougher, thicker, and of a yellowish-green colour. The gathering of the leaves requires great judgment, and is always entrusted to the most experienced hands. Reference has already been made to the gathering of the leaves at intervals to obtain uniformity of quality. As a rule the plant is cut down at once by severing the stem close to the ground. Only such plants as appear fully ripe are cut down, the rest being left for a short time longer, but the planter has always fear of frost before his eyes. Cut down in the early morning, the plant is carefully laid on the ground and exposed to the heat of the sun for the day, the juicy, brittle leaves thus becoming wilted, or flaccid, and bendable without breaking. Before evening the leaves are carefully collected and stored in sheds.

The Soverane Herbe (by) W. A. Penn 1902

Mr. Dennis describes making a tobacco 'hand' which is "performed by holding the plant, top down, with the left hand, while with the right hand the leaves are pulled off, taking care to have the stems all even in the hand, so that the ends are together. When 10-15 leaves have thus been grasped by the right hand, change the handful to the left hand, and with the right, select a leaf and wrap it around the stems at the end, so as to bind them altogether and cover up the ends, then split the other leaves apart with the finger, and pull the end of your wrapping-leaf through, and you have a 'hand' of tobacco. A small 'hand' of leaves, uniform in size and colour, will be found the most desirable shape to tie it in.

Tobacco: A Handbook For Planters (by) C. G. Warnford Lock 1886

CURING

Curing and Flavoring
If there's a lot of disagreement among growers on the best methods to raise their crop, there's even more controversy and strong opinions on how to cure the leaves and how to bring out their best flavor. Some growers rely strictly on enhancing the natural metabolic processes that occur as the living leaves slowly die while others employ elaborate methods involving stacking, pressing, heating, soaking, etc. All seek the same end – a lovely color, a fine aroma, a delightful taste, and a nice buzz (to be blunt). Modern gardeners with relatively small amounts of leaf to cure won't have to duplicate the more elaborate of these processes, but may nevertheless learn from the early growers and in some cases might be inspired to try out some ideas of their own. (So here I'll offer just a few representative excerpts on curing and flavoring from the dozens of old books that you'll be able to download and read at your leisure from the address at the end of Section Two.)

The famous Latakia comes from Syria; its place of origin is the Laodicea mentioned by John in the Apocalypse, Latakia being the modern form of the name. It is an ugly, dark tobacco, the leaves being strung and plastered together, as is all Syrian and Greek tobacco. The peculiar flavour of Latakia is due to its being cured over fires of camel-dung—the common fuel of Arabia. To smoke it unmoderated by a lighter tobacco is equivalent to drinking brandy neat.

The Soverane Herbe (by) W. A. Penn 1902

The open air method for chewing and pipe tobacco curing is achieved by hanging the plants on scaffolds in the field and exposing them to the ray s of the sun and a heated atmosphere, or else sheltering them in a shed, simply a roof, on long, strong posts, without ends or sides, open all round, allowing the warm Southern breeze to blow through and over the contents. This mode of curing their light tobaccos is very effective, and if the season be favorable, it cannot be improved upon.

The leaf produced in certain counties of North Carolina is a very light, mild and fragrant tobacco, and when thus cured the product is of a brilliant, golden color, with a polish or lustre. This, therefore, has become very celebrated, and is much sought after by manufacturers as an outside wrapper for their highest grade plug tobacco, and it commands the highest price of any brand of the kind in this country. This golden tobacco is also being manufactured into tine pipe smoking tobacco, and with cheroot manufacturers is also very greatly in demand.

A Practical Handbook for the Tobacco Planter (by) B. Rush Sensensy, M.D. 1875

The flavour of tobacco has long been known to be produced by fermentation, and now the microbe is known to be the cause of the heating and fermenting. The fragrance of tobacco is produced by the omnipresent and omnipotent microbe. The Havana flavour is produced by bacteria indigenous to Cuba, that of Manila by a Filipinos microbe, while Virginia, Turkish and all other varieties of tobacco are the work of other microbes. The susceptibility of tobacco plants to local conditions has long been known, Havana plants cultivated in Germany producing strictly Teutonic tobacco, and inversely the German plant transported to Cuba producing the finest Havana leaf.

The Soverane Herbe (by) W. A. Penn 1902

When the leaves are dry, which is seen when the stems become of a brown color, and break when bent, the next work is to make tobacco out of them, for up to now we have nothing but a tasteless dry weed. Its hidden qualities must be developed. This is done by a process of fermentation, the sweating of the tobacco. The leaves are broken one by one from the stalks, ill damp weather, (otherwise they would break,) stretched out nice and even, and, with the ends in the came direction, put up in heaps. These heaps, of which every workman makes one, are afterwards put into one or more large conical heaps, from four to six feet in diameter at the base and from one and a half to two feet at the top. These are covered with woolen blankets, straw mats, or any thing that will press the heap lightly, and shut out the air. In twenty-four to thirty hours a fermentation sets in, the heap gets warm, and when it is so hot inside that the hand cannot bear it very well, the heap is broken up and packed over again, pulling the tobacco that had been outside upon the inside, and vice versa, and treating the same way as at first. In such heaps the tobacco remains twenty to forty days, until all the heat is gone: then the heaps are again broken up in damp weather, the leaves tied up in bundles of one half to one pound in weight, stretched even and packed in boxes or hogs heads, pressed tightly and covered. Now the tobacco is done - is a salable article.

The process of sweating must be conducted with every possible care, for on this depends the color of the tobacco, and in a large degree its fine flavor. If the fermentation is too strong, the tobacco gets black and the flavor is driven out; if too little fermented, the color remains green and whitish yellow, and the flavor is not developed. Those who raise the plant principally to get wrapper for segars will need to sort it. Sorting is done right after the last breaking up of the heaps, and consists in laying the damaged leaves apart from the whole ones ; and these again are separated, according to color or other qualities, for wrappers, into two, three, or four different kinds, so that every variety is of the same quality and color.

First quality—Color, dark brown ; even over the whole leaf.

Second quality—Color, light brown ; even.

Third quality—Color, dark yellow ; even.

Fourth quality—Color, light yellow ; even.

Fifth quality—Color, green, black, whitish yellow, spotted.

The first four kinds include the larger leaves, while the smaller ones go into the fifth quality. Every kind is bundled by itself. This work is not difficult, and increases the price considerably. The first three sorts, and even the fourth, may be sold as wrappers, which bring the highest price. The fifth la mixed with the damaged leaves together, and sold for fillers or chewing tobacco and snuff.

Tobacco Culture: Practical Details (by) Orange Judd Company 1884

Let me call your attention to the celebrated fragrant Killikinick, the highly celebrated Indian luxury and remedy, possessing as it does, the remarkable power of protecting the system against taking cold after smoking it, making it invaluable for cubeb cigarettes, and a ready relief for all catarrhal affections. All practical tobacco men are more or less familiar with the brand Killikinick, though very few understand the origin of the name. It is an Indian name, and the North American Indians were wise, however, and availed themselves of this discovery hundreds of years ago. It is well known what inveterate smokers the Indians are, and still we never see any injurious effects of this habit upon them. This may be due, in part, to their vigorous constitutions and hardy nomadic life; but it is mainly due, I think, to the form in which they use their tobacco, and until they learn the habit from the whites they rarely or never use the pure leaf. Their "Killikinick " - the agreeable aroma of which, once inhaled in a wigwam or lumberman's cabin, can never be forgotten.

This is composed of equal parts of tobacco and the inside bark of a species of the cornus coricea, or swamp dogwood. Sometimes the admixture of tobacco in it is not more than a fourth. This bark is an astringent, and abounds in tannin, and therefore, in a great measure, neutralizes the effects of the tobacco. The fancy brands of smoking tobacco labeled " Killikinick," sold by tobacconists in papers is needless to say, is pure tobacco, and has no real claim to the name. The Indian name for the peculiar species of swamp dogwood which they use for smoking, is "Killikinick," and yellow sumac bark, or rhus glabra, hence the name.

Avalanche of Information (by) Dr. S. O. Bentley 1883

The changes which occur during the first period of the curing, and which are by far the most important, are dependent upon the life activities of the minute cells which make up the body of the leaf. If a ripe tobacco leaf is killed outright with chloroform or with heat and then placed under normal curing conditions, it does not develop the characteristic properties of a well-cured leaf. It is certain, therefore, that in order to secure a satisfactory cure the conditions must be such that the leaf will remain alive long enough to allow these necessary changes to take place. In the curing shed the leaf undergoes a slow process of starvation unless it is killed prematurely by injury, such as bruising, by heat, or by too rapid drying out. Of course, the leaf must have food in order to remain alive, and this comes from the reserve supply which has been stored up. We have seen that the ripe leaf is very rich in starch and that one of the important changes in the curing is the disappearance of this starch, which is consumed by the living portion of the leaf itself. Now, if the leaf is killed by bruising, rapid drying, or heating too high there is no means of removing this starch, and the tobacco is harsh, lifeless, and " strawy." The vitality of the tobacco plant is remarkable, and parts of the leaf will continue to live for several weeks in the curing barn under favorable conditions. After the starch is all used up it is probable that some of the nitrogenous constituents are attacked as a last means of prolonging the life of the residual living matter.

Principles and Practical Methods of Curing Tobacco (by) W. W. Garner 1909

Fermentation has two purposes. The first is to insure the proper texture, glossy appearance, and color to the leaf. It brings out the characteristic properties of the leaf, which are hardly apparent when the leaf is cut in the field. The best results are obtained when bulk fermentation is practiced. In this method, the leaves are assorted into piles, depending on what part of the stalk they have been taken from. Layer after layer of leaves are placed together, until piles of more than 1 meter are reached. The temperature in the pile gradually rises, and frequently thermometers are inserted to determine the exact degree of heat, which is never allowed to become excessive, or the tobacco will be injured. The piles are frequently turned over, to secure the proper heat and regulate the fermentation. No statement can be made as to how often the piles should be turned over, or when this should be done, as it depends upon the condition of the tobacco, especially as to how moist it was when placed in the pile. The leaves from the upper part of the stalk must be fermented more slowly than the lower leaves; consequently, the piles must be torn down and rebuilt more often.

Cultivation of Tobacco (by) Clarence Dorsey, 1903

We will now consider tobacco in a barn, without fire. It has been well ripened in the field, and during fine weather taken to the dry house where it has been hung up in tiers, one above the other, until the house has been tilled. It has not been hung too closely or crowded, so that it would "house burn " or rot, but just close enough so as to allow of a free ventilation throughout the mass. The fall and the winter have been favorable, and your crop has been curing nicely, so that along about February or March, (sometimes in January), you find it is all well and nicely cured and you are ready for stripping.

A Practical Handbook for the Tobacco Planter (by) B. Rush Sensensy, M.D. 1875

"Sweating" tobacco is a chemical process which the plant must undergo before it is ready for the manufacturer's use. With this process the grower ordinarily has nothing to do. The warehouse man or wholesale tobacco merchants buy from the planter in early Spring, and convey it to their large curing houses, where it is further sorted to suit their trade, and packed down again to be sweated during the summer months. Some planters, however, are now beginning to hold their tobacco from one season to another, just as farmers sometimes hold their grain crops for higher prices. In order to do this you will have to pack and sweat it, and I will explain how it is to be done. There are several ways.

Some packers bulk their tobacco on large piles of five or six tiers of hands, in a warm, dry room, allow it to remain there live or six weeks, in the meantime handling it often whenever it gets warm, placing the outer plants in the centre, and the inner plants on the outside of the heap, thus insuring it a uniform sweat. It is then taken down and packed in boxes, and allowed to stand in the warehouse for five or six months, when it is ready for the manufacturer. Some packers allow it to remain in bulk, conditioning for this length of time, and then pack for market. Others assort and stack it as soon as received from the grower, and allow it to go through the process of sweating in these same boxes or hogsheads. During the curing, if the tobacco be too dry, you may take a bucket of warm water and dip a broom into it, with which you may sprinkle the mass, turning it over and over to moisten the whole lot. In Cuba and among some packers in this country a fluid is specially prepared for this purpose. Sometimes it is water in which tobacco had been soaked. Among Cuban packers it is a common practice to use rum or a highly aromatic wine, peculiar to the island, to sprinkle and season their fine leaf. This is now much resorted to among tobacconists when they wish to disguise a rank and musty or ill flavored tobacco. A decoction is also much used to give the native brands of tobacco the peculiar and delightful aroma of the Cuban article. The materials much in vogue are the vanilla and tonka beans, the fluid extract of valerian and highly flavored herbs which are steeped in aromatic wine and then sprinkled upon the tobacco, which is to be made up. When your tobacco has been packed do not keep it in a damp place. It you have a good, close, dry house, keep it there or in your barn, on a floor, not upon the ground, as it will absorb moisture and mould. If you have been so unfortunate as to have kept it where it absorbed moisture and moulded, in this case it must be taken out and hung up to dry, and then re-packed.

A Practical Handbook for the Tobacco Planter (by) B. Rush Sensensy, M.D. 1875

There are two general methods of harvesting the crop and arranging it in the barn. In the one case the leaves are picked from the stalk as they ripen and are arranged on strings or sticks suitable for hanging in the curing shed. In the other method the leaves are not removed from the stalks, but the latter are cut off near the ground and suspended in an inverted manner in the barn. Of course all the leaves on the plant do not ripen at the same time, so that the tobacco is harvested at such time as will give the greatest number of the best leaves at the proper stage of ripeness. This necessitates a considerable sacrifice in both bottom and top leaves, since the former are overripe and the latter still immature, but the method saves labor.

Principles and Practical Methods of Curing Tobacco (by) W. W. Garner 1909

For those who are not "up to snuff" I will tell you how it is made. The process of manufacture is nearly as follows:

The leaf is stripped from the stem in large quantities, and steeped in water until thoroughly wet ; it is then placed in a kiln, where it is dried until it is simply flexible, loosing all that crispness which it originally had. From the drying kiln it is taken to a strong screw press and placed in an oblong box, where it is pressed until it becomes a solid block, this is done that it may present a hard unyielding surface to the knives of the cutter, beneath which it is next placed. It may be well to state that each manufacturer possessing a cutter has to give security to the amount of $3,000 for the payment of his producing tax.

The tobacco is cut closely by the machine, from which it is taken to the drying floor above ; here it is deposited in a heap to ferment, a process that requires about a month to perfect. The greatest caution and attention are required while the weed is in this state, to keep it from spoiling. Like bread, however, the nearer you can get it to spoiling, without actually doing so, the better it will be. It has to be turned and moved constantly until it is thoroughly fermented, when it is taken down stairs again and put through the mill, this mill consists of a series of conical hoppers, called " mulls," in which are placed four vertical iron rollers, which act as mill stones in grinding the tobacco. The manufacturer has to give security in $1,000 for each mull also, to insure the payment of his tax to the government.

The tobacco comes out of the "mull" in the shape of what is called "coarse meal," the grain being about twice the size of coarse Indian meal. After being wet and manipulated this becomes "Rappee" snuff without further grinding, and it is the cheapest kind. The whole mass is then put into barrels in a perfectly cool condition, it has no smell nor flavor whatever; after remaining in the barrels a short time it becomes heated, and in the course of ten days or two weeks it is taken out with a high flavor and strength. The longer it is kept in the barrels the darker it becomes in color, and it also gains additional strength. Salt is then mixed with it to cool it down and keep it. If "Scotch" snuff is desired it is made perfectly dry and ground in the mill again to make it of finer grain. This is the whole mystery of snuff-making.

Avalanche of Information (by) Dr. S. O. Bentley 1883

It is this curing, or fermentation, of tobacco which gives the leaf its well-known and varied flavours. There are various methods adopted, and by them the final flavour of the herb is determined. Tobacco-leaves simply dried have no more odour and taste than any other dry leaf. The gathered leaves are first dried. In Asia they are simply dried in the sun; in Europe in hot-houses of 70° or 80° Fahrenheit, while in America both methods are practised, the more common one being in artificial heat.

By the first or natural method the leaves are simply hung in well-lit and ventilated sheds, spitted on poles like herrings. Every tobacco-leaf thus has a hole at the base of the stalk by which it has been suspended. The reader may be again reminded that the leaves are bigger than cabbage-leaves, being a couple of feet long by one and a half broad. After six or seven weeks' suspension the leaves are thoroughly dried. The more common method is a combination of artificial and natural means. After being partially dried in the sun the leaves are finished off in sheds by the heat of smouldering fires of bark and rotten wood.

Then comes the process of 'sweating.' The leaves are heaped on the floor of the shed and covered with matting. The mass of tobacco gradually 'sweats,' or becomes damply warm, this being due to the evolution of heat and water. To prevent overheating the leaves are turned every twenty-four hours, thus insuring equable ' curing ' and guarding against 'firing,' which turns the leaves dark and black. In six or eight weeks' time the tobacco assumes a warm, brown colour, though it is still flavourless.

The essential fragrance of tobacco is produced by fermentation. To understand this process some knowledge must be had of the leaf. It consists of three parts—the upper skin, the lower skin, and the intervening cells. The upper cuticle is a thin, transparent, colourless, tough substance, very like waxed tissue-paper. The lower cuticle is a similar but coarser skin with tiny, short, bulbous protuberances. Between the two skins is a honeycomb-like collection of cells containing sap. It is this sap which gives the colour, flavour and taste to tobacco; the skin is merely an envelope, and, burnt, forms the ashes. At first in the growing plant the sap is a pale green; as the plant matures it becomes a bright emerald, and later of an olive shade. In the sweating process the sap is decomposed by the heat into a thick, viscid gum of a brown colour. The final process of fermentation evolves the flavour of the tobacco.

When by 'sweating' the leaves have become warmish brown, they are formed into bundles of six or ten leaves, secured by a leaf. These 'hands' are collected and stacked. The inherent heat and moisture of the closely-massed leaves sets up fermentation and the tobacco undergoes a radical change. To prevent the mass of tobacco reaching too great heat (90° is the limit), it is constantly stirred, the inmost hands being brought to the edge. Various mixtures are used to promote fermentation and produce certain flavours. With some choice tobaccos the Americans use cider, but the natures of the dressings are trade and firm secrets.

When to stop the process is a matter of the utmost importance. With some tobaccos a day and a half's fermentation suffices; require others much longer; in scarcely any two cases is the period the same. Fermentation must be stopped when the tobacco attains a certain temperature. To ascertain this the planter thrusts his hand into the heap. Experience and a keen judgment are the only guides. If the tobacco is heated too much the leaf becomes very dark and harsh in quality, while insufficient fermentation results in musty tobacco. Imperfect curing causes black leaves, produces ammonia products and imperfect combustion.

The Soverane Herbe (by) W. A. Penn 1902

No. 1 is my favorite flavor for Havana, and can be used for all the fine grades of stock. This in itself, being entirely inodorous, is not intended for a box flavor, but will yield the fine natural Havana aroma when burning, hence the advantage in using it on fine goods, as they never can be called doped or doctored goods. It is equally good for cheap stock, (.but it makes it too fine.) No. 1 consists in simply a strong infusion of the green old government Java coffee, the other fine grades would answer, such as golden Rio, Mocha or Cordova. To guarantee uniform results special care must be taken in preparing the coffee, and if the following directions are closely followed this entire list of formulas must lead to success throughout.

Notice: In preparing the coffee, first select only the best clean coffee, then dry in a stove oven, at a slow heat, not hot enough to burn or even brown, but only dry enough to grind in a clean mill, or if it can be ground or coarsely powdered, without drying, all the better. Be careful that no roasted coffee is present, as all practical cigar men understand how very sensitive tobacco is, and will so readily partake of any foreign odor, as paint, fish, coal oil, etc. To prepare the coffee take one ounce of the finely ground coffee to one pint of boiling water, and boil until the strength is entirely exhausted, then   strain and bottle for use. Any quantity can be made in this proportion, or as strong as possible, but the coffee should always be prepared fresh for use, unless it be preserved with alcohol and a little glycerine. For the No. 1 flavor take of the coffee infusion, 1 pint; nitrate of potash, 1 drachm; pure glycerine, 1 drachm; oil of bitter almonds, half drachm; alcohol, 98% or pure alcohol, to cut the oil, 1 ounce. Mix and apply to the filler and binder when ready to work up. Apply by sprinkling or blowing with an atomizer, and use freely, as you are not likely to get too much. When no odor is wanted the oil of bitter almonds can be omitted, and use the oil of Havana, half drachm. Or both oils together work well.

Avalanche of Information (by) Dr. S. O. Bentley 1883

Online Access To Master Tobacco Growers

Finally, after all the various processes you've gone through your leaves are ready for making into whatever kind of tobacco you want to end up with. You may want to be able to roll your own, or you may want to smoke your fine, aromatic leaf in a pipe.

You may want to make snuff, which when made from some of the Native American species can literally be a mind-altering experience, and can also be dangerous if over-indulged in. That's dangerous as in heart attack or stroke – so I really don't recommend snuff as a way to enjoy your fine crop of tobacco.

And as for making chewing tobacco – please just forget about it! Both snuff and chewing tobacco made from highly potent Native American varieties of tobacco can potentially overdose your system and especially your brain with such a powerful dose of nicotine that you risk having your nervous system simply shutting down.

In the books listed below, which you can access by going online to **www.archive.org** *you'll find hundreds of recipes for processing your own tobacco into any form you like, but because using these tobaccos in any way except very conservative smoking and perhaps a light, very light pinch of snuff, is so potentially dangerous I hesitate to offer even a few excerpts on these topics, which are nevertheless covered in exhaustive detail in these books.*

I hope, dear reader, that you will understand my reluctance to endorse any but the most conservative uses of natural Native American tobaccos, and that if you choose to indulge in any other practice that you will exercise the utmost caution and take all necessary steps beforehand to ensure that if you do get into trouble there will be someone nearby who can help.

I hope and trust that this warning will not in any discourage you from growing your own tobacco garden and enjoying the fruits of your efforts in moderation, for that is how Tobacco was used, for the most part, by the Native Americans. After all, one does n ot abuse that which is a gift from God, or from the Great Spirit as he is known among his People.

Go to **www.archive.org** *and enter any of these titles and/or authors in the search box and the book will pop up in multiple downloadable formats. You'll need access to a high speed connection because most of these books are quite large files in PDF format. If* you have a slow connection you will usually have a 'text-only' download format which will give you a readable text file that may have quite a few scanning errors but which will still be useful. I recommend that, if possible, you use the PDF format or, if you have a Kindle Reader, that format works well also.

Tobacco & Native American and Native Peoples Worldwide

Use Of Tobacco Among North American Indians (Ralph Linton) 1924

Aboriginal Tobacco (William Setchell) 1921

Tobacco Among The Karuk Indians of California (John Peabody)

The Tobacco Society of the Crow Indians (Robert Lowie) 1919

Use of Tobacco in New Guinea and Neighboring Regions Field Museum of Natural History) 1924

Tobacco and Its Use in Asia (Berthold Laufer) 1924

Use Of Tobacco In Mexico And South America (J. Alden Mason) 1924

Effigy Pipes in Stone (by) George E. Laidlaw 1923

The Introduction of Tobacco into Europe (Berthold Laufer) 1924

Old-Time Tobacco Growing Methods, Techniques & Secrets

A Practical Handbook for the Tobacco Planter (by) B. Rush Sensensy, M.D. 1875

A Treatise on the Culture of the Tobacco Plant (by) Jonathan Carver 1779

Principles and Practical Methods of Curing Tobacco (by) W. W. Garner 1909

Fertilizing Tobacco (German Kali Works) c. 1920

The Tobacco Growers Guide (by) James Mossman 1863

Tobacco Culture (by) German Kali Works c. 1921

Cultivation of Tobacco (by) Clarence Dorsey, 1903

The Soverane Herbe (by) W. A. Penn 1902

The Planters Guide for Curing and Cultivating Tobacco (by) Shelton Tobacco Curing Company 1871

Saxton's Handbook on Tobacco Cultivation (by) C. M. Saxton 1863

Tobacco: A Handbook For Planters (by) C. G. Warnford Lock 1886

Tobacco Culture in the West Indies (by) The German Kali Works, Havana, Cuba c. 1920

Avalanche of Information for the Manufacturer of Cigars and Smoking Tobacco (by) Dr. S. O. Bentley 1883

Tobacco And Its Adulterations (by) Henry P. Prescott 1858

Tobacco Culture: Practical Details (by) Orange Judd Company 1884

Tobacco Culture Adapted to the Northern Section of the United States (by) Chas. W. Cornell, 1864

Tobacco History & Lore

Original Contributions by James Thompson to "Cope's Tobacco Plant" (Magazine) 1889

Mark Twain's Sketches (Mark Twain) 1887

Nicotiana (or) The Smoker's & Snuff-Takers Companion (by) Henry James Miller 1832

Tobacco Jokes for Smoking Folks 1888

(Robert Louis) Stevenson and Margarita (by) Will H. Low 1922

St. Nicotine or The Peace Pipe (by) E. V. Heward 1909

A Counter-Blaste to Tobaccy (by) King James the First 1885

SECTION THREE: WHO ARE THE TRUE TERRORISTS?

My father's life was ended by a heart attack on Christmas Eve as he drove to the airport to pick up my sister. He died behind the wheel of his beloved Caddy Eldorado, and a few days after the funeral I cleaned that car out. My take for the job included a bottle of nitro pills and a spare pack of Camels from the glove compartment. It was years before the steering wheel of that car, warming as I drove, stopped giving off the odor of Old Spice and cigarette smoke from my dead fathers hands.

Dad was a two pack a day Camel smoker, a habit he had picked up as a young man hanging around the streets of Albany. Cigarettes were such an important part of his life that he would not give them up even when he had suffered several major heart attacks, and been diagnosed as having terminal leukemia. Of course, the fact that he lived twenty years after these grim pronouncements no doubt contributed to Dad's contempt for the suggestion that he stop smoking.

My mother's life ended in the 1990s, but it was over since the early 70s. She was all through raising her three kids, and my Dad was retired from the army with his heart and his cancer, when she set out in her mid-fifties to realize her life's ambition and become a newspaper editor. She was doing pretty good too, until her first stroke cut her down at 56. It was massive, and we all struggled with her as she came back.

She kept smoking - it helped calm her nerves- but she did switch to a Low Tar & Nicotine brand as a concession to her health. Her newspaper editor stood with her, and she began writing again. The second stroke finished her. She sank into medicated despair, still smoking, although now it was mentholated cigarettes, two packs a day, and she was lost to the world for many years. When she finally died after nearly 30 years of suffering, she was ready to go.

I knew that smoking was contributing to the health problems of both my father and mother, but I always felt that they were adults, and knew that they were potentially damaging their health with cigarettes, so who was I to lecture them or plague them with "I told you so's" after it happened.

Besides, I was a smoker for many years, quitting only when my son was born because of a feeling that quitting would symbolize a new commitment to life.

I never questioned the true nature of what caused their suffering and death because I assumed that I knew. It just never occurred to me that what my parents and I were smoking might not be tobacco at all. I had no idea that the industry was completely free of regulation controlling the materials used to make cigarettes. I didn't know that Mom and Dad were smoking "synthetic smoking materials" made from paper mill byproducts and recycled municipal waste.

After all, the tobacco industry seems regulated, doesn't it. You read all the time about government programs for the tobacco farmers, about taxes on tobacco products, and of course, not a day went by without one or more references in the newspapers and magazines to government studies on smoking & health and the "tobacco" industry. Then there's the US Surgeon General's warning label on every pack of cigarettes.

Surely all this means that cigarette contents are regulated, right? It must mean that cigarette manufacturers are not actually free to use anything they want to in cigarettes, including reprocessed industrial waste, tobacco trash from foreign processing plants contaminated with Class Six pesticides, industrial chemicals, human and animal waste, and other loathsome and dangerous substances.

Few of us realize that the person dying of smoking-related disease is most certainly dying of smoking, but probably not of the effects of smoking tobacco. The fact is that cigarettes stopped being real leaf tobacco years ago, and for the past several decades, they have been increasingly manufactured of synthetic substances, dangerous untested chemicals, and known disease-causing and lethal chemicals.

I have only recently discovered just how much of a victim my parents and I have been. Like us, you may be a victim yourself and not know it. I lost my father, and have seen my mother destroyed, and for a very long time, I simply thought that was the breaks, the way things were. I never considered that my parents suffering and death, and my own loss, might have been caused by institutionalized greed, and corruption of historical proportions.

Many, and perhaps most of the people lying in bed today sick with smoking-related disease were put there not by tobacco, but by the secret chemical experiments of unregulated, so-called "tobacco" companies. Out of all the millions of words written and spoken about the dangers of smoking, none of us have ever been made aware that these dangers probably have very little to do with smoking tobacco.

The words "tobacco" and "cigarettes" are used interchangeably by almost everyone who writes or talks officially about smoking-related disease, from the

American Cancer Society to the US Surgeon General, from the New England Journal of Medicine to the Tobacco Institute.

Note that the warning label on every pack of cigarettes in the country speaks of the dangers of cigarettes, and of smoking, but never once mentions tobacco. There is substantial evidence that the dangers of smoking cigarettes made with synthetic chemical materials are far greater than the dangers of smoking tobacco, though of course, smoking anything, even tobacco, is inherently dangerous and potentially harmful.

Few people dying of some dreadful disease brought on by the careless chemical experimentation of some giant company would lie silently, suffering disease and death without seeking fair treatment. The cry would be- get me a lawyer! Get me justice, even if it comes after my death!

Yet almost all of the folks suffering smoking-related disease are silent, accepting the blame for their disease, their suffering, and their death. These are the silent, smoking dead. The smoking dead, and their loved ones, are the victims of a corporate and government conspiracy of violence, greed and madness unparalleled in history, yet in what is one of the most remarkable phenomena in history, how few of the injured and killed seem to be crying out for justice, for relief, for revenge!

It is an easy matter to ignore the immense amount of cruelty and hate in the world. The details of human suffering are an affliction and a burden to every person who even begins to realize their magnitude and depth. Injustice marks our experience at all levels of existence, exploitation by the powerful and the malicious is rampant, and no person feels fully capable of protecting himself, much less making a difference in the course of human destiny.

With so many people dying each year, each of us knows somebody who has died because of cigarette smoking, or knows of a deformed child of a smoking mother or father. A great harm has been done to us, and that we have a remedy in the courts under existing law, if only we knew.

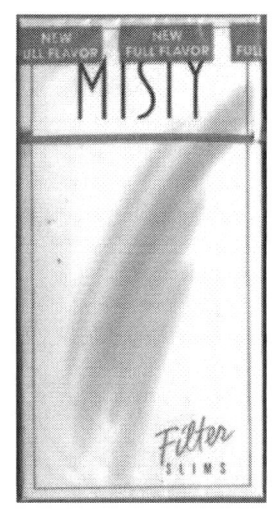

Hundreds of thousands a year go to death in silence, mourned by those who loved them, eulogized in their churches, going in great pain and suffering, and with many cries on their lips- except for that cry for justice we would expect from any other victim. If only I hadn't smoked, if only I'd quit, if only I had known, if only I had been stronger. The pathos goes on, and on, in cancer wards, lung clinics, and dark sickrooms around the country- people blaming themselves for suffering on a scale never before seen in history, year after year. They die bravely, horribly, painfully, shamefully- and utterly without justice.

They bring economic disaster upon their family and community as they lie dying, but they seek no relief. Full of remorse for wasted years, dreams unlived, opportunities now gone forever, they lie drugged and dying, cursing God, cursing their mother, cursing fate. With the cold grave before them, and the disease eating them alive, some few of the smoking dead may even curse cigarettes but even then so many, like my father, continue to smoke.

With so much suffering, tragedy, and dying going on all over earth, especially among the innocent and the powerless, why should we give more than a passing glance, unless we know and love him, to the poor jerk lying in the hospital bed dying of smoking-related disease? Since we all know that smoking causes horrible diseases, why be concerned with the fate of people who do this terrible thing to themselves? The victims in bed cry out in fear, and in mortal pain, but they truly believe that this disease and suffering is the result of their own behavior, and is their own fault, and that they have nobody to blame but themselves. They wouldn't know who else to blame if they were inclined to do so- we all know cigarettes are dangerous, and can kill you, don't we?

If you are dying of a smoking-related disease right now, then one of the few choices left to you is whether or not to fight against those who have caused you pain and suffering, taken a great toll on your family, friends, and business associates, and placed you among the Smoking Dead. You do not deserve to die carrying the added burden of blaming yourself for your suffering.

The fact is, you have been cruelly murdered, by criminal corporations who are clearly liable for the suffering and death they have knowingly caused.

You can't be blamed for not seeing through the veils of deception which the tobacco companies have in place around the thing that's killed you- the cigarette, or perhaps the pipe, or snuff, or some other killer product of this criminal industry. Everyone has been deceived, from the Surgeon General to the Cancer Society, from the media to the academics, from the regulatory agencies to the Congress.

There's a general presumption that the smoking dead deserve their fate. Not that there isn't a lot of sympathy for the individual dying bravely of lung cancer, or emphysema, but even these folks who are victims usually blame the smoking, accepting what they believe to be their responsibility.

Smoking victims today line up silently at the door to the tomb just as cooperatively as the Indian youth in Aztec times lined up at the base of the sacrificial pyramids. The young people at the base of the bloody pyramid believed that their death would feed the Gods, and that if the Gods were not fed, the world would end. It amazed the earliest of

Europeans, the few who saw it; it amazes those few who think about it today. It is difficult to imagine a society in which, many times a year, thousands of young people would line up at the base of a pyramid, waiting patiently and cooperatively for their turn to climb the steps, lie on the alter, and have their hearts cut out.

Those few events documented from the European point of view express amazement at the evident willingness and docility of the waiting youngsters. They speculate on drugs, spells, and other explanations for the inexplicable. These young people grew up in special villages, attended by special priests, had all the pleasures of the mind and body, and there they stood, young hearts waiting to be cut from their living flesh. How to explain that? The smoking dead believe that they have caused their own death, and therefore accept it as quietly as the pain will allow, and as uncomplainingly as the young people in line at the base of the pyramid, waiting to be fed to the hungry, bloody Gods at the top.

They believe that they are responsible for a variety of reasons- they had adequate warning, they always knew smoking would kill them, their doctor warned them, they read plenty of articles about smoking & health, they never thought it would happen to them and that was foolish, and so on.

The smoking dead think that they have been killed by tobacco, and by their own habit of smoking tobacco. They know that tobacco is grown by hundreds of thousands of farmers, and that the tobacco companies make cigarettes and all kinds of other tobacco products, and they know that even though tobacco is bad it has always been grown, sold, and smoked, and probably always will be. The smoking dead agree with those who point out that many people smoke for a long and healthy lifetime, and believe that they are simply those who took their chances and lost.

Four hundred thousand people a year dead of smoking in America alone is pretty savage bookkeeping, but the Smoking Dead are more numerous than even that. They include not just those dying of smoking-related disease, who number over one million a year worldwide, but also those stillborn or born defective because of smoking by their mother, those developing disease and disability because of environmental smoke, and the many others whose lives will be shortened and made more painful and nasty by smoking and its consequences.

The smoking dead have been done a terrible, systematic, deliberate wrong. They have been abused, exploited, sickened, mocked, fooled, taunted, experimented on, and poisoned by people and organizations driven by immense greed, by a form of corporate insanity, and by an anachronistic freedom from accountability rare in any society at any time, much less in our own highly regulated times.

If I could say only one thing to my fellow human beings the smoking dead, I would say this: You are responsible, but you are not to blame. It was your behavior and your habit that made you sick, that will kill you- but it is not your fault. Wake up, before you die, and realize that you are among the ultimate victims in history! Then, if you can, or if you can mobilize those around you to help, get yourself together and take action!

You have been grievously injured, and you have been deceived from the very fundamentals to the most exotic aspects of your disease and its causes by ignorance, to some degree, but largely by a carefully organized conspiracy, and your death is the direct result of their actions, not your own. You are not guilty of causing your own death by smoking, and you have the right to go after these killers with any resources you have.

You greatest resource is the truth that you did not cause your disease, but that the cigarette companies certainly did, and did so in deliberate pursuit of enhanced profitability. You must realize that they meant to cause you this harm, because doing so meant a more profitable business for them. Also, you must realize that they have been protected and shielded by our government from people like you and me who they have injured, and that government totally sanctions this massive homicidal conspiracy.

Next, you must decide not to take your murder lying down, and, finally, you should go talk to a good attorney. Working with your attorney, and perhaps with other victims joining in a class legal action, you will have an excellent chance of proving that the cigarette company which sold you your brand of smokes over the years, willfully and negligently manufactured an unreasonably dangerous product.

The Problem With The Lawyers

Lawyers for people injured by cigarettes and other products, such as snuff, have traditionally operated under the assumption that they were fighting for clients injured by tobacco and tobacco products. Consequently they have spent immense amounts of their time and resources trying to prove a case against tobacco and tobacco products, and because of this fundamental flaw, they have lost every time.

In most cases, the lawyers have focused on Nicotine addiction as a primary culprit, usually attempting to show in court that their clients were addicted to nicotine, and therefore were unable to stop using the product in question. After attempting to establish this fact- never very successfully- the lawyers have usually gone on to attempt to prove that the cigarettes, or snuff, or other "tobacco" product in question was dangerous to their client's health, usually by dragging in some variation of conventional scientific and medical evidence which supported their case.

The cigarette industry has used its historical exemption from product content regulation to produce consumer goods which it has every reason to know are unreasonably harmful and dangerous. Even the most cursory search of the cigarette patent literature turns up plenty of evidence that the cigarette companies have known what they were doing in manufacturing an unreasonably dangerous product. The patent literature shows the industry experimenting with and using materials and chemicals which are known to present severe health hazards under conditions of slight, but chronic exposure. The patent literature also reveals an industry blatantly using highly toxic, cancer-causing materials in manufacturing, knowing that these materials remain in the final product. Full copies of these and hundreds of other "tobacco" product-related patents are public record.

While the patent literature reveals unequivocal evidence that the cigarette manufacturers have been pursuing development of unreasonably dangerous synthetic, chemicalized products, the agricultural /industrial literature surrounding tobacco production reveals another source of unreasonable danger which the cigarette companies and the US government have known about, and deliberately ignored for many years. This is the area of agrichemical contamination of tobacco used in manufacturing. While the use of synthetic smoking materials in cigarettes has risen dramatically over the past ten years, there is still a great deal of tobacco also used in manufacturing.

However, very little of this tobacco is real leaf; most of it is ground up stalks and stems, reconstituted into thin sheets which are shaved to resemble actual tobacco leaf when used in cigarettes. And as mentioned, most of it is of foreign origin, even when it says something like "Pure Virginia Tobacco" on the pack. That just means that there is some Virginia-type tobacco parts in the cigarette- probably from Zaire, Syria, or some other Third-World dictatorship friendly to chemical companies and other giant multinationals.

The reconstituted "tobacco" made from this imported trash is highly contaminated with some of the most powerful, toxic, carcinogenic agricultural chemicals in the world. The presence of any one of these chemicals on any food, drug or cosmetic product sold in the US would bring on an immediate ban and seizure by Federal, State and local health authorities. The manufacturing plant responsible for the contamination would be closed immediately. Billions of dollars in lawsuits would follow, and those injured by the chemical contamination would be assisted by their government in obtaining justice from the guilty manufacturer.

The cigarette industry is totally exempt from any law or regulation which exposes them to this sort of legal action. They are fully insulated from the oversight of any government agency, with regard to the materials used in manufacturing their product, or its contamination with dangerous, even totally banned chemicals.

Some of the most dangerous of these chemicals are pesticides applied during agricultural production and subsequently during storage. The bulk of these pesticide residues occur on foreign-grown tobacco which comprised over 40% of the actual tobacco used in the average US cigarette in 1994, up from 6% in 1970. Many of these pesticides are so dangerous, even at trace levels, that they are banned for any use at all throughout the US, and their presence in any regulated food, drug or cosmetic product is strongly prohibited.

Tobacco products sold in the US, however, are specifically exempt from inspection for, or regulation of pesticide residue content, by any agency of government at any level. As of 1985, manufacturers of cigarette products were banned from importing tobacco contaminated with residues of pesticides banned for use on tobacco in the US. However, this carefully worded ban includes only those pesticides banned for use on tobacco in the US- and did nothing about the vast chemical soup coming in from the Third World on tobacco scrap, stems, and leaf.

Some of the pesticides which published responsible research shows are or have been routinely present in cigarettes sold in America today include: BHC, Parathion, Paraoxon, Disulfoton, Dioxin, Dimethoate, Demeton, Malathion, Diazinon, Aldrin, Endrin, Dieldrin, DDT, Toxaphene, Heptachlor, Chlordane, Lindane, Leptophos, Monocrotophos, Methomyl, Aldicarb, Carbaryl, and Carbofuran. There are many other such dangerous pesticides in cigarettes; it's just that there is no government agency responsible for checking on them, and the cigarette industry is under no obligation to either report this contamination or to do anything about it.

Many of these pesticides present in tobacco products have established, unequivocal causal impact on human health at the levels found in tobacco products, when ingested in chronic, sub-lethal doses, as in habitual smoking behavior or regular exposure to side stream smoke. These established effects are predominantly irreversible, and include carcinogenicity, neurological damage, fetal damage, DNA and chromosome damage, reproductive system damage, respiratory damage, and numerous other organ & system-specific damage. The effects of these pesticides are, in many cases, known to be cumulative, additive, and synergistic, and to demonstrate enhanced impact when consumed along with tobacco smoke. The irony is that cigarettes and other tobacco products manufactured in the US for sale in the European Economic Community market are subject to stringent regulation by EEC government health authorities with regard to pesticide residue content. That's because the governments of Europe have been enforcing strict laws against pesticide contamination for over 20 years. This regulatory environment is based on qualified scientific and medical assessment of the added, increased risk to public health presented by pesticide residues in tobacco products.

US government agencies, including USDA and US Department of Commerce, participate in preparation and enforcement of standards for US tobacco growers in production of tobacco meeting these EEC regulations. They are aware of the dangers described by European health authorities, and spend our tax money helping the giant tobacco companies test their export cigarettes for pesticide contamination. But they do this while allowing these same companies full license to poison Americans.

It's not just the government which has dropped the ball. You will look in vain for any research by any of the well-publicized health groups and foundations on the subject of the hazards of smoking pesticides, recycled municipal waste, military nerve gas, or any of the other ingredients of modern cigarettes. The health effects of the pesticide residues present in tobacco products have not been studied by any US government agency or by any major private US foundation for their health effects on humans when consumed by smoking, and the scientific/medical literature in this area is very thin. (The single exception to this bleak picture is work done by Dr. Dietrich Hoffman at the American Health Foundation in Valhalla, NY.) EPA-mandated product safety data sheets on many of these pesticides, however, warn specifically against respiratory exposure, and against smoking in any environment in which they are present. In addition, there has been extensive EPA study of the combustion of pesticides and the resulting byproducts, which has resulted in published warnings concerning exposure to such combustion due to danger to human health.

In addition to the established presence of known pesticides in tobacco products, considerable evidence suggests that pesticides of unknown character and effect are routinely formulated and applied in the field in foreign countries to tobacco which is then brought into the US and manufactured into tobacco products for US consumption. In addition, there is considerable evidence of over-application and misapplication of pesticides in foreign countries on tobacco which is subsequently brought into the US for manufacture and consumption.

Tobacco product manufacturers have known of the presence of these pesticide residues in their products for many years, and qualified industry-employed scientists have raised the issue of the potential for negative human health effects of these pesticides in a wide variety of technical and scientific literature. It can be shown that the tobacco manufacturing industry has been in a position to know of the established negative health impact of these pesticide residues for many years, and that in no instance has it taken ameliorative action with regard to products intended for the US market, while taking extensive ameliorative action with products intended for the EEC market.

The story of chemicalized, synthetic tobacco is only a part of the description of the wholesale slaughter which has been done by the cigarette companies worldwide, with the full knowledge and cooperation of governments and regulatory agencies.

It is clear that there is nobody in authority who can, or will stop the killing. It is also clear that the only way to bring these corporate murderers to justice is to sue them effectively.

If you are among the millions of victims of this brutal conspiracy, then it is your responsibility to take what action you can, because if you don't, nobody else in government, the health professions, or any other institution in our society is going to lift a finger.

If you have been injured by cigarettes, or snuff, or some other "tobacco" product, then you have been injured by an unreasonably dangerous product, which the manufacturers had every reason to know was unreasonably dangerous, because they deliberately made it that way. If you are a smoker, you have been deliberately deceived, misled, and kept uninformed in ways intended to prevent you from making an informed decision on whether or not to smoke. If you are not a smoker, but have to breathe air full of cigarette smoke, you have been deliberately deceived, misled, and kept uninformed about the true nature of the dangers involved. In either case, you have been injured in a way which seems to satisfy the most basic requirements of a successful lawsuit involving product liability.

The fact that only a few of the recent tobacco products liability lawsuits has been partially "won" by the victim should not discourage you at all. These poor people have not had the benefit of the necessary knowledge it would have taken to win. They have not known the true facts behind their disease, and their lawyers have been swinging blind.

Finally, to answer the question contained in the title to this section – who are the true terrorists? What is a terrorist, and a terrorist organization? Aren't terrorists individuals and organizations who willfully murder people and destroy lives without compunction in order to achieve their goals – whatever those goals may be? Whether the goal is political, religious of economic, terrorists are wanton killers unmoved by the suffering they inflict on other, innocent people.

There is no doubt that 9/11 was caused by terrorists, and they destroyed thousands of lives. It doesn't diminish the value of each of those lives to point out that 3000 lives were taken, and thousands of families were destroyed, by the terrorists of 9/11 while every year in America alone the cigarette companies kill 400,000 and destroy millions of lives in pursuit of profit.

If our political 'leaders' were truly dedicated to a war on terror, meaning a war on those who wantonly kill huge numbers of innocent people then surely the government would be closing down the cigarette industry and jailing its leaders. We all know why this is not happening, and never will happen. There can be no doubt, Jesus weeps.

Maybe It's Not The Tobacco Killing People

A proposition for reasonable people to consider - what if it hasn't been the tobacco in cigarettes that's been killing cigarette smokers?

This isn't a trick question, or a joke.

What if the combinations of pesticide residue contaminants on the tobacco and reconstituted tobacco portions of cigarettes and other so-called tobacco products are enough in themselves to explain a large proportion of cigarette-related disease and death?

Then what if residues from chemicals which are known carcinogens like benzene, hexane, and phosgene, used in the processing of industrial waste into synthetic smoking materials for cigarette manufacturing, and for manufacturing into smokeless and pipe "tobaccos", are enough to explain a large portion of the remaining cigarette-related death and disease?

I've been tracking the activities of the cigarette industry for almost thirty years and while my research resources have been limited, I've pieced together enough of a picture to convince me that it may very well not be the tobacco at all that's killing many, or even most smokers.

This section of Cultivators Handbook of Natural Tobacco is dedicated to raising the question of whether smoking-related disease and death can be largely prevented without having to try to change the desire to inhale volatilized plant materials for chemical satisfaction, an activity which appears to be hardwired into the pleasure centers of the brains of a significant portion of the human race, and just as firmly hardwired into the aversion centers of the brains of everyone else. If this is so, then a home-grown crop of natural tobacco produced without pesticides and processing chemicals from plants that are not industrially created hybrids but pure, native strains, should be inherently much safer to smoke than the products sold in the billions of units worldwide by the killer tobacco corporations.

If it isn't the tobacco that's killing people, then almost all of the millions of deaths to come over the next 20-50 years from cigarettes and other so-called tobacco products are preventable by requiring that all tobacco products be manufactured from natural and uncontaminated tobacco.

It's important to know from the beginning, and to keep in mind as you review what I've assembled here as evidence, that American cigarettes stopped being 100% real leaf tobacco decades ago, and instead are manufactured using a combination of materials, including:

√ Real US-grown tobacco leaf - this kind of component is very uncommon in US cigarettes.

√ Foreign-grown tobacco leaf - this component makes up most of any actual leaf tobacco used in US cigarettes, but leaf itself is uncommon.

√ Reconstituted smoking materials made from ground-up foreign tobacco stems, stalks, and waste and a wide range of additives, glues, fungicides, etc. Use of this *tobacco sheet* became very common in US cigarettes beginning in the late 1970's and accelerated in the late 1980's. Because of the industry's secret status and lack of research into the question, nobody knows which US brands, many using images and words like "true tobacco taste" that imply that there's actually tobacco in the pack, are composed mostly or exclusively of this kind of reconstituted tobacco. We do know that Winston was the first to invent this scam as early as the 1950s.

√ Synthetic smoking materials are made from materials like recycled paper mill waste, food processing waste, and recycled municipal cellulosic waste. Appropriately this stuff, rolled out into slabs before being shaved to resemble real tobacco, is called "Sheet" – and that's exactly what it is. Pure Sheet. This material is extremely common in US cigarettes, especially the Low T&N brands. Again due to secrecy and lack of regulatory oversight, nobody knows which brands are partly or exclusively made from these synthetic smoking materials.

The giveaway to both synthetic and reconstituted tobacco is that the leafy material in the cigarette tube has no natural leaf ribs which, if they are present, can be easily detected with any magnifying glass.

With the limited exception of US-grown tobacco, all of the other three materials used to manufacture cigarettes are normally and commonly contaminated with residues of pesticides which in themselves are well-established causal agents for breast, lung, and other cancers, for nervous system degeneration, for fetal malformation and irreversible genetic damage. In the 1985 Food Security Act the US government put a limited set of regulations in place to deal with pesticide residues on tobacco, requiring that imported

Flue-Cured and Burley leaf tobacco be certified to have been grown using only pesticides registered under the US Federal Insecticide, Fungicide and Rodenticide Act. As we'll see this is actually tricky wording, allowing enormous amounts of tobacco waste and scrap to slip through unregulated, and begging the question of what smoking even regulated pesticides does to human health.

The unbelievable fact is that very few of the common pesticide contaminants of tobacco appear to have ever been tested for their health effects when consumed by smoking. This isn't to say that the pesticides haven't been studied for their human health effects - they certainly have. The EPA, the FDA, the USDA, and others have all done extensive work with the tobacco pesticides. There has been a significant amount of published research on the human health effects of chronic sub-lethal exposure, and of exposure by inhalation, to many of the common tobacco product pesticide contaminants. There have also been oral/dermal toxicity studies which have shown many of the common tobacco contaminants are far more toxic when ingested orally than when absorbed through the skin, which implies similar toxicity when they are smoked. However, I've searched in vain for literature references to studies on what happens to these pesticides when they are volatilized by dry distillation and inhaled in combination.

In the 1990s, US medical/scientific teams reported a series of findings that ought to bring the issue of pesticide contamination of cigarettes into sharp focus:

At least four of the pesticides commonly contaminating US cigarettes, when ingested together even in trace amounts, become extremely potent chemical agents capable of causing cancers, birth deformities, and genetic damage even at trace levels. A study by Dr. John MacLachlan of Tulane University, reported in *Science, June, 1996,* which had nothing to do with tobacco or cigarettes in particular, demonstrates that the extremely small dosages of pesticide residues on US cigarettes, which the industry has been debunking as negligible for decades, turn out to radically enhance each other's toxic, fetus-damaging, and cancer-causing properties when consumed together. The combinant effects of trace pesticides in this study were on the order of 1:1600, so those tiny traces of Endosulfan, Dieldrin, Disulfoton etc which in themselves may or may not be harmless, are beyond doubt serious health risks when consumed together - as they are when smoking pesticide-contaminated cigarettes or inhaling contaminated second-hand smoke.

The risks of inhaling the raw pesticides are great enough, but those risks are compounded by the presence of xenobiotic combustion by-products. For example, DDT has been a common contaminant of US cigarettes since the 1950s, and when DDT is burned it creates among other compounds a chemical named benzo-a-pyrene. This benzo-a-pyrene has been known for at least 35 years to cause lung cancer as fast as anything known to the industrial world, and it has shown up in assays of cigarette smoke streams since at least the early 1950s. For many years scientists have been trying to link benzo-a-pyrene to the lung cancer they know it causes. In 1996 a team led by Mikhail Denissenko reports in *Science, October 1996* that they have traced this chemical step-by-step from the cigarette smoke stream to a human chromosome site called P53 where the mutations leading to human lung cancer are stimulated by BAP's presence.

Finally, researchers at National Cancer Institute reported in *JAMA* on *Nov. 12, 1996* that in women with a weak gene, called NAT2, that defends against toxins and carcinogens, the risk of breast cancer from smoking a pack of cigarettes a day increases 400% over women with a normal NAT2. This research shows that a sizeable proportion of women, about 50% of all white women and nearly 40% of all Black, Hispanic and Asian women inherit this weak NAT2 gene, increasing their risk of breast cancer from exposure to toxic and carcinogenic chemicals - such as the raw and combusted pesticide compounds found in cigarette smoke – but quite possibly not in naturally-raised tobacco smoke. A worthy research topic, perhaps?

For other angles on this increasingly likely link between environmental pesticides and human cancer, with strong implications for women smokers, see:

Davis D.L., Bradlow H.L., Wolff M., Woodruff T., Hoel D.G., Anton-Culver H. 1993, *Medical hypothesis: Xenoestrogens as preventable causes of breast cancer.* Environmental Health Perspectives v101 n372 p. 7

MacMahon, B. , *Pesticide Residues And Breast Cancer?* Journal of the National Cancer Institute: JNCI
April, 1994 v 86 n 8, p.572

Hunter, D. J., Kelsey, K. T., *Pesticide Residues and Breast Cancer: The Harvest of a Silent Spring,* Journal of the National Cancer Institute: JNCI
April 1993 v85 n8, p.598

Soto, Ana M., Chung, Kerrie L., Sonnenschein, Carlos, *The Pesticides Endosulfan, Toxophene, and Dieldrin Have Estrogenic Effects on Human Estrogen-Sensitive Cells* Environmental Health Perspectives: EHP
April 1994 v102 n4 p. 380

Pesticides Currently On US Tobacco Products

This list of tobacco pesticides is taken from current figures published by North Carolina State University as part of an effort to inform North Carolina tobacco growers about the safe application of pesticides to tobacco crops. Note that this list is only partial, and refers only to some of the pesticides registered for use on tobacco in the US, not to the dozens of compounds being prepared and applied by illiterate fieldworkers in the tobacco companies' third world growing operations.

Note that the table refers only to the LD 50 of the parent compounds, and not to the compounds created by the dry distillation of these parents during smoking. Its also important to keep in mind that LD 50 refers only to the chemical's ability to poison an individual, not its ability to give them cancer, destroy their genes, or cripple their babies. More about all that later.

LD 50 in mg per kg body weight

Common Name	Trade Name	Oral Exposure	Skin Exposure
acephate	Orthene	866	10,250
carbaryl	Sevin XLR Plus	725	>2000
carbofuran	Furadan	11	10,200
chloropicrin	Chlor-O-Pic100	250	----
Chlorphyrifos	Lorsban	96 to 270	2000
Chlomazone	Command	1,406	>2000
Diazino	Diazinon	300 to 400	3,600
dichloropropene	Telonell, Telone C-17	224	333
disulfoton	Di-Syston	2 to 10	6 to 20
endosulfan	Thiodan, Endocide +	30	359
ethoprop	Mocap	46.7	369
Fenamiphos	Nemacur	5	80
ferbam	Carbamate	> 17,000	---

Flumetralin	Prime+	3,100	---
Fonofos	Dyfonat	8 to 17.5	25
isopropalin	Paarla	>5,000	---
malathion	Cythion, Malathion	1,000	4,100
maleic hydrazide	Several	3,900	---
metalaxyl	Ridomil	669	3,100
methomyl	Lannate	17	5,880
napropamide	Devrinol	4,640	---
oxamyl	Vydate	5.4	2,960
parathion	Several	2	73
pebulate	Tillam	921 to 1,900	4,640
pendimethalin	Prowl	2,679	>2,260
trichlorfon	Dylox, Proxol	250	>2,100

A Piece Of Good Advice

The Soil & Water Conservation Service, other USDA agencies, other government agencies, and university scientists all agree that people applying these pesticides are at risk. The literature is full of warnings such as this one.

"An LD50 is used to measure pesticide toxicity to humans and other mammals. An LD50 is an amount of a substance that will cause death in 50 percent of a target population. The lower the number, the more acutely (short-term) toxic. Care should be taken to minimize exposure to humans and wildlife from all pesticides. However, extreme caution should be taken with pesticides that have low LD50's such as Temik, Di-Syston, Nemacur, or Parathion."

"Protective clothing should always be worn when handling pesticides. Rubber gloves, boots, and goggles or face shields should always be worn when mixing pesticides. A respirator also should be used when handling pesticides that have a strong odor and are easily detected by smell. This is especially true with fumigants such as Telone C- 17 or Chloropicrin."

The really interesting aspect to all this material is that you will search in absolute vain for any reference to hazards to the smoker created by these pesticides. You read reams of materials about operator safety, environmental protection, keeping costs down and profits up, how to use these sprays and granular materials most effectively, what bugs, snails, molds and fungii are controlled by which chemicals - and not a whisper about the exposure of the smoker. Can it be that these folks think all this stuff simply disappears? That's highly unlikely, at least in the case of NCSU, University of Kentucky, and the others which are heavily involved in tobacco crop science and other related disciplines, because they all have conducted studies of pesticide residues in cigarettes, cigars, and other tobacco products, so they have to know that many of these pesticides are extremely persistent and do not disappear.

Pesticides mean tobacco profitability

Pesticide contamination of tobacco products goes back to the beginning of pesticide use on agricultural crops. Since tobacco and cotton have always been the most profitable crop per-acre they have always received the bulk of the pesticides. The careful planning that went into making so-called tobacco products exempt from regulation under the Federal Pure Food, Drugs and Cosmetics Act of 1951, which regulates the safety of consumable products sold in the American marketplace, means that tobacco products have never been regulated or inspected for pesticide contamination except in gradual, limited ways beginning in approximately 1985. This in turn means significantly greater profit margins for the cigarette manufacturers, who can use tobacco grown in the cheapest parts of the world, sprayed with lightly regulated or unregulated chemicals to prevent as much insect destruction as possible, and brought into the US under the most favorable duty treatment for processing using unregulated chemicals and filler materials into tobacco sheet.

Many people aren't aware that tobacco products, including cigarettes, cannot be regulated by the U.S. government, or by the states, whose Pure Food, Drug & Cosmetic laws are carefully modeled on the federal law, which takes precedence. This means that the health authorities of your state have no authority at all to regulate tobacco products even if you demonstrate to them that there are banned pesticides in those products which are known human carcinogens in the dosages experienced by smokers and their families, and by the public in second-hand smoke. I know because I live in Texas and I've tried it in testimony before the Texas Department of Health, the Texas Legislature, the Texas Attorney General - the states have no right to regulate cigarettes.

The fact that tobacco products, including some cigarette brands, ceased to be actual "tobacco" products many years ago does not seem to affect their continued exemption, which was based on the original argument that tobacco was neither a food, nor a drug, nor a cosmetic and therefore should be - and was- made exempt from regulation under the Act. They maintain this image with great care, because it enables them to continue to operate under cloak of secrecy.

Most recently in an enormous 2000 page document developed by the tobacco industry to oppose proposed FDA regulations, the companies argued that "like manufacturers of other consumer products based on agricultural commodities" they have to "design and manufacture their products so that they economically and reliably meet consumer preferences".

The simple fact that the industry takes so much trouble, as you'll see throughout this section, to ensure that it can keep on freely using pesticides has not received much attention in the great debate over the hazards of smoking, but as someone said - follow the money. And the money trail points directly to the fact that the ability to use pesticides free from regulation during production seems to be as much of a profitability factor as margins on the manufactured product itself, if you judge by the activities of the industry over the years.

Many of the pesticides contaminating American tobacco products have never been registered in the US, because so few US cigarette brands actually contain American tobacco. When US brands of cigarettes claim to contain Virginia tobacco, they imply that it has been grown in Virginia, but Virginia-type tobacco is grown worldwide from

Bangladesh to Zimbabwe to China, and becomes US cigarettes only after being drenched with unregulated mixtures of insecticides and fungicides in its tropical growing environment. While the leaf portions of this so-called Virginia tobacco must conform to US pesticide regulations, the stems, stalks and trash from processing don't, and many of the chemicals used on tobacco translocate to the stems, stalks, and roots.

Finally, when tobacco pesticides are sprayed they are routinely mixed with chemicals called "adjuvants". These chemicals are designed to make the spray go further, last longer, and cling to the plant better, and there is no regulatory control over these chemicals at all. In the US, manufacturers of these pesticide adjuvants must meet EPA manufacturing regulations, but there is no testing I'm aware of for their ultimate health impact on the smoker. However, the really hazardous picture emerges when you consider that overseas, where most of the tobacco consumed in the US is grown, there is no way to know what producers are using as adjuvants, which in the past have included a wide range of hazardous substances including benzene and asbestos.

For an interesting discussion of some of the issues around exposure to unregulated pesticide formulations see: Davis DL, Blair A, Hoel DG. (1992b). *Agricultural exposures and cancer trends in developed countries.* Environmental Health Perspectives 100:39 44.

The next question is usually - so what happens to all that tobacco grown in America?

The answer is that a lot of it winds up in European cigarettes. US-grown tobacco is actually relatively free of pesticide residues compared with the tobacco from third world sources, especially those which have come to be recognized as serious killers, so American tobacco goes into cigarettes manufactured for European markets where relatively strict regulations apply to tobacco products. Cigarettes manufactured for Europe must, by and large, be cleaner, must actually contain tobacco, must not contain a number of additives common in the US, and must be inspected and regulated by the health authorities- none of which applies in the US.

It isn't as if US government officials were unaware of the concern of European health officials over the health risks presented by pesticide residues on tobacco. They are very concerned about pesticide residues when they affect the export of American tobacco, as the following comments demonstrate.

"Despite lower maleic hydrazide (MH) residues on U.S. tobaccos, German tobacco industry officials continue to express concern that the residue levels are excessive. The German cigarette industry is currently operating under an unofficial agreement with the

German health authorities that limits the MH residues in finished cigarettes to less than 80 parts-per-million (ppm). US flue-cured tobacco imports from the 1980 and 1981 crops averaged 150 ppm in the most recent tests. Blending down MH residues on US tobaccos is becoming more difficult because of increased use of MH in other tobacco producing countries. German imports from Korea, Argentina, the Philippines, and Guatemala contain varying levels of MH residue. Industry officials also report that MH is being used in India and Zimbabwe, but no samples have been tested thus far. (in) USDA World Tobacco Situation March, 1982

The reason that American tobacco is cleaner than third-world tobacco is that gradually over the years certain insecticides have been banned for use on tobacco in the US, including most of the organo-chlorines like DDT, Endrin, Dieldrin, Heptachlor, Toxaphene. DDT, which gives of benzo-a-pyrene when burned, and Endrin, which is extremely carcinogenic and generates lethal combustion by-products, were almost universal contaminants of American cigarettes and tobacco products throughout the 1950's, 1960's, and most of the 1970's. When these potent pesticides were finally banned for use anywhere in the US, the giant American tobacco companies moved most of their own growing operations into the third world - so that they could keep right on spraying with DDT, Endrin, Aldrin, Dieldrin, Toxaphene, BHC, and the rest of the pesticides that continue to contaminate much of the world's tobacco supply. The most heavily contaminated tobacco leaf, of course, can't be sold in either Europe or the US, but that doesn't mean it is tossed and burned - it simply winds up in places like Latin America, Africa, the Middle East, Asia, and Russia, packaged as American cigarette brands promoting the happy illusion to young smokers that they are part of the sophisticated, sexy, successful American scene.

Contamination Of Third World Tobacco

One of the major problems for smokers of tobacco grown in many poor countries is that the people applying the pesticides on these valuable export tobacco crops not only don't read or speak English but are likely to be illiterate in their own language. This means that when the time comes to load up the sprayer with bug-killing chemicals and head out into the fields, the guys mixing the chemicals may very well have no idea what's in the barrels they're mixing from.

If this sounds far-fetched, consider this piece from Progressive Farming (1/82)

"It's hard enough to get farmers in this country to apply pesticides properly. A field study conducted by the University of Nebraska found that "The biggest problem of agricultural chemicals is the people applying them". This study of 95 Nebraska farms by agricultural engineers from the University found that "six out of ten missed their estimated application rates by more than 10%. The average over-application rate was 35%, and the maximum 85%.

Farmers using granular products didn't do any better. Actually 60% of the users made application errors greater than an acceptable 10%. One in three over-applied by an average of 40%. "Reasons for the errors ranged from not reading label instructions to not knowing how much liquid was in the sprayer tank.

This study was conducted with American farmers in a region where the educational level of farm-owners is 13.5 years of school. These folks aren't dummies, yet they regularly over-apply dangerous chemicals. They are literate, understand chemicals to a degree, have access to government and industry information and assistance, and are checked carefully to make sure that their crops are within acceptable residue levels. Still, they over-apply by enormous amounts.

So what can we really expect from farm workers and independent farmers in developing nations?

Consider this piece from Nature (9/92)

"*Both farmers and extension agents in developing countries must normally rely on pesticide company salesmen for information on how to use agricultural chemicals - much as physicians in western countries rely on pharmaceutical company salesmen for information about new drugs.*"

Smoking-Related Disease And Agrichemicals

For thousands of years the Native American peoples used tobacco, but many individuals smoked only for ceremonial reasons, and nobody ever noticed a difference in life expectancy rates between smokers and non-smokers. Within a single lifetime after tobacco was discovered in the Americas by European explorers its use had spread everywhere on earth, but tobacco pipe and cigar smokers didn't suddenly start dying by the millions in their mid-lives the way cigarette smokers do now. In fact for several hundred years tobacco smoking was, whether viewed as a pleasure or an obnoxious vice, not viewed as an automatic death sentence the way it has so obviously become today.

Tobacco smoking has always offended many different people and institutions, and in the early days its use was vigorously opposed. Laws were passed in most major societies forbidding tobacco use, up to and including a law calling for summary execution on the spot for tobacco smoking in 18th century Turkey. Nothing ever worked. Tobacco's enormous appeal has made it arguably the most heavily consumed substance after food in almost every society worldwide for hundreds of years. But for all these years, not enough more tobacco smokers died compared to non-smokers for anybody to seriously notice the difference.

Of course some people who smoked died, sometimes horribly, of the results of their behavior - but it wasn't just plain inevitable. Until cigarettes. Or more specifically, until cigarette manufacturers began using chemical and industrial technologies to manipulate both the product itself and consumer behavior in pursuit of even greater profitability. Just in case anyone hasn't noticed, cigarette smokers didn't start dying in remarkably large numbers until sometime after the 1950s.

In other words, smoking-related disease rates really start climbing about 20 years after the beginning of (1) intensive use of pesticides in tobacco production and (2) heavy, unregulated use of chemical and materials technologies in cigarette manufacturing processes.

While the debate over smoking and health has raged for many years now, it actually turns out that it isn't necessary to decide whether tobacco kills cigarette smokers. That can be decided later, after a generation or two have had a chance to smoke contaminant and additive-free 100% tobacco products. Isn't it enough to know that specific pesticide contaminants are present in sufficient concentrations in cigarette industry products to explain 100% of the primary and secondary smoking-related disease rates, along with the other relevant morbidity and mortality indices?

The Cigarette Pesticides

The pesticide residues which have contaminated generations of cigarette brands in the US include known supertoxins, carcinogens, neurotoxins, compounds specifically designed to produce genetic damage in fetal insect life forms, and pesticides designed to damage female insect reproductive systems. The actual amount of exposure received per cigarette by smokers to these chemicals is tiny - never enough to have any immediate effect, or to be detectable by taste or smell - the cigarette companies even back in the 1950s the companies were spending millions making sure that pesticide residues aren't detectable by the smoker through what they call "off-flavor".

Insecticide Residues as a Source of Off-Flavor in Tobacco, Townes, H.K., Tobacco Science, 146 (26): pp 24-26, 1958

However, long-term exposure, puff after puff, to exquisitely tiny amounts of these pesticides burned in combination with each other, and to their combustion by-products, does create a syndrome called "Chronic sub-lethal exposure".

Medical and scientific literature, and pesticide industry technical literature are each quite clear on the effects of chronic sublethal exposure to pesticides such as Toxaphene, Heptachlor, DDT, BHC, and Dieldrin known to have been in generations of American cigarettes - such exposure unequivocally causes the diseases which kill cigarette smokers. The intended victims of these chemicals are bugs which damage valuable tobacco crops, especially in third-world countries. However, since the cigarette industry uses heavily contaminated foreign tobacco waste, stems and stalks as raw materials for its high technology manufacturing processes, literally dozens of these pesticide residues are gasified and inhaled hundreds of times a day by cigarette smokers, and often their families, friends, and coworkers.

A number of the pesticides present in cigarettes are known to cause cancer, neurological disease, miscarriage, and genetic damage more frequently, more quickly, and more severely in African-Americans and Hispanics than in whites, especially when these pesticides are inhaled.

Krieger NK, Wolff MS, Hiatt RA, Rivera M, Vogelman J, Orentreich N. (1994). *Breast cancer and serum organochlorines: A prospective study among white, black, and Asian women*. J Natl Cancer Inst 86:589-99.

Rios R, Poje GV, Detels R. (1993). *Susceptibility to environmental pollutants among minorities*. Toxicol And Health 9(5):797-820.

The Low Tar Game - And You're It

But it's not just chronically lethal pesticide residues which cigarette smokers encounter as hazards. Some of the additives in cigarettes are deliberately designed in cigarette company laboratories to addict smokers to that particular brand, while others are designed to regulate the rate at which the smoker lights up and puffs. Another class of additives is designed to raise the burning temperature of the cigarette, thereby turning more of the "tar" into gas, which lowers the "T&N" rating of the brand since tar particles and not tar gasses are used to obtain the rating.

It's probably coincidental that by imposing tar and nicotine limitations on cigarettes the government gave the industry its greatest marketing tool ever and actually increased the danger of the resulting cigarettes to smokers, but that's what happened, just as it is probably coincidental that the cigarette companies cite the Surgeon General's warning on the pack as "fair notice" to cigarette smokers about the hazards of using the product.

If you are told often enough that you are badly injuring yourself by your behavior, and you don't see it happening, then it's natural to listen to a friendly demon who just happens to be sitting right there on your shoulder whispering in your inner ear

"Of course, you're too special for anything bad to happen to you. Not to you, my dear - oh no. All those terrible stories are about other people, the unlucky ones, the ones who aren't young, and beautiful, and special, like you."

The cigarette companies, ever pleased to tap into or create human weaknesses, evidently concluded long ago that the way to deal with those not fully convinced by that soothing voice in their inner ear, placed there with consummate craft by psychic surgeons unlike any the world has ever seen before, was to put the issue of danger right out front and then trivialize it using known psychological processes.

To accomplish this the industry needed a line, a hook, and just by coincidence the FTC, which has no authority to regulate the industry with regard to content, imposed what looked like regulations on the output of the cigarette -the smoke stream. The "Low Tar &

Nicotine Derby" has been the greatest aid to market segmentation that any industry has ever seen. It has allowed the cigarette companies to create brands which appeal to specific kinds of health fears and concerns, and to create other brands for those macho folks who want a real man's smoke - no filter, heavy on the T&N.

The clear intent of low tar and nicotine cigarette brand advertising is to convey that they are less risky because they are lower in harmful stuff. In the beginning of the Derby that may have been true - cigarette manufacturers in the early 1970's when this all began first responded by using various chemical treatments to puff-up the tobacco in their cigarettes, meaning less tobacco per cigarette and therefore less T&N per cigarette.

However things quickly got trickier because cigarettes began being made not from tobacco, but from synthetic ingredients which could impregnated with precisely measured amounts of nicotine. The problem was that pesky tar, and the solution was to raise the burning temperature of the cigarette so that more of the stuff that makes tar at low temperatures is turned to gas and therefore isn't trapped as particles by government tests. The tar chemicals still wind up in the smoke, and in the lungs, because while cigarette filters are pretty good at trapping particulate matter they are terrible at stopping gasses, and the hazards presented by this gasified tar are different, and possibly worse such as vinyl chloride and hydrogen cyanide, than those created by the original tar. Of course, that's not what's important or relevant. The point is, turn the tar into gas, which isn't measured and - voila! - you've got a low tar cigarette brand.

One of the major classes of gas-phase cigarette smoke are the hydrazine analogues, produced as the result of pesticide combustion. As early as 1977 cancer researchers were writing about this class of chemicals in serious tones, such as

" *Studies on the tumorigenic activities of hydrazine analogues are aimed at revealing the environmental significance of this class of chemicals in cancer causation. To date (1977) 37 such compounds have been shown to produce tumors of intestines, blood vessels, lungs, liver, kidneys, breast, and central and peripheral nerve tissues of laboratory animals. Interestingly enough, nearly all of the hydrazines studied were tumor inducers. Since the human population is environmentally exposed to approximately half of the hydrazines studied thus far that induce tumors in experimental animals, it seems justifiable to warn against further use of these hazardous compounds*"
B. Toth et al., Cancer Research, Vol. 37, October, 1977 page 3499

These researchers weren't writing about the hydrazines liberated by pesticide combustion in cigarette smoke - they were writing about exposure to hydrazine compounds in the environment - anywhere, anyhow. And smokers have been exposed to an additional 20 years of hydrazines, among many other classes of extremely dangerous chemicals, since this was written.

By the way, speaking of nasty things that come across in the gas, those filters are tricky little high technology items too. For example, if you examine many filters you'll see a pattern of holes everywhere but at the tip of the filter. This means that when the laboratory testing machines grip the filter to obtain smoke for a T&N rating, they grip it right at the tip and so the smoke that goes into the machine is modified by air being drawn through all those holes further down the filter. However, when a person smokes that filter cigarette, especially a person with larger lips and fingers, a great many of those tiny holes get covered up, and the actual smoke stream that smoker gets is hardly low T&N. That's how the cigarette companies can produce a brand which they can claim is Low Nicotine and still deliver the buzz to the smoker - because the smoker covers up the air holes in the filter that dilute the laboratory smoke stream and gets a much more concentrated smoke.

Cigarette technology, by the way, offers a rich trail of evidence once you understand what you're looking at. For example the development of the longer, slimmer cigarette has little to do with fashion and a lot to do with the fact that you can burn the smoking materials at a higher temperature in a longer, thinner tube and turn more of the tar into gas, while controlling the nicotine as just described, resulting in a Low Tar & Nicotine, (high gas and buzz) cigarettes for all those health conscious women who smoke.

There are three core facts to keep in mind as you leave this section of the book behind:

1. The US Surgeon General's warnings refer to smoking, and to cigarettes, but never to tobacco for a very good reason. Few is any brands of cigarettes on the US market contains 100% natural, uncontaminated tobacco – although a few claim to do so, if you can trust the manufacturers.

2. Only one of the several dozen heavy-duty pesticides known to contaminate cigarettes since the 1950's has ever been tested in a published study for human health impact when consumed by smoking. That chemical, maleic hydrazide, technically not a pesticide but a specialty chemical designed for use specifically to save money in tobacco production, has been shown to cause cancer of the mouth and throat when ingested by smoking.

3. None of the contaminated foreign tobacco waste used to make reconstituted tobacco, and none of the unregulated materials used to make synthetic tobacco, have ever been tested for human health impact when consumed by smoking, although tobacco

substitute materials are known to contain processing chemical residues which in themselves are cause for severe health risk to consumers.

My hope is that with the help of this information, one or more people will be able to prove in a court of appropriate jurisdiction that these companies have truly been engaged in monstrous criminal behavior which renders them liable by all criteria of product liability law. All it will take is for one of the millions of us who have been injured to win such a case in the appropriate court, presenting proper evidence and obtaining a full public airing of the real facts, and the game will begin to be over for some of the most fantastic criminal conspiracies in history.

Speaking of history, let's now move to the last section of this book where we'll take a look at the experiences of people who enjoyed the noble weed for many centuries before it was finally co-opted by the predecessors of today's industry.

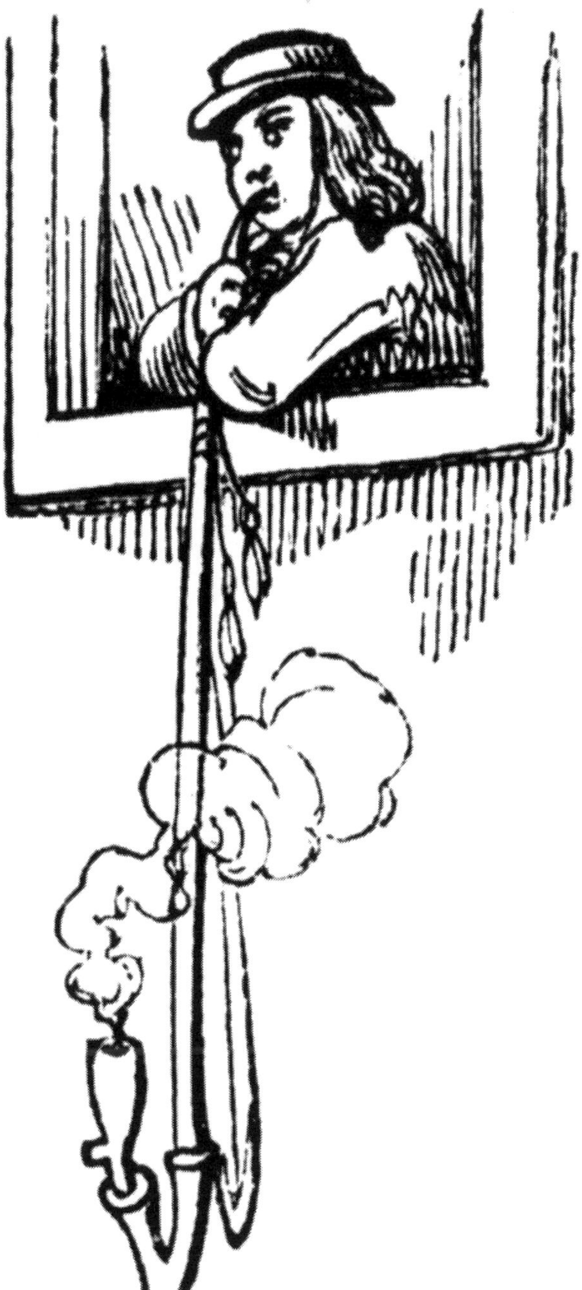

SECTION FOUR: Native Natural Tobacco and the European Mind
(With grateful acknowledgement to my old friend Richard Erdoes who did much of the original research for this section.)

Love It or Hate It
Europeans came to the Americas prepared to find uncivilized inhabitants and these expectations colored their observations from the very beginning. Columbus and his companions were the first Europeans to encounter Tobacco and the Admiral's journal describes what no European had ever seen before.

> " Among other evil customs, they (the Indians) persist in one which is very pernicious, that of smoking, called by them tobacco, for the purpose of producing insensibility. This they effect by a certain herb, which, as far as I can learn, is of a poisonous quality. The chiefs, or principal men, have small hollow sticks, about a span long, made in a forked manner, the two ends of which are inserted into the nostrils, while the other extremity is applied to the burning leaves, which are rolled up in the manner of pastilles. They inhale the smoke till they fall down in a state of insensibility, in which they remain as if intoxicated.

It didn't take long for familiarity with the pleasurable state that smoking native natural tobacco produced to flourish, and for smoking to evolve into a commonplace habit among white people in the New World. Early writers like Lescarbot found that their countrymen were rapidly succumbing to this New World practice

"Our Frenchmen who visited the savages are for the most part infatuated with this intoxication of petun [tobacco], so much so that they cannot dispense with it, no more than with eating and drinking, and they spend good money on this, for the good petun which comes from Brazil sometimes costs a dollar (ecu) the pound."

John Hawkins observed disdainfully in 1564 that the French in Florida used tobacco for the same purposes as the natives. A. Thevet, who visited Brazil in 1555-56, characterized the Christians living there as "marvelously eager for this herb and perfume." Gabriel Soares de Souza (Noticia do Brazil, written in 1587), a Portuguese farmer, who lived in Brazil for seventeen years from about 1570, wrote that tobacco leaves were much esteemed by the Indians, Mamelucos (Africans), and Portuguese, who "drank" the smoke by placing together many leaves wrapped in a palm-leaf - an early and no doubt rather harsh version of the cigar.

The earliest English account of the use of tobacco was by John Sparke the Younger, in an account published by Hakluyt in 1589, where he writes that John Hawkins, ranging along the coast of Florida for fresh water in July, 1565, came upon the French settlement there under Laudoniere, and found that

> "The Floridians when they travell have a kind of herbe dryed, which with a cane, and an earthen cup in the end, with fire, and the dried herbs put together, do sucke thoro the cane the smoke thereof, which smoke satisfieth their hunger, and therewith they live foure or five days without meat or drinke, and this all the Frenchmen used for this purpose: yet do they horde opinion withal, that it causeth water and fleame to void from their stomachs."

In "Treatise of Brazil," written in 1601 and published by House of Purchas, also describes the mode of cigar smoking in Brazil and winds up by saying,

> "The women also doe drinke it, but they are such as are old and sickly, for it is verie medicinable unto them, especially for the cough, the head-ache, and the disease of the stomacke, and hence come a great manie of the Portugals to drinke it, and have taken it for a vice or for idlenesse, imitating the Indians to spend daies and nights about it."

Arguably the best-known of the early tobacco literature is King James' "A Counterblaste to Tobacco. Imprinted at London by R. B. Anno 1604." The king's name does not appear as author, however, the author refers to himself as King throughout the work. Perhaps the best comment on James' effort was by William Bragge (Bibliotheca Nicotiana, 1880) who noted that "he most Quixotically broke his lance against one of the great appetites of man."

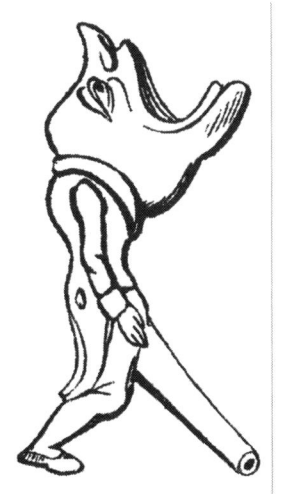

King James Sees The Devil

King James condemns the use of tobacco from a wild combination of ecclesiastical, political, economic and racial motives as can be seen in his initial exhortations

"And now good Countrey men let us (I pray you) consider, what honour or policie can move us to imitate the barbarous and beastly maners of the wild, godlesse, and slavish Indians, especially in so vile and stinking a custome? Shall wee that disdaine to imitate the maners of our neighbour France (having the stile of the first Christian

> Kingdom) and that cannot endure the spirit of the Spaniards (their King being now comparable in largenes of Dominions, to the great Emperor of Turkie)?
>
> Shall wee, I say, that have bene so long civill and wealthy in Peace, famous and invincible in Warre, fortunate in both, we that have bene ever able to aide any of our neighbours (but never deafed any of their eares with any of our supplications for assistance) shall we, I say, without blushing, abase our selves so farre, as to imitate these beastly Indians, slaves to the Spaniards, refuse to the world, and as yet aliens from the holy Covenant of God? Why doe we not as well imitate them in walking naked as they doe in preferring glasses, feathers, and such toyes, to gold and precious stones, as they do yea why do we not denie God and adore the Devill, as they doe?"

King James didn't buy any of the arguments being made for tobacco's miraculous healing powers and argues that its popularity is due more to imitation and fashion. He also notes that people are smoking themselves to death these days – a clear indication that immoderate behavior with the potent early natural tobaccos of commerce was dangerous.

> "For such is the force of that natural Selfe-love in every one of us, and such is the corruption of envie bred in the brest of every one, as we cannot be content unlesse we imitate every thing that our fellowes doe, and so proove our selves capable of every thing whereof they are capable, like Apes, counterfeiting the maners of others, to our owne destruction."
>
> "The argument that people have been cured of diverse diseases by taking tobacco is fallacious and rests on a confusion of cause and effect; the disease takes its natural course and declines, but it is not tobacco that wrought this miracle. If a man smoke himself to death with it (and many have done), O then some other disease must beare the blame for that fault. "

He rejects the notion of tobacco could act as a cure for all that ails you.

> "O omnipotent power of Tobacco!" he exclaims, "And if it could by the smoke thereof chace out devils, as the smoke of Tobias fish did (which I am sure could smel no stronglier) it would serve for a precious Relicke, but for the superstitious Priests, and the insolent Puritanes, to cast out devils withal!."

The King believes that tobacco use is undermining the physical as well as the moral health of the country.

> "In the times of the many glorious and victorious battailes fought by this Nation, there was no word of Tobacco. But now if it were time of warres, and that you were to make some sudden Cavalcado upon your enemies, if any of you should seeke leisure to stay behinde his fellows for taking of Tobacco, for my part I should never bee sorie for any evill chance that might befall him. To take a custome in any thing that cannot bee left againe, is most harmefull to the people

The King notes that smoking in public had increased to the point that people were forced to take it up in a strange kind of self-defense

> "partly because they were ashamed to seeme singular, and partly, to be as one that was content to eate Garlicke (which hee did not love) that he might not be troubled with the smell of it, in the breath of his fellowe.
>
> "Moreover, which is a great iniquitie, and against all humanitie, the husband shall not bee ashamed, to reduce thereby his delicate, wholesome and cleane complexioned wife, to that extremitie, that either shee must also corrupt her sweete breath therewith, or else resolve to live in a perpetual! stinking torment."

The English social class system operated at full strength when it came to King James' ideas about who should and who should not be allowed to indulge in tobacco.

> "and is now at this Day, through evell Custome and the Toleration thereof, excessivelie taken by a number of ryotous and disordered Persons of meane and base Condition, whoe, contrarie to the use which Persons of good Callinge and Qualitye make thereof, doe spend most of there tyme in that idle Vanitie, to the evill example and corrupting of others, and also do consume that Wages whiche manye of them gett by theire Labour, and wherewith there Families should be releived, not caring at what Price they buye that Drugge, but rather devisinge how to add to it other Mixture, therebye to make it the more delightful to their Taste, though so much the more costly to there Purse; by which great and imoderate takinge of Tabacco the Health of a great number of our People is impayred, and theire Bodies weakened and made unfit for Labor, the Estates of many mean Persons soe decayed and consumed as they are thereby dryven to unthriftie Shifts onelie to maynteyne their gluttonous exercise thereof, besides that also a great part of the Treasure of our Lande is spent and exhausted by this onely Drugge so licentiously abused by the meaner sorte, all which enormous Inconveniences ensuinge thereuppon."

The close of James' Counterblaste is perhaps the best known part of the document

> "Have you not reason then to bee ashamed, and to forbeare this filthie noveltie, so basely grounded, so foolishly received and so grossely mistaken in the right use thereof ? In your abuse thereof sinning against God, harming your selves both in persons and goods, and raking also thereby the markes and notes of vanitie upon you: by the custome thereof making your selves to be wondered at

by all forraine civil Nations, and by all strangers that come among you, to be scorned and contemned. A custome lothsome to the eye, hateful! to the Nose, harmefull to the braine, dangerous to the Lungs, and in the blacke stinking fume thereof, neerest resembling the horrible Stigian smoke of the pit that is bottomelesse."

King James' attitude was reflected in the ruling monarchs of much of the rest of Europe. In France of this same period men were challenged to duels for calling another person a tobacco drinker. In Berlin in the mid-1600s smoking was punished with jail and the pillory. In 1624 the Pope officially threatened the users of snuff with excommunication- it seemed that their sneezing was entirely too similar to a sexual orgasm.

This, by the way, is the origin of the blessing which accompanies a sneeze - the Vatican declared that anyone who sneezes suffers a momentary lapse in consciousness during which demons or the devil himself may enter, unless that momentarily disconnected soul is protected by the blessing of someone in the vicinity - even a total stranger. It's also the reason, of course, for making marriage a holy, sanctified state - so that people can have orgasms and be protected from demons during their out-of-body moments - protected by god, so to speak.

Didn't Work Then, Doesn't Work Now

The Ottoman Turks were among the more extreme of official reactions - they imposed the death penalty for smoking. The Turks have always enforced their drug laws with extreme penalties and have used pain as an instrument of political rule.

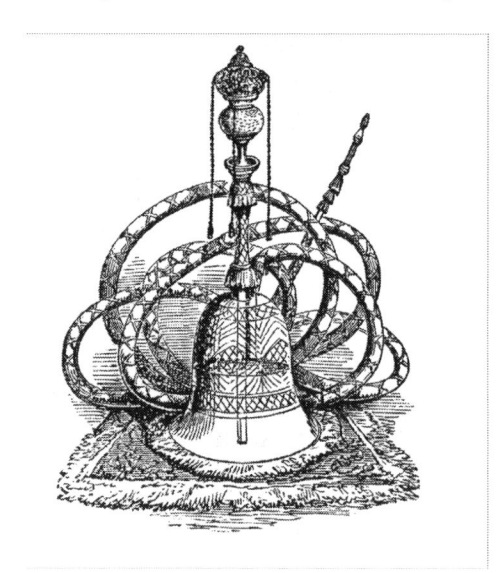

"It was chiefly for tobacco that he made many heads fly. He caused two men in one day to be beheaded in the streets because they were smoking tobacco. He had prohibited it some days before because, as it was said, the smoke had got up into his nose. But I rather think that it was in imitation of his uncle Sultan Amurat (1623-40), who did all he could to hinder it as long as he lived. He caused some to be hanged with a pipe through their nose, others with tobacco hanging around their neck, and never pardoned any. I believe that the chief reason that Sultan Amurat prohibited tobacco was because of the fires, that do so much mischief in Constantinople when they happen, which most commonly are occasioned by people that fall asleep with a pipe in their mouth."

As anti-smoking campaigns go, this was serious, yet the Turks kept right on smoking along the rest of the world.

The 17th century Czar Alexis of Russia decreed that smokers should be whipped, have their noses slit, and then be transported to Siberia. In Austria, smokers were heavily fined for the first offense, pilloried for the second, whipped and jailed for the third. Smokers were frequently suspected of being poisoners and witches. Many a witch burned at the stake owned her fate to having been discovered using tobacco. Even in the enlightened 19th century, in many countries and kingdoms, it was still forbidden to smoke in public, or on the street, or even inside one's own home - if one happened to be a woman.

The Clergy were against smoking from the very first as American parsons thundered from their pulpits against Satan's *little soul destroyer, the cigarette*. Girls who smoked and went dancing with young men, preachers of the twenties sermonized, were *fast girls on the road to damnation*, who would automatically become prostitutes. The prohibition movement fought not only against "**Demon Rum**" but also against "**Devil Tobacco**." Young ladies were instructed to tell suitors who indulged in either

> "You may not see me, John, while the breath of alcohol and tobacco is on your lips. But I shall pray for you, pray to God to deliver you from these evil habits. And, if a year from now, you can say that in that time you have totally abstained, then, John, with the permission of Papa and Mama, you may call on me again."

Carrie Nation not only smashed saloons with her hatchet, she also snatched cigars from the mouths of passersby, screaming "*You rum-soaked, beer swilling Tobacco fiend, how do you dare corrupt children's morals by smoking this horrid thing?*" While preachers and moralists condemned smoking for its sinfulness, doctors lectured on the baleful effects of tobacco on the brain, the lungs and the nervous system, calling it a drug worse than opium.

None of this could stem the triumphant march of tobacco, just as today's warnings, printed on every pack of cigarettes, that the Surgeon General has declared cigarettes dangerous to the user's health have not have a significant impact on smoking. For every blast against the "**Filthy Weed**," there was a panegyric to the "**Plant Divine**."

Tobacco Inspires Poetry & Song

Philosophers praised it as a sovereign aid to thinking and contemplation. Poets waxed lyrical over the "Royal Herb's Virtues."

Said Charles Lamb in his sad **Farewell to Tobacco**
*For thy sake, Tobacco, I
Would do anything but die.*

Lord Byron wrote
*Sublime Tobacco, which from East to West
Cheers the tar's labor or the Turkman's rest.*

Spenser spoke of "*Divine Tobacco*".

Ben Jonson "*lusted after the Tawny Weed*".

Sir Arthur Helps exulted "*What a blessing smoking is it - the greatest that we owe to the discovery of America!*"

In Spenser's *Fairy Queen* (1590) he makes Belphoebe include it with other medicinal herbs gathered to heal Timais (Book III, Canto VI, 32). This is the earliest poetical allusion to tobacco in English literature.

> Into the woods thenceforth in haste shee went,
> To seeke for hearties that mote him remedy;
> For she of hearties had great intendiment,
> Taught of the Nymphe which from her infancy
> Her nourced had in trew nobility:
> There, whether yet divine Tobacco were,
> Or Panachea, or Polygony,
> She fownd, and brought it to her patient deare
> Who al this while lay bleding out his hart-blood scare.

William Lilly, the Euphuist and court-poet to Queen Elizabeth, a great smoker himself, wrote a play **The Woman In the Moone** (1597), in which Pandora wounds a lover with a spear and sends her servant for herbs to cure him:

> Gather me balme and cooling violets,
> And of our holy herb nicotian,

And bring withall pure honey from the hive,
To heale the wound of my unhappy hand.

In an ode to "Virginia's Kingly Plant," a poet using the alias "Old Salt," wrote

> Philanthropists, no doubt
> With good intentions ripe,
> Their dogmas may put out
> And arrogantly shout
> The evils of the pipe.
> Kind moralists with tracts,
> Opinions fine may show,
> Produce a thousand facts -
> How ill tobacco acts
> Man's system to o'erthrow.
>
> Learn'd doctors have employed
> Much patience, time and skill,
> To prove tobacco cloyed
> With acrid alcaloid
> With power the nerves to kill.
> E'en Popes have curst the plant;
> Kings bade its use to cease
> But all the Pontiff's rant
> And Royal Jamie's cant
> Ne'er made its use decrease.
>
> Oh tell me not 'tis bad,
> Or that it shortens life.
> Its charms can soothe the sad,
> And make the wretched glad,
> In trouble and in strife.
> 'Tis used in every clime,
> By all men, high and low
> It is praised in prose and rhyme,
> And can but end with time,
> So let the kind herb grow!
>
> Tis a friend to the distress'd,
> Tis a comforter in need
> It is social, soothing, blest;
> It has fragrance, force, and zest
> Then hail the kingly weed!

Distinguished People Who Inhaled

In history, perhaps the most distinguished people since Sir Walter Raleigh have been on the side of Tobacco. Louis XIV, James I, Napoleon, Swinburne, Rousseau and Voltaire have been enemies of smoking but Ben Jonson, Milton, Spenser, Tennyson, Scott, Thackeray, Carlyle, Kingsley, Lamb, Prince Bismarck (who gave his last cigar, on a battlefield, to a wounded soldier), and particularly the jolly King Edward VII., have all been great smokers.

Carlyle admired Tobacco as the friend of silence. Byron and Robert Burns chewed tobacco. General Gordon was said to have had but one fault - he smoked too much. His enemy and conqueror, the Mahdi of the Sudan, on the other hand, punished smoking with eighty lashes of a hippopotamus whip. He said that smoking was against the Koran. Field Marshall Lord Wolseley gave his cigarette-case to the hero who mended the boiler of Lord Charles Beresford's Nile boat, and then gave up smoking. Frederic the Great took enormous quantities of snuff, and had boxes on all his chimney-pieces; seeing a page help himself, he gave him the box, "for I think it is too small for the both of us." Bonnie Prince Charlie broke the stem of his only "cutty," in the Highlands, and repaired it by inserting the quill of a bird's feather - "a desperate expedient in a desperate strait", as he described it.

Empress Elizabeth of Austria, reputedly the most beautiful European woman of the 19th century, was a chain-smoker, addicted to perfumed cigarettes. The Princesses of France, daughters of the Sun King, borrowed pipes from the officers of the Swiss Guards. The Prussian General Moltke was nervous before the battle of Sedan, but calmed himself when, offering a cigar to Bismarck, saw the Iron Chancellor thoughtfully fingering each cigar in turn and, after what seemed a long time, finally choosing the best. General Moltke was then reassured that the battle would be won.

President Franklin D. Roosevelt smoked cigarettes in long holders, clenched between his teeth at a rakish angle. Sir Winston Churchill was never seen without chomping on his Havana Cheeroot. Of Paley it is recorded that "he would smoke any given quantity of tobacco and drink any quantity of punch while conversing like a being of a higher sphere". Charles Lamb pitied Socrates "whose pot was unaccompanied by a pipe."

Thackeray hoped to live to see a Bishop "loll out of the Athenaeum with a cheeroot in his mouth, or, at any rate, a pipe stuck in his shovel hat." A certain Sir Frederic Porson, then in his seventies, in thirty six hours was said to have used half a pound of snuff, a big bundle of cigars, assisted by two bottles of Trinity ale, six of claret, two of brandy, and some trifles of light wines. During a lecture given on his 70th birthday, Mark Twain declared

> I have made it a rule never to smoke more than one cigar at a time. I have no other restrictions as regards smoking. I do not know just when I began to smoke, I only know that it was in my father's lifetime, and that I was discreet. He passed from this life when I was a shade past eleven ever since then I have smoked publicly. As an example to others, and not that I care for moderation myself, It has always been my rule never to smoke when asleep, and never to refrain when awake. It is a good rule. I mean for me; but some of you know quite well that it wouldn't answer for everybody that's trying to get to be seventy.

> I smoke in bed until I have to go to sleep. I wake up in the night, sometimes once, sometimes twice, sometimes three times, and I never waste any of these opportunities to smoke. This habit is so old and dear and precious to me that I would feel as you, Sir, would feel if you should lose the only moral you've got - meaning the chairman - if you got one. I am making no charges. I will grant, here, that I have stopped smoking now and then, for a few months at a time, but it was not on principle, it was only to show off; it was to pulverize those critics who said I was a slave to my habits and couldn't break my bonds.

Finally, it is said that many heroes of the American Revolution in their younger years made money smuggling tea, rum, molasses and tobacco - just about anything on which the British Government had placed a tax.

The longevity of some famous smokers is something to behold. Hobbes lasted to ninety-two.

Izaak Walton gave up smoking at age 91 and promptly died. One tobacco addict, R. Faviot, lived to be 104, Jane Garbut, who smoked pipes incessantly, gave up the ghost at the age of 110. Heinrich Hartz, a Silesian patriarch and chain-smoker supposedly reached an age of 142 years. Winston Churchill, who not only smoked one cigar after the other all his life, but who also imbibed great quantities of brandy, made it safely past the ninety year mark.

Some who sang Tobacco's praises, condemned it at the same time. Robert Burton remarked

> Tobacco, divine, rare, super excellent tobacco, which goes far beyond all panaceas, potable gold, and philosopher's stones, a sovereign remedy to all diseases . . . but as it is commonly abused by most men, which take it as tinkers do ale, 'tis a plague, a mischief, a violent purger of goods, lands, health, hellish, devilish and damned tobacco, the ruin and overthrow of body and soul.

Others were pure and direct in their attribution of all kinds of virtue to the noble weed, such as Sir James Barrie, who wrote:

> When Raleigh, in honour of whom England should have changed her name, introduced tobacco into this country, the glorious Elizabethan Age began. I know, I feel, that with the introduction of tobacco, England woke up from a long sleep. Suddenly a new zest had been given to life. The glory of existence became a thing to speak of. Men who had hitherto only concerned themselves with the narrow things of home, put a pipe into their mouths and became philosophers. Poets and dramatists smoked until all ignoble ideas were driven from them, and into their place rushed such high thoughts as the world had not known before. Petty jealousies no longer had hold of statesmen, who smoked and agreed to work together for be public weal. Soldiers and sailors felt, when engaged with a foreign foe, that they were fighting for their pipes.
> from *My Lady Nicotine* London, 1890.

How Tobacco Arrived & Conquered

John Gerard (The Herball of Generall Historie of Plantes, 1597) writes that

> "there be two sorts or kindes of Tabaco, one greater, the other lesser; the greater was brought into Europe out of the provinces of America, which we call the West Indies: the other from Trinidada, an ilande neere unto the continent of the same Indies. Some have added a third sort, and others making the yellow Henbane *Nicotiana rustica* for a kinde thereof. Being now planted in the gardens of Europe, it prospereth very well, and commeth from seede in one yeare to beare both floures and seede. The which I take to be better for the constitution of our bodies then that which is brought from India [America]; and that growing in the Indies better for the people of the same countrey: notwithstanding it is not so thought nor received of our Tabackians; for according to the English proverbe; Far fecht and deere bought is best for Ladies."

The tobacco of Trinidad is mentioned in 1595 by Robert Dudley (**Voyage to the West Indies**, p. 22):

> "The daie followinge, beinge Sondaie, in the morninge came the savages with two canowes aborde us, as they had promised our men, bringinge such commodities with them as their islande did afforde, saving they brought neither golde nor pearle, of the which theare are great store within the ilande, but tobacco, nutes

and such kinde of fruites, the which they exchanged for knives, bugles, beades, fishinge hookes and hatchetts."

George Waymouth, who visited Virginia in 1605, wrote

"They gave us the best welcome they could, spreading deere skins for us to sit on the ground by their fire, and gave us of their tobacco in our pipes, which was most excellent, and so generally commended of us all to be as good as any we ever tooke, being the simple leafe without any composition, very strong and of a pleasant sweete taste: they gave us some to carry to our captaine, whom they called our Bashabe, neither did they require any thing for it; but we would receive nothing from them without remuneration."

George Percy, who visited Southern Virginia in 1606, describes an entertainment given in his honor

"After we were well satisfied they gave us of their tabacco, which they tooke in a pipe made artificially of earth as ours are, but far bigger, with the bowle fashioned together with a piece of fine copper."

Many of the English colonists in Virginia quickly took up pipesmoking. Thomas Hariot in **A Brief and True Report of the New Found Land of Virginia** (1588) was plainly taken with the properties of tobacco

"which is sowed a part by it selfe and is called by the inhabitants Uppowoc. In the West Indies it hath divers names, according to the several places and countries where it groweth and is used: The Spaniards generally call it Tobacco."

"We our selves during the time we were there used to suck it after their maner, the leaves thereof being dried and brought into powder. They use to take the fume or smoke thereof by sucking it through pipes made of claie into their stomacke and heade.

Since our returne wee have found manie rare and wonderful experiments of the vertues thereof; of which the relation woulde require a volume by it selfe: the use of it by so manie of late men and women of great calling as else, and some learned Phisitions also, is sufficient witnes."

The healing powers of tobacco were celebrated in an poem by John Davies in 1598 (**Works of Marlowe**, ed. of F. Cunningham, p. 268), beginning

Homer of Moly, and Nepenthe sings
Moly the gods' most sovereign herb divine Nepenthe,
Helen's drink, most gladness brings,
Heart's grief expels, and doth the wits refine.
But this our age another world hath found,
From whence an herb of heavenly power is brought
Moly is not so sovereign for a wound,
Nor hath Nepenthe so great wonders wrought.
It is tobacco, whose sweet subtle fume,
The hellish torment of the teeth doth ease,
By drawing down, and drying up the rheum,
The mother and the nurse of each disease.

Both sides of the controversy are skilfully represented in Ben Jonson's **Every Man in His Humor (**Act III, Scene 2), acted on the 25th of November, 1596, and printed in 1601. Bobadilla pleads thus in favor of the case:

"Signior beleeve me, (upon my relation) for what I tel you, the world shall not improve. I have been in the Indies (where this herbe growes) where neither my selfe, nor a dozen Gentlemen more (of my knowledge) have received the taste of any other nutriment, in the world, for the space of one and twentie weekes, but Tabacco onely. Therefore it cannot be but 'tis most divine.

"Further, take it in the nature, in the true kinde so, it makes an Antidote, that had you taken the most deadly poysonous simple in all Florence, it should expell it, and clarifie you with as much ease, as I speak. I could say that I know of the vertue of it, for the exposing of rewmes, raw humors, crudities, obstructions, with a thousand of this kind; but I professe my selfe no quack-salver: only thus much: by Hercules I doe horde it, and will affirme it (before any Prince in Europe) to be the most soveraigne, and pretious herbe that ever the earth tendred to the use of man."

Then Cob represents the other side as follows:

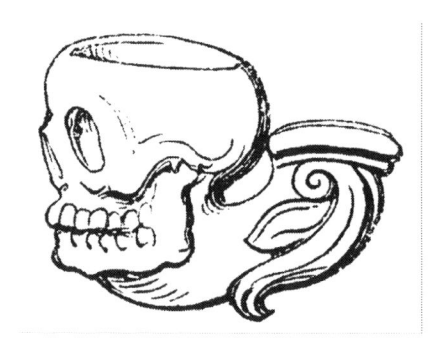

"By gods deynes: I marke what pleasure or felicitie they have in taking this roguish Tabacco; it's good for nothing but to choake a man, and fill him full of smoake and imbers: there were foure died out of one house last weeke with taking of it, and two more the bell went for yester-night, one of them (they say) will ne're scape it, he voyded a bushell of soote yester-day, upward and downward. By the stockes; and there were no wiser men then I, I'ld have it present death, man or woman that should but deale with a Tabacco pipe; why, it will stifle them all in the end as many as use it; it's little better than rats bane."

Meanwhile the raves received by this novel experience seemed to be outweighing the abuse. Catherine de Medici ordered that, "in honor of her sovereign self," the new intoxicating plant should be called "Herba Regina" - the Queen's Herb, which gave tobacco a mighty royal pat on the back. Meanwhile, the Papal Legate, Santa Croce, who already had brought a piece of the true cross from the Holy Land to Rome, also introduced tobacco into Italy.

In July 1586, some of the Virginia colonists returned to England and disembarked at Plymouth smoking tobacco from pipes, which caused a sensation. William Camden (1551-1623) a contemporary witness, reports that:

> "These men who were thus brought back were the first that I know of that brought into England that Indian plant which they call Tabacca and Nicotia, or Tobacco, which they used against crudities being taught it by the Indians. Certainly from that time forward it began to grow into great request, and to be sold at an high rate, whilst in a short time many men every-where, some for wantonness, some for health sake, with insatiable desire and greediness sucked in the stinking smoak thereof through an earthen pipe, which presently they blew out again at their nostrils: insomuch as tobacco-shops are now as ordinary in most towns as tap-houses and taverns. So that the Englishmen's bodies, (as one said wittily) which are so delighted with this plant, seem as it were to be degenerated into the nature of Barbarians, since they are delighted, and think they may be cured, with the same things which the Barbarians use."

The Kingly Weed was brought to England in 1565 by Sir John Hawkins. Soon Sir Francis Drake's sailors also arrived smoking Caribbean tube pipes. In 1585 Drake introduced Sir Walter Raleigh to the habit. There is an amusing story of Sir Walter smoking inside London's Mermaid Tavern, and an eager, horrified tapster, knowing nothing of tobacco and thinking Sir Walter to be on fire, emptying a keg of cold ale upon the person of the intrepid sailor.

Sir James Barrie wrote that "the Elizabethan Age might be better named the Beginning of the Smoking Era". It was from 1583, when Drake returned from Virginia, that the habit of smoking began to conquer England. It was taken up with an "enthusiasm unknown on the Continent." This, it was believed, was due to tobacco used at court, as well by persons in high places known for their wit and learning.

Tradition says, that in the time of Queen Elizabeth, "Sir Walter Raleigh used to sit at his door with Sir Hugh Middleton and smoke. The custom was thus sanctioned, through the public manner in which it was exhibited and the passers-by inhaling the aromatic flavor, imitated the example."

King James didn't like Raleigh at all anyway, and this kind of public flaunting of the King's wishes was probably what led to Raleigh's execution. Not that Raleigh wasn't warned. In his 1604 Counterblaste James wrote, without much subtleness

"Now to the corrupted basenesse of the first use of this Tobacco, doeth very well agree the foolish and groundlesse first entry thereof into this Kingdome. It is not so long since the first entry of this abuse amongst us here, as this present age cannot yet very well remember, both the first Author, and the forme of the first introduction of it amongst us. It was neither brought in by King, great Conquerour, nor learned Doctor of Phisicke. With the report of a great discovery for a Conquest, some two or three Savage men, were brought in, together with this Savage custome. But the pitie is, the poore wilde barbarous men died, but that vile barbarous custome is yet alive, yea in fresh vigor: so as it seemes a miracle to me, how a custome springing from so vile a ground, and brought in by a father so generally hated, should be welcomed upon so slender a warrant."

Smoking quickly became the universal habit. Not only regular tobacconists, but also innkeepers, grocers, chandlers and apothecaries sold the tawny weed. Tobacco, in the earliest days, was also known as "Sotweed."

Tobacco became the chief import from the New World. Europeans began to cultivate it in Santo Domingo in 1531, in Cuba in 1580, in Brazil in 1600, at Jamestown in 1612, in Maryland in 1631. It was grown in England, France and Spain, but the European varieties were scorned by the connoisseurs such as Francis Bacon, in whose "*Sylva Sylvarum: or a Natural History*" (IX, 855) we find this passage

> "Tobacco is a thing of great price, if it be in request: for an acre of it will be worth (as is affirmed) two hundred pounds by the year towards charge. The charge of making the ground and otherwise is great, but nothing to the profit. But the English tobacco hath small credit, as being too dull and earthy; nay, the Virginian tobacco, though that be in a hotter climate, can get no credit for the same cause: so that a trial to make tobacco more aromatical, and better concocted, here in England, were a thing of great profit. Some have gone about to do it by drenching the English tobacco in a decoction or infusion of Indian tobacco; but those are but sophistications and toys; for nothing that is once perfect, and hath run his race, can receive much amendment. You must ever resort to the beginnings of things for melioration."

William Barclay in **Nepenthes, or the Vertues of Tabacco**, Edinburgh, 1614 recommends exclusively tobacco of American origin

"Albeit this herbe disdaines not to be nourished in many gardens in Spaine, in Italie, France, Flanders, Germanie and Brittaine, yet nevertheless only that which is fostered in India [America] and brought home by Mariners and Traffiquers is to be used. But avarice and greedines of gaine have moved the Marchants to apparel! some European plants with Indian coats, and to enstall them in shops as righteous and legittime Tabacco. So that the most fine, best and purest is that which is brought to Europe in leaves, and not rolled in puddings, as the English Navigators first brought home."

The ready acceptance of the new habit throughout the Old World caused astonishment. In the words of Peter Parley

"The habit of tobacco-smoking is more perfectly artificial than almost any other in which man indulges; and there are few which are more repulsive to the natural taste. It is generally disagreeable to those who do not practice it; those who do, have, in the first instance, acquired it with effort and difficulty' and many of those who try are unable to acquire it at all. Now, the wonder is, how it happens that a habit of this description should exceed all others in the extent of its diffusion. It embraces the circumference of the globe, it comprehends every class of people, from the most savage to the most refined, and includes every climate, from Siberia to the equator and from the equator to the extreme south.

"In Spain, France, and Germany, in Holland, Sweden, Denmark, and Russia, the practice of smoking tobacco prevails amongst the rich and the poor, the learned and the gay.

"In the United States, smoking is often carried to a reprehensible excess. If we pass to the East, we shall find the practice almost universal. In Turkey, the pipe is perpetually in the mouth, and the most solemn conferences are generally concluded with a friendly pipe, employed like the Calumet of Peace among the Indians. In the East Indies, as well as the West, not merely all classes, but both sexes, inhale the fragrant steam. In China the habit equally prevails. What renders the habit the more surprising is the comparative recent period within which it has become thus extended. A hundred and fifty years is a short time for a habit to gain all but universal prevalence."

A Blessing For Many; A Curse For Some

When smoking was still a brand-new fad, King James I was astonished and offended at the wide and swift acceptance it had gained in such a short while.

And for the vanities committed in this filthy custom, is it not great vanity and uselessness that at table, a place of respect, of cleanness, and of modesty, men should not be ashamed to sit tossing off tobacco-pipes, and puffing off the smoke one to another, making the filthy fumes thereof to exhale across the dishes, and infect the air, when very often men that abhor it are at their repast? . . But not only meal time, but no other time, nor action, is exempted from the publick use of this uncivil trick. Is it a great vanity that a man can not welcome his friend now, but straightway they must be in hand with tobacco? No, it has become, in place of a curse, a point of good-fellowship and he that will refuse to take a pipe with his fellows is accounted peevish, and no good company yea, the mistress can not in more mannerly kind entertain her servant than by giving him, out of her fair hand, a pipe of tobacco.

James was not the only ruler who made laws against smoking. The "Terrible Turk," Ammurath the Fourth, had smokers dragged from their hiding places in their homes and strangled for their neighbors amusement and edification. In Boris Godunow's Russia, the admirers of the heavenly herb had a pipe-stem run through the cartilage of their noses. Urban VII issued a Bull against the habit, while the Calvinists at Geneva declared that smoking was one of the sins forbidden by the decalogue, though it is hard to see how they could quote scripture to support this idea.

Laws and sermons - tobacco triumphed over them all.

While Royal Jamie ranted, Sir Walter Raleigh founded a veritable smoking club of the wits and sages of the age, who smoked their pipes and discursed at the Mermaid Tavern. Around Sir Walter's social board assembled more genius and talent than the world had ever witnessed before. Among the constant members were Selden, Beaumont, Fletcher, Ben Jonson, and Shakespeare. The mystery is that tobacco is never once mentioned in all of the Great Bard's works. On one of their meetings, Ben Jonson, curling an extra whiff of smoke around his jolly shining face, exclaimed "Tobacco, I do assert, and will affirm it before any prince in Europe, to be the most sovereign and precious weed that ever the earth tendered to the use of mans.

Tobacco inspired, within the short space of a century, almost two hundred treatises in English, many of them "exceedingly learned, and of rare literary excellence." Some extravagantly extolled its virtues, while others as violently declaimed against and deprecated its use. Among the earlier pamphlets were *A Chew of Tobacco for fine gentlemen in Livery*, "A right pleasant and veritable discurse, touching choice, rare, and curious particulars concerning the historic of the "Holy Herb."

It is only natural that a nation of gardeners like the English would have tried every way possible to grow their own tobacco, considering how expensive it was. There were many attempts to grow tobacco, as well as to create tobacco substitutes, and different kings took different approaches to this activity.

By various acts passed in the reign of Charles II (1660-85), the planting of tobacco was forbidden in England in favor of the colonies, on forfeiture of forty shillings for every rod of ground thus cultivated, excepting in physic gardens, where it was allowed in quantities not exceeding half a pole of ground.

Justices of peace were empowered to issue warrants to constables to search after and destroy the plants. It appears that walnut-tree leaves were used as a substitute for tobacco; for the cutting of such leaves, or any other leaves (not being tobacco leaves) or coloring them so as to resemble tobacco or selling these mixed or unmixed for tobacco was forbidden under a penalty of forfeiting five shillings a pound.

In J. W. Gent (**Systema Agriculturae; the Mystery of Husbandry Discovered**, 2d ea., 1675, p. 156) we find the following passage

> "The Statute-Laws are so severe against the planters of tobacco, but it is a plant so much improving land, and imploying so many hands, that in time it may gain footing in the good opinion of the landlord, as well as of the tenant, which may prove a means to obtain some liberty for its growth here, and not to be totally excluded out of the husbandmans farm.
>
> The great objection is the prejudice it would bring to navigation, the fewer ships being imployed; and the lessening his Majesties revenue. To which may be answered, that there are but few ships imployed to Virginia, and if many, yet there would be but few the less; for it's not to be imagined, that we should plant enough to furnish our whole nation, and maintain a trade abroad also:
>
> And in case it should lessen the number of ships for the present, they would soon encrease again, as the trade of Virginia would alter into other commodities, as silk, wine and oyl, which would be a much better trade for them and us.
>
> And as to the lessening his Majesties revenue, the like imposition may be laid on the same commodity growing at home, as if imported from abroad, or some other of like value in lieu of it. Certain it is, that the planting of it would imploy abundance of people in tilling, planting, weeding, dressing and curing of it.
>
> And the improvement of land is very great, from ten shillings per acre, to thirty or forty pound per acre, all charges paid: before the last severe laws, many plantations were in Gloucestershire, Devonshire, Somersetshire, and Oxfordshire,

to the quantity of many hundreds of acres.

"Some object, that our English-tobacco is not so good as the forreign; but if it be as well respected by the vulgar, let the more curious take the other that's dearer. Although many are of opinion that it's better than forreign, having a more haulgust, which pleaseth some; if others like it not, they may in the curing of it make it milder, and by that means alter or change it as they please: It hath been often sold in London for Spanish tobacco.

The best way and manner of planting and curing it, would be easily obtained by experience: many attempting it, some would be sure to discover the right way of ordering of it, and what ground or places' it best affects. But that which hath been observed is, that it affects a rich, deep and warm soil well dressed in the spring before planting time: The young plants raised from seed in February or March, on a hot bed, and then planted abroad in your prepared ground, from whence you may expect a very good crop, and sometimes two crops in a year. The leaves, when gathered, are'first laid together on heaps for some time, and then hang'd up (by threads run through them) in the shade, until they are through dry, and then put up and kept, the longer the better. In this, experience is the best master.

There were two reasons, besides the pleasant narcotic effect, for the swift and wide acceptance of the new craze. The first was that people believed smoking to be healthy - a defense against infection from the ever-prevailing epidemics of the time. Plague was warded off "by ye chewing of rhubarb, lovage, and muche Tobacco." Some plague doctors went about with a beak-like mask. Smoldering inside the beak, which was pierced with a number of small holes, were burning tobacco leaves supposedly protecting the wearer against the noxious vapors of the plague. For centuries snuff was believed to be a "sovereign remedie for the dripping and clogging of ye nose." Up to the 19th century infusion of tobacco enemas were given to surgery patients, instead of the chloroform of later days, "to prevent troublesome muscular spasms, and induce a state of tranquility and a reasonable insensibility to pain." In 1704, the Fugger Newsletter reported "The plague has broken out in Hungary, killing people left and right. One tries everything to stop this epidemic, even going so far as allowing smoking on the street."

An advertisement, appearing in a 1727 Hamburg newspaper, let the public know that

"At Peter Heuss' Shop, next to the bank, is sold Tobaco de Becco, a lovely, pleasant and mild Toback to smoke, the very essence of Toback, fit for all royal courts and highest personages. It has found great universal applause from dissolving corrosive phlegm, stopping nose-dripping and headaches, clears the eye-sight, strengthened hearing, cures toothaches within minutes, and subdues by reason of its balsamic oil and fragrance all pains of the human body, renders the heart merry and drives away melancholy, and does not dry out the body as other tobaccos do.

A gentleman can smoke this Tobaco de Becco all day long without the slightest ill effects. The pound twelve Marks good Hamburg currency, the half pound six marks. The Tobaco is Sealed with a fine red seal depicting a West-India Merchant Man, and the package can be sent easily everywhere by horse courier."

The second reason for the tolerance of the "filthie, stinking weed" was, of course, the enormous profits derived from it. It was Tobacco which kept the American colonies going. Hard cash being scarce to non-existent, tobacco was made legal tender just about everywhere. One 19th century historian wrote:

> "So prominent is the place that tobacco occupies in the early records of the middle Southern States, that its cultivation and commercial associations may be said to form the basis of their history. It was the direct source of their wealth, and became for a while the representative of gold and silver; the standard value of other merchantable products; and this tradition was further preserved by the stamping of a tobacco-leaf upon the old continental money used in the Revolution.

A Good Woman Was Worth A Lot Of Tobacco

The wives of a number of the first colonists of Virginia, it will be remembered, were exported from England at the price of one hundred pounds of tobacco each and as the "Governors of the Colony" selected young women "who were well recommended for their virtues, education, and demeanor," the demand increased, and higher prices still were gladly given for such agreeable "help mates." Among other things illustrative of the times, a minister's salary was recorded as paid in tobacco, and the claim had priority over all other debts; and whoever was absent from the church without a valid excuse was fined a pound thereof and if absent a month, fifty pounds and for abusing the minister the penalty was forfeiture of the whole crop"

In 1643, at Lancaster, Pennsylvania. the tailor Noah Rogers received eighty pounds of prime tobacco for a fine, embroidered gentleman's suit, and sixty pounds for a lady's dress. A pound of first quality Virginia was worth two prime beaver pelts or five gallons of Monogahela Rye.

Governments quickly caught on to the fact that so-called "sin taxes" filled the royal exchequers as nothing else. Sinfulness and filthyness could be overlooked as long as the sinner could be made to pay for it - to pay mightily every time he indulged his habit. Tobacco taxes became the subject of parliamentary battles. Lord Chesterfield was politically ruined for stubbornly resisting Walpole's increased excise tax on Tobacco and wine.

In many countries the sale of tobacco became a government monopoly. The first year the monopoly was established in France it brought in 150,000 livres. Twenty years later the sum was four million livres. Louis XIV. detested snuff, but tolerated its use, even at court, because the income derived from it financed his war in the Low Countries.

It was easy and profitable to tax tobacco, said a French minister, because it "is an article of first necessity, the delight of the rich, and the comforter of the poor." As Edward Lowell wrote in his *On the Eve of the French Revolution*

"Of all known stimulants, tobacco is perhaps the most agreeable and the least injurious to the person who takes it but no method of taking it has yet been devised which is not liable to be offensive to the delicate nerves of some bystander. It is probably on this account that a certain discredit has always been attached to this most soothing herb, and that it seldom gets fair treatment in the matter of taxation. Over a large part of France, containing some 22 million of inhabitants, tobacco had been subject to monopoly for a hundred years when Louis XVI. came to the throne, yet the use of the article had become so general that this population bought fifteen million pounds yearly, or between five eights and three quarters of a pound per head. Of this amount about one twelfth was used for smoking in pipes, and the remainder was consumed in the pleasant form of snuff.

3 Livres 15 sous a pound was the price set by the government and collected by the (tax) farmers, and yet, at this great price, the tobacco was often mouldy."

In "The Honestie of this Age, Prooving by good circumstance that the world was never honest till now", by Barnabee Rych Gentleman, Servant to the Kings most Excellent Maiestie" (1614) we find this calculation of the economic impact of tobacco on early London.

> "There is not so base a groome, that commes into an Alehouse to call for his pot, but he must have his pipe of tobacco, for it is a commoditie that is nowe as vendible in every Taverne, Inne, and Ale house, as eyther Wine, Ale, or Beare, and for Apothicaries Shops, Grosers Shops, Chaundlers Shops, they are (almost) never without company, that from morning till night are still taking of Tobacco, what a number are there besides, that doe keepe houses, set open shoppes, that have no other trade to live by, but by the selling of Tobacco.

> I have heard it tolde that now very lately, there hath bin a Cathalogue taken of all those new erected houses that have set uppe that Trade of selling Tobaceo, in London and neare about London: and if a man may beleeve what is confidently reported, there are found to be upward of 7000 houses, that doth live by that trade. I cannot say whether they number Apothicaries shoppes, Grosers shops, and Chaundlers shops in this computation, but let it be that these were thrust in to make uppe the number: let us now looke a little into the *Vidimus* of the matter, and let us cast uppe but a sleight account, what the expence might be that is consumed in this smoakie vapoure.

> "If it be true that there be 7000 shops, in and about London, that doth vent Tobacco, as it is credibly reported that there be over and above that number: it may well bee supposed, to be but an ill customed shoppe, that taketh not five shillings a day, one day with another, throughout the whole yeare, or if one doth take lesse, two other may take more: but let us make our account, but after 2 shillings six pence a day, for he that taketh lesse than that, would be ill able to pay his rent, or to keepe open his Shop Windowes, neither would Tobacco houses make such a muster as they doe, and that almost in every Lane, and in every bycorner round about London. Let us then reckon thus, 7000 halfe Crowns a day, amounteth just to 319,375 pounces a yeare. *Summa totalis,* All spent in *smoake."*

Nicolas Aubrey, writing at about the same period informs us

> "Tobacco was sold then for its wayte in silver, I have heard some of our old yeomen neighbours say, that when they went to Malmesbury or Chippenham Market, they culled out their biggest shillings to lay in the scales against the tobacco; now, the customes of it are the greatest his majestic hash."

Pipes & Other Great Inventions

Pipes and pipe-like tubes are occasionally found by old world archaeologists and seem to have been used for smoking something -something, but what? It could not have been tobacco, indigenous to America and only first encountered by Columbus and his men in 1492. One American, writing in 1855, mused

> "How did the people of all time, up to 1500, manage without the "weed." What was Caesar's "way" when for the moment annoyed? - did he bite his fingers, pace his room, or rap his knuckles on his armor? Napoleon, under such circumstances took snuff. It would seem that the portrait of Diogenes, housed in his tub, was never complete, because he had not a rude pipe sticking through the opening, while the blue smoke curled about his independent head. Yet this might have spoiled his best accredited saying, because his telling Alexander to "get out of his sunshine," is more sublime than saying that "he did not care a whiff of tobacco smoke for any king in pagandom," as is daily observed by kindred philosophers in these modern times."

The first users of tobacco were pipe-smokers. Ralph Lane, the first Governor of Virginia, is credited with having invented the long-stemmed clay pipe. He gave one to Sir Walter Raleigh who brought it to London in 1586. Hundreds of clay pipes have been dug up during excavations at Jamestown. The earliest settlers were already heavy addicts to the kingly plant.

The fashion of using the pipe, it is said, was not established until Raleigh set the example. Good Queen Bess, fond of fun and novelty, allowed Raleigh to smoke in her presence, and even went so far as to use a walnut shell and straw to take a few puffs herself. Raleigh, reputedly, made a bet with the Queen, offering to give the exact weight of all the smoke rising from her pipe. He accomplished this by first weighing the tobacco and afterward the ashes, explaining that the difference between the two was the weight of the smoke. After Paying the wager, Elizabeth told Sir Halters "That although she had known many laborers who had turned gold into smoke, he was the first she had found who could turn smoke into gold."

The pipe-makers' guild was incorporated at London as early as 1619. By 1650 all classes smoked long pipes. The so-called "Church Warden Pipe" was popular in Holland and colonial America.

An early treatise on pipes has this to say about the Dutch Church Warden pipe

> "Everyone is familiar with the Holland pipe, so perfectly identified with the old Knickerbockers. It is the cheapest and best pipe ever used. These are made of fine clay and have always been preferred to any other of similar material the world

over."

Gouda, the seat of their manufacture, is one of the handsomest town in the Netherlands, and soon after the introduction of tobacco into Europe, its inhabitants commenced making these pipes, and eventually created a trade that, in 1720, demanded sixty millions of pipes, and employed many thousands of operatives.- One advantage of this type, from the point of view of the industrious Hollanders, was that they were so breakable, keeping the folks in old Gouda Town forever gainfully employed.

For a long time it was believed that ancient Britons during the time of the late Roman Empire had been smokers, because in England, as well as Ireland, clay pipes were sometimes dug up together with Roman relics. These "Elfin" or "Fairy" pipes, however, turned out in the end to have been made in the 17th century.

Long-stemmed, white clay pipes were also used in Frederic William's Tabak Collegium. It was a kind of smoking club in which that ruler, father of Frederic the Great, could let himself really go. Surrounded by his general officers, the *Soldier King* could indulge his love of puffing and beer-swilling, while swapping coarse, scatological anecdotes and playing sadistic practical jokes on some unfortunate courtiers. Great entertainment was to be had by getting the victim drunk to the point of insensibility and then putting him to bed together with a pig, or even wild boar. One man awoke from his stupor to find a live bear sharing his blanket. The poor man was badly mauled even though the beast's claws had been clipped.

As American as apple pie was the true American pipe, so much used in "the West, and immortalized from its being the favorite of General Jackson, while occupying the White House. It consists of a piece of dried sweet corn cob, with the pith removed, to form the bowl, the stem, a joint of the cane, or reed. This rural pipe is undoubtedly the most agreeable of all others, for a new one is used at every sitting, and the cob, from its dryness and sponginess, draws out, in the process of combustion, all the pernicious oil of the tobacco, and the pith actually increases the fragrance of the tobacco itself."

The corncob pipe was made famous worldwide by General Douglas McArthur, whose trademark it became. The general always posed with a corncob on dramatic occasions - such as him wading ashore during the invasion and reconquest of the Philippines during World War II.

In the course of time, each nation created its own kind of pipe. The Germans evolved the painted porcelain bowl and their pipes were made the subject of immense and learned studies. German pipes consisted of four parts - the "Kopf," or Head, containing the tobacco. The Kopf often had a "Decker" or lid of silver or some other metal. Then came the "Abguss," or drain, that served to catch the "pernicious oil. which might otherwise spoil the taste the "Rohr," or stem and, finally the "Mundstuck," or mouth-piece. This scientific wonder was invented by an Austrian physician around 1800 and, at first, became a favorite of hunters and outdoorsmen. For this reason the pipe bowl was often painted with the images of rutting stags, pheasants, hunting dogs, and the like. In Germany this became a military smoking utensil. Soldiers of certain regiments could purchase pipes with the name or number of their unit and, usually, a soldier in full parade uniform of the particular outfit. Occasionally naked ladies were encountered on these pipe bowls.

The Hungarians became famous for their red clay pipes, favored throughout the old Austro-Hungarian Empire. Ulm, in Bavaria, produced pipes with hardwood bowls. The pipe-makers of Dorsetshire, England, produced a type of white, glossy clay. In a class by themselves are the "Meerschaums," meaning *Ocean Foam*. They were popularly supposed to have been made of some mystical stuff floating on the surface of the sea, but are actually made of a certain ivory colored clay which is found in several parts of Europe.

In its original state Meerschaum is white and soft and can be cut like hard cheese. Great care and artistic talent was spent on large Meerschaums whose bowls were carved into fanciful Turks' Heads; sinuous, high-bosomed Mermaids; the likenesses of popular heroes, generals and rulers; and a thousand other figments of their makers imagination. Frequently ornamented with gold and silver, some Meerschaums have fetched high prices at auctions of artistic artifacts.

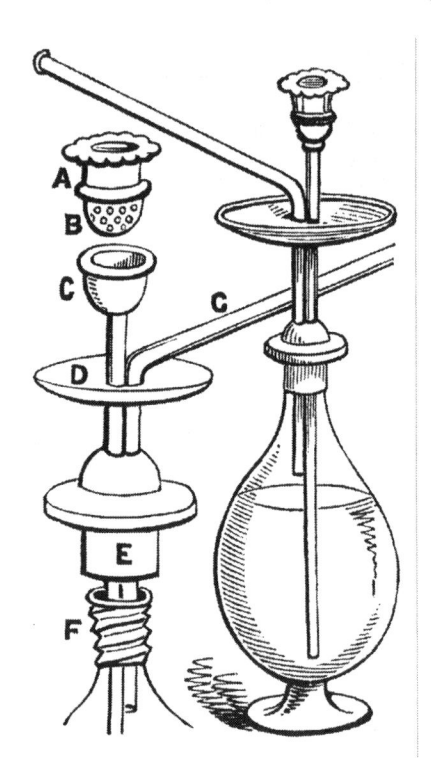

The pipe of pipes is the near-eastern Hookah - in the words of a Victorian travelers

"In this magnificent instrument, the Oriental Hookah, the smoke is sublimated and cooled by passing through water. Thus relieved of every foreign substance, the Persian drinks it in as the breath of heaven".

In many parts of the East it is the mark of signal hospitality to place the hookah in the center of the apartment, and pass the long, flexible tube from guest to guest, each one taking a whiff in turn. Sometimes the liquid contained in the bowl is rosewater, in such case, the smoke not only loses its solid particles but also acquires additional fragrance. The ornamentation, in diamonds and other precious stones, on some of the hookahs belonging to princes, exceeds beliefs in many instances even surpassing all the other crown jewels in value.

Our age sometimes prides itself on having seen and done everything, but the Anal Hookah, as a friend with a dark sense of humor called this approach, appears to have been first developed in the 16th century by the Dutch as a means of bringing drowning victims back to life.

The then-newly discovered Tobacco was being used for many experimental medical applications during the early days in Europe, and the tobacco smoke enema for drowning victims was one of the more useful treatments of its time and appears to have been used successfully in dozens of drownings in the Netherlands alone.

I've tried to picture how this remarkable discovery was made. It must have been a tragedy involving a drowning in one of the Dutch canals, with everyone standing around crying and yelling "Can't somebody do something!" Nearby stood a Dutchman - perhaps a physician himself - smoking his pipe and feeling quite moved by the scene. If he was like most Dutch people I know, he was a very private person and would never even allow another person's lips to touch his pipe, making what must have happened next a remarkable act of compassion.

In a moment of pure selflessness - or maybe he just needed a good excuse to buy a new pipe, though that would be unlike most of my Dutch friends of today - he must have walked up to the crowd gathered around the drowned person and said something like - "Ahem, er um, well, if nobody has any objections, I could try blowing a little tobacco smoke up this poor soul's rectum. My first puff in the morning certainly wakes me right up."

The crowd must have been stunned, then someone must have cried out "Just do it!" - and the rest was medical history, at least for a few decades, at least in The Netherlands. Hence also, possibly, the origins of the phrase – "Blowing smoke up his ass."

The Dutch might have invented it and used it to good effect, but the rest of the queasy world was evidently not ready for the Tobacco smoke enema even to save lives, since I've seen no evidence of it around emergency rescue vehicles and lifeguard stands.

Many modern smokers prefer a pear-shaped or bulldog-shaped bowl made from the seasoned roots of the Mediterranean Brier plant. Just as tobacco itself, snuff, or the lordly Havana Cigar, the brier pipe has also inspired its share of poetry.

> Let the toper regale in his tankard of ale,
> Or with alcohol moisten his thrapple,
> Only give me I pray, a good pipe of soft clay,
> Nicely tapered and thin in the stapple
> And I shall puff, puff, let who will say enough,
> No luxury else I'm in lack o',
> No malice I hoard, 'gainst Prince, Duke or Lord,
> While I pull at my pipe of Tobacco.
> Should my recreant muse - sometimes apt to refuse
> The guidance of bit and of bridle,
> Still blankly demur, spite of whip and of spur,
> Unimpassioned, inconstant, or idle;
> Only let me puff, puff, till the brain cries enough,
> Such excitement is all I'm in lack o',
> And the poetic vein soon to fancy gives rein,
> Inspired by a pipe of Tobacco.
> And when with one accord, round the jovial board,
> In friendship our bosoms are glowing
> While with toast and with song we the evening prolong,
> And with nectar the goblets are flowing;
> Still let us puff, puff - be life smooth, be it rough,
> Such enjoyment we're ever in lack o'
> The more peace and goodwill will abound as we fill
> A jolly good pipe of Tobacco.

This is a type of my old pipe. I fill it with tobacco then light the stuff, now (puff, puff, puff), of comfort there's no lack, O! (puff) 'tis, indeed, a friend in need that (puff) drives away trouble. Like (puff) a wife, it cheers our life and (puff) makes pleasures double. One who is sad it (puff) makes glad & (puff) makes life worth living. All strife it heals and friendship seals and (puff) ing. When I'm pipe I smoke for (puff) my pose to splendours the rings which hazy, and (puff) I (puff, puff), though old and lazy. No cabbage leaf brings me to grief, nor cigarette so nasty. My pipe so sweet though not so neat, gives (puff) a joy more vasty. My pipe's my yoke; its fragrant smoke in solitude I'm snuffing. Tho' I decry all else, yet my dear pipe I'm ever puffing. makes hearts forgiv- 'dead broke' my nor care a continental, woes soon (puff) trans- oriental. I watch ascend blend with atmosphere so dream of bliss supreme

Up Your Nose

During the Age of the Baroque and Rococo snuff was lord. Throughout the 18th century its use was universal. Snuff came in the form of *rappee* and needed a grater to render it usable. Snuff-taking originated in France, and was the fashionable craze at the court of Louis le Grand. To refuse a pinch was taken as an insult and some men were killed in duels over this.

An early author figured that at the time consumed by a ceremonious snuff-taker varies from one-tenth to a quarter of his whole existence.

> "We knew one of these happy individuals, who occupied five minutes and twenty seconds going through the entire operation. This included the taking out of the box, the tapping on one side, the opening, the handing around, the pinch seized and placed, the box returned, the handkerchief produced, flourished, and then returned to the pocket."

The Earl of Stanhope made the following curious calculation. He said that

> "every inveterate and incurable snuff-taker, at a moderate computation, takes one pinch every ten minutes. Every pinch, with the agreeable concomitants, consumes a minute and a half. Deducting a minute and a half out of every ten, and allowing sixteen hours to every snuff-taker's day, it amounts to two hours and twenty-four minutes out of every day, or one day out of ten, and thirty-six and a half days in a year."

In other words, a snuff addict wasted about a tenth of his whole life upon the pursuit of his habit. For the modern smoker, the snuff habit is unexplainable. Good fine-powdered snuff when sniffed up into the nostril, instantly produces a strong, almost unbearable irritation of the nasal organ followed by violent sneezing. Snuff-taking surely is the untidiest form of using tobacco. Historians have always described the clothing of heavy users, such as Frederic the Great/as disfigured by being covered with snot and snuff. It took hardy men with iron constitutions to acquire the habit. Heavy snuffers had permanently inflamed eyes, a sore proboscis, and a weak, damaged sense of smell.

Some, who did not want to suffer, but still wanted to be fashionable, only pretended to take snuff. What they really sniffed was a mild concoction of cinnamon and cream.

Snuff was for intellectuals, dandies, arrivists, the gentry, and royalty. It was called "the vice of the scholar." It was the very thing, the stimulant to witty conversation.

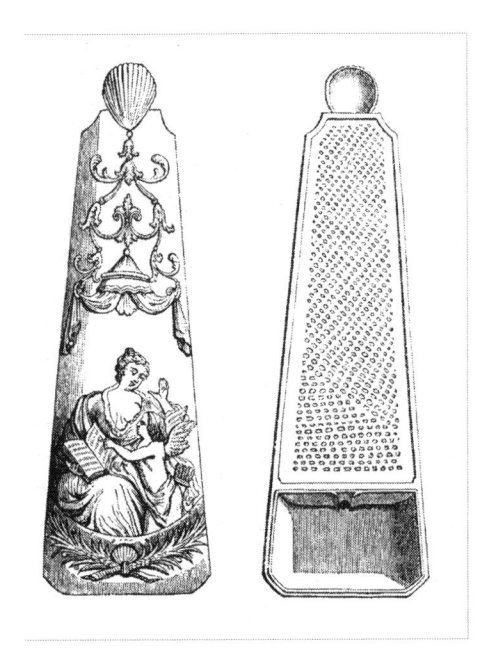

For as long as snuff reigned - longer than a century - the pipe was looked upon as vulgar, the Pastime of the lower classes. As to sociable snuffing, Alexander wrote

At every word a reputation dies.
Snuff, or the fan, supply each pause of chat,
With singing, laughing, and all that.

Robert Leighton wrote the ode to the "Snuffle Auld Man"

And now but his nose is a troublesome member -
Day and night, there's nae end to its snuffle desires
It's wide as the chimlie, it's red as an ember,
And has to be fed like a dry-whinnie fire.

It's a troublesome member, and gie's him nae peace,
Even sleepin', or eatin', or sayin' the grace.
The kirk is disturbed wi' his hauchin and sneezin',

The dominie stoppit when leadin' the psalm

The minister, deav'd out o' logic and reason,

Pours gall in the lugs that are gapin' for balm.

The auld folks look surly, the young chaps jocose,
While the bodie himsel' is bambazed wi' his nose.

Among the devotees of snuff were Frederic the Great, Count Mirabeau, Voltaire, Talleyrand and other notables. In America, it was Pierre Lorillard, 1742-1776, who turned colonial noses to snuff and thereby made a huge fortune. The enterprising Frenchman set up his Tobacco Manufactory at New York, on Chatham Street, near the gaol. His trademark was an Indian Sachem puffing on a pipe, leaning on a barrel of "Best Virginia." It became famous the world over. Lorillard advertised

"Tobacco Snuff of the best Quality and Flavor, Cut tobacco, kitefoot ditto, common smoking ditto, Segars, Ladies Twist, Pigtail in small rolls, Plug, Hogtail, Prig or Carrot ditto, Maccuba Snuff, Scotch Snuff, London Getleman's ditto, Rappee, Strasburg French Snuff, Common Rappee ditto, Scented Snuff of different kinds, and Jolly Tar's Twist."

The recipe for Lorillard's own best snuff was to use the best and strongest Virginia Tobacco, trimming off the stems and steeping these coarse scrap materials in good Jamaica Rum. The Tobacco was made into powder and aged for four months. Generous quantities of vanilla, tamarind, salmoniac and camomile flowers were added to the mixture called *Best Paris Rappee Snuff.*

In 1792 the younger Lorillard brothers moved to the Bronx, setting up their snuff mill on the banks of the Bronx River. It still exists as part of the New York Botanical Garden. Their *acre of roses*, whose flowers were used to give fragrance to their snuff, actually gave birth to the garden. In 1830, the enterprising Lorillards made a contract with the U.S. Mail for national distribution of their product and for postmasters to stock and sell their wares by mail order. Premiums and prizes were wrapped inside their products and happy winners received lamps, shoe laces, silk stockings or neckerchiefs. They even wrapped $100 bills at random in packages of cigarette tobacco named "Century," in order to celebrate the hundredth anniversary of the firm in 1860. The enterprise eventually grew into the giant American Tobacco Company which, under the Anti-Trust law, the Supreme Court in 1911 split up into American Tobacco, Liggett & Myers, and P. Lorillard. When snuff-taking went out of fashion, the firm concentrated on chewing tobacco and cigarettes, their most successful brands being *Beech Nut*, for chewing, its name sprawled over innumerable barns throughout rural America , and Kent and Old Gold cigarettes.

Pierre Lorillard had his yacht berthed at Newport, saw his colt, Iroquois, win the English Derby, and introduced fashionable society to the Tuxedo, named after his 7,000 acre estate and sporting club in Orange County, New York. Thus humble snuff gave rise to a huge commercial empire which has evolved into the multinational cigarette industry of today.

It also gave rise to the craft of snuff-box making which gave employment to the miniature painter, the jeweler, the gold and silversmith, the enameller, the gem cutter, even the sculptor. Humble folks contented themselves with boxes of silver, brass, tortoise shell, porcelain or crystal, but even for them, the possession of a fine snuff box was a status symbol.

A connoisseur wrote about these boxes

> "Ever since snuff became the fashion the box used to hold it has been made by Royalty the evidence of esteem. If a crowned head desires to acknowledge an obligation to an individual, it is generally done by the presentation of a gold snuff-

box set with diamonds. Following the Battle of Waterloo, the House of Commons, in one year, appropriated twenty-two thousand five hundreds pounds for snuff-boxes alone, intended as complimentary presents to be bestowed upon diplomats and soldiers engaged in the events consummated on that field of blood".

Napoleon very characteristically complained of the time wasted in opening them, so he placed his snuff, without covering, in his vest-pocket. Frederic the Great, who was an inordinate snuff-taker, had his "Westentasche" lined with tin, and he strewed the powder over his person and face with a most profuse hand. He also had a collection of over 300 precious snuff-boxes. While General Jackson was president, he received from England the present of a porcelain box, of which he seemed very proud. Inside of it was a paper, stating that it was offered as a grateful memorial from a British soldier for the kind treatment he had received while he was the general's prisoner. The tobacco-box of Sir Walter Raleigh is still in existence, and it is of no ordinary dimensions, being seven inches in diameter and thirteen in height.

The biggest boxes were the "Mulls" - silver-mounted, hollowed-out Rams Heads, filled with snuff, placed by Scottish Lairds in the center of the table for everyone to help himself. Up to 1900, the Czars of Russia still made presents of enameled snuff boxes to their favorites. These masterworks usually bore the giver's likeness on the lid, set in diamonds, sapphires, and emeralds.

One of them was valued at a quarter million gold rubles.

While snuff-taking was the accepted social amusement of men, it was resented when practiced by women. In 1775, the editor of the "Spectator" printed this complaint from a London gentlemen

> "I have writ you four times, to desire you would take notice of an impertinent custom of the women, the fine women, have lately fallen into, of taking snuff. This silly trick is attended with such coquet air in some ladies, and such a sedate masculine one in others, that I cannot tell which most to complain of, but they are to me equally disagreeable. Mrs. Santer is so impatient of being without it, that she takes it as often as she does salt at meals, and as she effects a wonderful ease and negligence in all her manner, an upper lip mixed with snuff and the sauce, is what is presented to the observation of all who have the honor to eat with her. The pretty creature, her niece, does all she can to be as disagreeable as her aunt; and if she is not as offensive to the eye, she is quite as much to the ear, and makes up all she wants in a confident air, by a nauseous rattle of the nose, when the snuff is delivered, and the fingers make the stops and closes on the nostril."

An early Victorian writer thundered

"Of all the detestable, obnoxious, offensive, unnecessary, and abominable imitations which dear woman is guilty of inheriting from fallen, depraved, corrupt, and wicked man, that of snuff-dipping stands preeminent. How the second edition of angels - the ne plus ultra of heaven's best workmanship - the idol of man, the diamond of song - the gem of prose, and the crowning glory of humanity, can concentrate a table spoonful of pulverized poison, that would kill a rattlesnake, and prove certain death to every living creature except the tobacco worm, is to us at variance with all philosophy, reason, scripture, taste, and refinement, and utterly incomprehensible."

Perhaps the best thing that can be said about snuff is that in a time of open sewers, when pigs roamed in the gutters of big cities, and chamber pots were emptied into the streets - it totally destroyed the sense of smell of the user.

The (Dis)Graceful Art

The Duke of Marlborough was the first distinguished man who rendered chewing tobacco famous - the next celebrity of historic interest was a goat belonging to the crew of Decatur's flagship. This animal took his quid as regularly as any of the old salts and, being possessed of a long, gray beard, his cud-chewing moved it from side to side, causing constant amusement to all who witnessed it.

Though practiced by sailors the world over, chewing tobacco was especially an American habit. Several 19th century presidents could not exist without their plugs. Modern baseball players chew during games. The Bull-Durham Bull with its huge, dangling testicles, still can be found emblazoned on the side of American barns. Frontiersmen, sodbusters, miners, and railroaders chewed. Davey Crockett chewed up a storm. Hand in hand with chewing went the incessant spitting of brown tobacco juice. The walls of railroad stations, eating establishments and hotel lobbies were stained with it. This led to the invention of the cuspidor, also known as spittoon or goboon. They were found everywhere, placed for the *aiming convenience of fastidious gents*. Lincoln had several spittoons placed throughout the White House for the use of his distinguished political friends. Westerners walked about with a "chew of baccer" wedged in their cheeks resembling nut-gathering chipmunks. They prided themselves with being able to hit a fly on the wing at a distance of ten feet.

The story is told of a sourdough sitting in a saloon expertly spitting gobs of 'ambeer' at bugs crawling on the floor without availing himself of the proper facilities. A bar attendant discreetly placed a cuspidor in front of the gentleman, moving it from time to time, trying to make him use it, until the exasperated customer finally lost patience and threatened "Iffen yer don't take that goldurn thing away I'm li'ble to spit in it."

The Gentleman's Smoke

The pipe and snuff were ultimately eclipsed by the more gentlemanly cigar. Cigar smoking is an ancient New World custom. Columbus encountered Indians smoking crude cigars. The word came from the Spanish *Segar* - from the Cuban cigar-shaped cicada. The first real cigar was brought to the American Colonies by General Israel Putnam - "Old Put" - in 1762, after a British campaign in Cuba. Old Put ran a brewery and tavern in Connecticut and introduced his customers to the new smoking article. In 1810 cigars were made in Connecticut and New Orleans. Long thin cigars had previously been made, from 1789 on, in Pennsylvania. These were the Stogies, named for the Conestoga wagons. A short, stumpy cigar, the cheeroot, also made its appearance. By 1830, the cigar had conquered America and "civilized" Europe. Cigars became the mark of a gambler, military officer, and business man. The politician's smoke-filled room - filled with cigar smoke - became proverbial.

At first, cigars were sold loose, from a barrel. For the first hundred years they were made strictly by hand. It was not until 1919 that the first cigar machine was installed, at great cost, at Newark, New Jersey. Special types evolved - straight, blunt Londres, Perfectos, pointed at both ends, long, thin "Panetelas;" short and stubby "Breves," the thick and straight "Corona"" and the long Perfecto called "Imperiale," the creme de la creme.

American Civil War generals made the cigar popular. Grant had a cigar planted permanently in his mouth. The habit eventually killed him. Though Spanish and Cuban ladies puffed their elegant slim "Cigarillos," the cheroot was thought to be offensive to women. In 1830, the Prussian Government enacted a law that cigars , in public, be smoked in a sort of wire-mesh contraption designed to prevent sparks setting fire to ladies' "crinolines" and hoop skirts. During the Edwardian age it became the custom , after a dinner party, for men and women to immediately separate, the male guests going into the smoking room to light their odorous cigars, the ladies retiring to the salon to talk about things concerning women, or to listen to piano or song recitals.

Gentlemen did not smoke in the presence of ladies either:

> It seems I've given great offence
> To her I hoped to call my bride
> This coming summer. Apologize!
> Such recompense I fain would make
> But am denied. Some glad new-comer,
> Who doesn't smoke, may win her while enraged.
> I try to smile, and say, "I'm disengaged.
>
> Cigar in mouth, one day last week,
> I ventured in the parlour bright,
> Where she sat tatting.
> She started, flushed, and tried to speak,
> Then cried, "At once, Sir, quit my sight,
> Nor stand there chatting.
> Disgusting creature! I'm so enraged,
> Consider, Sir, that we are disengaged!"

Arguably one of history's most famous cigar-smokers at the moment is Fidel Castro. There have been reports that the CIA has tried for decades to poison his cigars by putting something into them which would make the hair of his beard fall out, thus destroying his charisma.

The plot has not completely succeeded to date since he's still bearded, although these days his beard definitely has more of a terminal Ho Chi Minh look than it ever has since the Agency began work in the early 1960s.

I would say that the chemicals, or whatever they're using, are definitely taking their toll and that within another 5-10 years Fidel will be hairless. After so many failures its really encouraging to see at least one CIA plot actually generating some results - keep up the good work guys!

A Long Way, Baby?

It has only been in comparatively recent times that the problem of women taking to the weed, or of men smoking in the presence of the gentler sex, has been resolved by means of the cigarette. Now here was, finally, a dainty thing, unlike the crude, vulgar *chew of baccer*, or malodorous stogie, which looked chic and feminine between a lady's lips.

It was first encountered by British officers, during the Crimean War, in the form of "Papirossi," loose tobacco rolled by their Turkish allies into any paper that came handy. Both the English and the French, as well as their Russian foes, quickly adopted the "little cigar." When the men went home they brought the cigarette with them. That was in 1856. Cigarette smoking soon overwhelmed all other forms of tobacco taking as a result of clever advertising. The art of selling went hand in hand with the improvements of cigarette manufacture.

The invention and spread of the radio gave the cigarette a giant push. Flappers began to smoke as part of the women's liberation of the twenties. Slogans came into use - "They satisfy!" (Chesterfields), "I'd walk a mile for a Camel" (Camels), "It's toasted," (Lucky Strike). Old Gold held contests with $ 200,000 in prizes. Winners had to write an essay "The increased popularity of Old Golds in My Community as a Result of the Old Gold Contest." Sales doubled.

Philip Morris concentrated their creative effort upon a dwarf dressed up as a hotel bellhop, interrupting radio serials with a piercing, ear-splitting "Call for Philip Mor-or-ris!" Famous sportsmen were paid to endorse various brands of cigarettes. Joe Louis said "When my nerves fail during a match, I go for that little pack." The earliest network news star John Camron Swayze assured Americans that "When you're nerves are shot, Camels set you right", and early diet advice included "Reach for a Lucky instead of a Sweet". Some brands were even outright therapeutic - "We help to keep you regular."

A Novel Strategy for Natural Tobacco Growers

PLEASE NOTE: A lawyer friend of mine insists that I tell you that this section is not intended to give you financial or tax advice, nor to suggest that any of the strategies described will work in your individual situation.

To determine whether or not the strategies described might work for you, you should consult both a tax attorney and an accountant. (There – happy now Frank?)

For years as I drove through the southern US I wondered why so many obviously decrepit farms had so many equally decrepit tenant farmer shacks. I used to think surely nobody could make a living on most of these places – washed-out cotton fields, hard clay soils bearing scrawny corn and sorghum crops at best. I calculated that there must be hundreds of thousands of dirt poor tenant families living in miserable shacks like these all across the American south – and I could never figure out why. How could these folks possibly benefit from living in these places and working that obviously useless land, and how could the landowner possibly afford to keep the land, much less maintain the tenants?

It wasn't until I began reading the tax laws because of some new family responsibilities that I came across a little piece of the IRS Code - and I finally understood. This is the part of the code describing agricultural business expenses and it mentions, barely in passing, that as long as a legitimate sharecrop agreement exists between a landowner and a tenant farmer living on and working the land, then the housing, utilities and tools provided by the landowner are a full business deduction to the landowner and are not taxable as income to the tenant farmer/sharecropper.

To be specific, in Chapter 5 of IRS Publication 225, the Farmer's Tax Guide you'll find this language describing what you, the owner of agricultural business, can do about deducting your tenant house expenses:

Tenant House Expenses

"You can deduct the costs of maintaining houses and their furnishings for tenants or hired help as farm business expenses. These costs include repairs, heat, light, insurance, and depreciation.

"The value of a dwelling you furnish to a tenant under the usual tenant-farmer arrangement is not taxable income to the tenant. "

That's it. Pretty simple. Here's how it works, according to language elsewhere in the IRS code. The landowner and the tenant farmer must have a "legitimate share-crop agreement", meaning that the tenant will work the land according to the landowner's wishes and direction and will make every effort to produce a crop.

As long as the farm is in business intending to make a profit through farming it is a legitimate agricultural operation. Whether or not the farm makes a profit in the first several years is not as important as whether or not farming is taking place in anticipation of having a profitable operation. This means that a startup family farm, or a newly re-incorporated one, bears a lot of costs prior to turning a profit, including costs related to providing tenant housing.

Once the expenses of providing one or several tenant farmers with housing, utilities and tools are removed from the farm's bottom line the individual family farm has a lot more flexibility in how they will make a living. Business strategies like boutique wineries, production of gourmet food products and specialty products like organic tobacco, as well as specialty restaurant supply business, all become more viable for more family farms. Small family farms also benefit greatly from worldwide market access through the Internet, access to fast shipping, and a widespread growing appreciation of quality food.

This arrangement is unique to agriculture, and is specific to the tenant/sharecrop relationship only. If an employee of any other kind of business is provided housing by their employer as part of their employment agreement, they have to declare the fair market value of that housing on their income taxes and pay tax on it as if it was cash income.

Finally the reason for all those tenant houses across the South became clear – all those washed-out farms are owned by people like lawyers, judges, real estate investors, and other absentee landowners who have streams of income from their business or profession that they want to protect. So they place a fair market value of maybe $500/month on each of the houses they provide their tenants, plus another $200/month for utilities and tools, and they take $700 a month in expenses against their other income, while their tenants get to live poor but without owing taxes on their living.

But here is where this little provision gets interesting for anyone struggling to start a small family farm or keep one alive – there is no restriction on the legal or blood relationship between a landowner and their tenant farmer/sharecropper. In fact the IRS recognizes specifically that a tenant/landowner relationship can exist between parent/child, child/parent (the child owns the farm and the parents are the tenant farmers) spouse/spouse, and any other two or more parties.

The same laws that have worked for generations to benefit wealthy southern landowners and enslave poor tenant families can be used in completely legitimate, creative ways to benefit multi-generation families who want to live together on the land. These laws can even benefit couples, since the IRS specifically says that there is no restriction on the relationship between the land owner and the tenant farmer as long as that legitimate sharecrop agreement exists.

So just because benefits under the owner/tenant system have historically accrued only to the landowner, and because the system has been used primarily to exploit poor workers, in the right hands and with the right plan, the owner/ tenant relationship has powerful implications for successful small-scale farming with significant financial, environmental and social benefits.

Now, if you marry the concept of new uses for the tenant-sharecropper laws with the concept of TLC as an economic resource, you begin to see new economic opportunities for the skills and resources represented by many small family farms and their extended family members, and their communities.

For example, let's say that I'm your elderly parent, and that you own a 25 acre farm that produces a crop of hay every year but not much else. You decide that if someone were to live on the place full-time and manage a high-tech solar greenhouse you could produce a good additional income for the farm and begin the transition to becoming a specialty exotic plant/natural tobacco farm that markets its products on the internet. I'm ready to retire and your mother and I like the idea of living near our grandchildren and having a business for ourselves too.

So I become your tenant farmer/sharecropper, and the housing you provide to me, as well as my utilities and the tools of the trade, etc. are not required to be declared as income. That means as your tenant farmer/sharecropper I owe no tax on any of what you provide to me in the way of housing, utilities & tools – including a farm vehicle. Of course the fact that I was able to loan you the cash to build both the tenant house and the greenhouse & infrastructure doesn't alter our tenant sharecrop arrangement.

You on the other hand get to deduct the fair market rental value of the nice 3/2 solar electric house you provide for me, plus the interest on the loan, as well as all of the other expenses like my farm vehicle, the high technology solar greenhouse where I raise ½ acre of organic natural tobacco and other specialty herbs and flowers, the solar electric system running the agricultural portions of the property and tenant house - all as a business expense of yours. Your business plan is to have your herbs raised, processed, packaged and marketed by your tenant farmer, primarily through mail order and the internet channels to retail customers. Considering the potential demand worldwide for hand-raised native, natural tobacco products, this venture should produce a very nice cash flow.

Even if I don't make you enough money with my sharecropping activities, as long as I'm following your directions and those directions are intended to produce a profitable specialty farming operation, you get to write off all your expenses off against any other income you may have that you would otherwise have to pay taxes on.

Of course there are lots of other parts of the IRS code that bear on what you can and can't do if you are in the business of farming or ranching, but as long as you are or can be in compliance with those parts of the law then the potential benefits of the tenant housing provision can be available to you.

INDEX

additives ... 53
Adulteration ... 51
Algonquians ... 23, 24
alkaline ... 34
American Revolution ... 174
aroma ... 39, 41, 50, 53
aromas ... 44, 45
Austria ... 170, 173
Bismarck ... 173
black henbane ... 18
Blossoms ... 20
Boron ... 40
box ... 173, 192, 194, 195
Bragge ... 166
Brandy ... 47, 173, 174
Brazil ... 165, 166, 179
buffalo rib ... 20
bug problems ... 37
bug spray ... 38
Bull-Durham ... 196
Burley ... 33, 36, 42, 43, 45
Calcium ... 39
Calumet ... 180
Caraway ... 46
Carib ... 13, 14
Carlyle ... 173
Carrie Nation ... 170
Cayuga ... 18
Chamomile ... 46
Charles Lamb ... 171, 173
chewing tobacco ... 13, 51, 54, 194, 196
chlorine, ... 29
CIA ... 198
Cigar ... 47, 197, 198
Cigarette ... 199
cigarettes ... 170, 173, 194, 199
cigars ... 170, 173, 197, 198
cinnamon ... 192
Civil War ... 197
Clergy ... 170
Clove ... 46
coca ... 13
Columbus ... 13, 14, 165, 187, 197
commercial snuff ... 51, 53
container ... 29, 31, 35, 37, 51, 53, 54

containers ... 29, 31, 36, 37
corn ... 19, 20, 188
corncob pipe ... 188
Counterblaste ... 166, 168, 179
Cuba ... 179, 197
cultivation techniques ... 26
Davey Crockett ... 196
deadly nightshade ... 18
deficiencies ... 39
deficiency signs ... 39
devil ... 52, 169
Elizabethan ... 175, 178
England ... 179, 188, 189
English 13, 17, 166, 168, 171, 175, 176, 179, 180, 181, 182, 183, 194, 199
Europe ... 51, 169, 175, 177, 180, 181, 188, 189, 197
fertile plug ... 27, 35
fertilizers ... 27, 30, 36
Fidel Castro ... 198
flavor ... 17, 26, 39, 45, 49, 50, 178
flavors ... 42, 44, 45
Florida ... 165, 166
flower buds ... 41
flowering spikes ... 41
flowers. 16, 17, 26, 38, 45, 46, 194
fluorescent fixtures ... 32
food processor ... 49, 54
French ... 19, 165, 166, 185, 193, 199
George Percy ... 176
George Waymouth ... 176
Geranium ... 46
German ... 188
Grain Alcohol ... 47
growing conditions ... 26, 34
growing tobacco ... 25, 26, 27
growlights ... 29
Hakluyt ... 166
Halide lighting ... 32
harvest ... 20, 21, 42, 43
Hawkins ... 165, 166, 178
herbal tobacco ... 21
herbs ... 25, 33, 38, 46, 51, 166, 171

Hidatsa ... 19
Hobbes ... 174
Holland ... 180, 187
hookah ... 189
Hopi ... 23
humidity ... 36
Hungarian ... 189
indoors 27, 29, 31, 32, 33, 35, 37, 39
Izaak Walton ... 174
jimson weed ... 18
John Davies ... 176
Juniper ... 46
Kickapoo ... 19
King James ... 166, 168, 169
laws ... 26, 181, 182
leaf. 24, 39, 40, 43, 44, 45, 46, 48, 49, 50, 51, 52, 166, 184
Lemon ... 46
Lescarbot ... 165
Lord Byron ... 171
Lord Chesterfield ... 185
Lorillard ... 194
Louis XIV ... 173, 185
Magnesium ... 39
Mamelucos ... 165
Manganese ... 40
marigolds ... 38
Marijuana ... 25, 27
Mark Twain ... 174
Meerschaum ... 189
mid-rib ... 48
Milton ... 173
misting ... 36, 49
Molasses ... 45
Moltke ... 173
mulch ... 29, 37
Napoleon ... 173, 187, 195
Native American ... 12, 14, 15, 16, 18, 19, 21, 22
Native American tobacco use ... 12
natural tobacco 24, 28, 47, 48, 49, 51, 54
Nicolas Aubrey ... 186
Nicotiana attenuata ... 16
Nicotiana biglovii ... 17
Nicotiana chinensis ... 16

Nicotiana clevelandi 17
Nicotiana fructicosa 17
Nicotiana multivalvis 16
Nicotiana palmeri 16
Nicotiana persica 17
Nicotiana quadrivalvus 16
Nicotiana rapanda 17
Nicotiana rustica 16
Nicotiana tabacum 15, 17
Nicotiana trigonophylla 16
Nicotine 12, 15, 24, 39, 50, 175
Nitrogen 39
Orange 46, 194
organic natural tobacco ... 202
Ottoman Turks 169
Papirossi 199
Pennyroyal 46
pests 27
Peter Parley 180
pH 28, 34, 39
Philip Morris 199
Phosphorous 39
Pipes 187
Plains tribes 23
Pope 169
Potassium 39
potato 34
Potawatomi 19
potency 26, 30, 41, 51
potting soil 28
psychoactive 15, 51
quid 196
Raleigh 175, 179, 187

rappee 192
ribs 48, 49, 50
Robert Burton 174
Robert Dudley 175
Robert Leighton 193
Rocky Mountains 13, 23
rosemary 38
Rum .45, 47, 50, 51, 170, 174, 194
Russia 170, 180, 181, 195
Russian 199
rustica ... 16, 17, 31, 33, 43, 45
sandy loam 34
Sassafras 46
Sauk 19
sawdust 53
seedlings 29, 30, 31, 35
Seneca 19
share-crop agreement 200
Siberia 170, 180
signs of maturity 43
Sioux 21
Sir James Barrie 175, 178
sneezing 52, 169, 192
snuff 18, 39, 44, 45, 46, 51, 52, 53, 169, 173, 183, 185, 187, 191, 192, 193, 194, 195, 196, 197
snuff-boxes 195
soil .17, 20, 28, 29, 31, 34, 35, 36, 37, 39, 43, 49, 183
Solanaceae 18
Sotweed 179
Spaniards 13, 167, 176

Spanish 14, 17, 183, 197
sucker 40, 41
sulphur 34, 40
sunflower 20
Surgeon General 170
Swiss 173
Talleyrand 193
tenant farmer 200
Thackeray 173
Tionontati 19
Tobacco beds 34
tobacco products 47
tomato 34
top leaves 39
Turkey 16, 180
Vanilla 46
veins 40, 43, 48, 52
Virginia 15, 17, 172, 176, 178, 182, 184, 185, 187, 193, 194
Vitamin C 47
Vodka 47
Voltaire 173, 193
Walter Raleigh .173, 178, 181, 187, 195
water ... 16, 22, 23, 27, 28, 29, 32, 36, 37, 38, 39, 43, 46, 47, 50, 52, 166, 189
William Barclay 179
William Lilly 171
Winston Churchill 173, 174
Yaqui tobacco 17

Other books by Bill Drake

The Cultivators Handbook of Marijuana, self-published 1969; Whole Earth Catalogue edition 1975 – 1988; Ronin Books edition, 1992 (In print - available online)

The Connoisseur's Handbook of Marijuana, Straight Arrow Books (Rolling Stone) 1971 (Out of print)

The International Cultivators Handbook of Hashish, Cocaine and Opium, Wingbow Press 1974 (Out of print – updated second edition coming 2010)

Marijuana Foods, Simon & Schuster edition 1981-84; Ronin Books edition, 1996 (In print – available online)

Managing Children's Education in Expatriate Families, eBook available online, 2008

Personal & Family Security Planning For Expatriate Living, eBook, available online 2009

"Cultural Dimensions of Expatriate Life" eBook series, available online for all major ebook reading devices, 2008-10.

The series of full-length eBooks currently includes Australia, Chile, the Czech Republic, Egypt, Germany, Greece, Guatemala, Japan, Malaysia, Nicaragua, Nigeria, Portugal, Senegal, Singapore, South Korea, Spain, Thailand, The Netherlands, The UK, and Turkey

www.cultivatorshandbook.com

Made in the USA
Lexington, KY
25 July 2011